Child Development

AT THE INTERSECTION OF

Emotion and Cognition

APA HUMAN BRAIN DEVELOPMENT SERIES

MICHAEL I. POSNER, SERIES EDITOR

Child Development

AT THE INTERSECTION OF

Emotion and Cognition

EDITED BY

Susan D. Calkins and Martha Ann Bell

AMERICAN PSYCHOLOGICAL ASSOCIATION

WASHINGTON, DC

Published by
American Psychological Association
750 First Street, NE
Washington, DC 20002
www.apa.org

To order
APA Order Department
P.O. Box 92984
Washington, DC 20090-2984
Tel: (800) 374-2721; Direct: (202) 336-5510
Fax: (202) 336-5502; TDD/TTY: (202) 336-6123
Online: www.apa.org/books/
E-mail: order@apa.org

In the U.K., Europe, Africa, and the Middle East, copies may be ordered from
American Psychological Association
3 Henrietta Street
Covent Garden, London
WC2E 8LU England

Typeset in Goudy by Stephen McDougal, Mechanicsville, MD

Printer: Maple-Vail Book Manufacturing, York, PA
Cover Designer: Berg Design, Albany, NY
Technical/Production Editor: Harriet Kaplan

The opinions and statements published are the responsibility of the authors, and such opinions and statements do not necessarily represent the policies of the American Psychological Association.

Library of Congress Cataloging-in-Publication Data

Child development at the intersection of emotion and cognition / edited by
Susan D. Calkins and Martha Ann Bell. — 1st ed.
    p. cm. — (Human brain development series)
  Includes bibliographical references and index.
  ISBN-13: 978-1-4338-0686-5
  ISBN-10: 1-4338-0686-X
  ISBN-13: 978-1-4338-0687-2 (e-book)
  ISBN-10: 1-4338-0687-8 (e-book)
  1. Emotions. 2. Cognition. 3. Child development. I. Calkins, Susan D.
II. Bell, Martha Ann.
  BF511.C45 2010
  155.4—dc22   2009023621

British Library Cataloguing-in-Publication Data
A CIP record is available from the British Library.

Printed in the United States of America
First Edition

CONTENTS

CONTRIBUTORS

Laura Marie Armstrong, The Pennsylvania State University, University Park

Martha Ann Bell, Virginia Polytechnic Institute and State University, Blacksburg

Clancy Blair, New York University, New York, NY

Susan D. Calkins, University of North Carolina at Greensboro

B. J. Casey, Cornell Medical Center Sackler Institute, New York, NY

Pamela M. Cole, The Pennsylvania State University, University Park

Kirby Deater-Deckard, Virginia Polytechnic Institute and State University, Blacksburg

Tracy Dennis, Hunter College, City University of New York, NY

Denise R. Greene, Roanoke College, Salem, VA

Mark H. Johnson, Birkbeck College, University of London, England

Amanda C. Kesek, University of Minnesota, Minneapolis

Marc D. Lewis, University of Toronto, Toronto, Ontario, Canada

Stuart Marcovitch, University of North Carolina at Greensboro

Michelle M. Martel, University of New Orleans, New Orleans, LA

Megan M. McClelland, Oregon State University, Corvallis

Frederick J. Morrison, University of Michigan, Ann Arbor

Paula Y. Mullineaux, Virginia Polytechnic Institute and State University, Blacksburg

Joel T. Nigg, Oregon Health and Science University, Portland

Molly Nikolas, Michigan State University, East Lansing

Caroline K. Pemberton, The Pennsylvania State University, University Park

Claire Cameron Ponitz, University of Virginia, Charlottesville

Michael I. Posner, University of Oregon, Eugene

Li Qu, Nanyang Technological University, Singapore
Ross A. Thompson, University of California, Davis
Christy D. Wolfe, Bellarmine University, Louisville, KY
Philip David Zelazo, University of Minnesota, Minneapolis

FOREWORD

In this volume, Susan D. Calkins and Martha Ann Bell have made significant progress with an old issue in philosophy and psychology: How are our emotions and thoughts related? Can there be pure cognitive and pure affective psychology, or are the interactions of sufficient importance that their constituents cannot be examined separately?

Traditionally, science has analyzed the complexities of everyday life by separating them into simple, isolated components. This approach can be useful in scientific discovery. For example, studies of the role of the amygdala in fear by LeDoux[1] show how single emotions can be fruitfully isolated and studied. Similarly, the presence of proto-arithmetic operations in infancy shows that aspects of cognition can be isolated by appropriate experimental studies.[2,3]

Nonetheless, as this volume shows, cognition and emotional development influence each other in important ways. For example, Zelazo, Qu, and Kesek (chap. 6) show that emotional contexts can impair or enhance executive functioning, and a specific example is provided by Blair and Dennis (chap. 2), who show how excessive emotional arousal can limit cognitive performance. Conversely, Cole, Armstrong, and Pemberton (chap.4) describe how language—a cognitive skill—affects the development of emotional regulation.

In addition to demonstrating the two-way influences of emotion and cognition, the chapters explore possible mechanisms for these influences. For example, Bell, Greene, and Wolfe (chap. 7) propose a model that focuses on attentional control and self-regulation. Lewis (chap. 10) proposes a model linking desire and concept development, with dopamine playing a key role

---

[1]LeDoux, J. (2007). The amygdala. *Current Biology, 17*, R868–R874.
[2]Berger, A., Tzur, G., & Posner, M. I. (2006). Infant babies detect arithmetic error. *Proceedings of the National Academy of Sciences, 103*, 12649–12553.
[3]Wynn, K. (1992, August 27). Addition and subtraction by human infants. *Nature, 358*, 749–750.

as mediator. Deater-Deckard and Mullineaux (chap. 8) discuss the role that genes play in shaping both reactive temperament, such as negative affect, and self-regulatory ability.

Our increasing knowledge of the anatomy and mechanisms of cognitive and emotional control makes their joint regulation a topic of central importance. Nearly all of the chapters in this volume provide evidence from current studies, and in their afterword, Calkins and Bell consider how these findings may be amplified in the future.

The joint consideration of cognitive and emotional control can be approached at the psychological, biological, and behavioral levels. This volume provides a solid account of current efforts to achieve this integration.

Michael I. Posner
Series Editor

Child Development

AT THE INTERSECTION OF

Emotion and Cognition

1

INTRODUCTION: PUTTING THE DOMAINS OF DEVELOPMENT INTO PERSPECTIVE

SUSAN D. CALKINS AND MARTHA ANN BELL

The field of developmental psychology has made substantial theoretical and empirical contributions that extend into the more applied areas of behavioral science, such as child mental health and school performance. Clinical scientists, practitioners, and educators have looked to the field to address basic issues that have implications for children's everyday functioning, and considerable developmental research has been translated into practice that has improved the quality of life for children in their homes, with their peers, and in their schools.

Traditionally, researchers in the field of developmental psychology have made these important contributions even as they have segregated themselves into those who focus exclusively on emotional development versus those who focus on cognitive development. Early work in these distinct research areas examined normative developmental processes using cross-sectional studies to elucidate the developmental achievements of infancy, early childhood, middle childhood, and adolescence (Bjorklund, 1987; Brainerd, 1977; Izard & Malatesta, 1987). More recent work has examined the degree to which functioning in a particular domain early in development influences functioning in that and related domains, as children manage the transitions that characterize development. So, for example, research that has examined the origins of the social skills children exhibit in kindergarten has focused largely on emotional predictors and processes, such as emotionality, emotion regulation, and emotion understanding, that have been implicated in early childhood social competence (Eisenberg et al., 1995; Fabes & Eisenberg, 1992). In contrast, research on early academic success has emphasized cognitive precursors, especially processes associated with metacognition (e.g., Bransford, Brown, & Cocking, 1999; Gaskins, 1994), strategy use (e.g., Griffin, Case, & Siegler, 1994; Pressley, 1995), and other skills central to executive functioning, such as memory and problem solving (e.g., Stipek & Ryan, 1997).

The notion that emotion and cognition are biologically based psychological phenomena that may be mutually influential is not new. Early emotion research and classic emotion theorists (i.e., William James, Walter Cannon, Philip Bard) attempted to address the biological, physical, and mental manifestations of emotion. Schacter's work on emotional appraisal theory (Schacter & Singer, 1962) and Zajonc's (1980) view of the primacy of affect are salient examples of approaches that address the explicit role of emotion versus cognition in psychological phenomena. There is clear value in studying these processes separately, to both understand basic functions and their development and to assess their implications for later outcomes.

However, a more integrated view that acknowledges the mutual influences of both sets of processes may be more fruitful when considering the complex developmental skills that clearly draw on both domains. Indeed, little research has explored the combined contributions of emotional and cognitive processes to the development of the social and academic skills necessary for school success and mental health, despite recent acknowledgment that such integration will likely yield the most complete understanding of early adjustment (Bell & Wolfe, 2004; Blair, 2002; Gray, 2004; Ladd, Birch, & Buhs, 1999) and be of the greatest benefit to the design and implementation of educational practice and interventions.

Despite the lack of empirical work that crosses the two domains, it is clear that research that integrates cognition and emotion is essential to any comprehensive conceptualization of development (Gray, 2004; Rothbart, 2004). Although traditionally considered separate processes, cognition and emotion are dynamically linked, at the level of both biology and behavior, both "in the moment" and across development, working together to process information and execute action (Blair, 2002; Cacioppo & Berntson, 1999). Cognitive processes of thinking, learning, and action can be viewed as regulators of a child's emotion behaviors. Likewise, emotions can be understood as organizers of behavior, essentially modifying a child's thinking, learning, and action (Cole, Martin, & Dennis, 2004). Thus, cognition and emotion represent inseparable components of the developmental process (Bell & Wolfe, 2004).

There has been much conceptual work proposing the integration of cognition and emotion (e.g., Bell & Deater-Deckard, 2007; Fox & Calkins, 2003; Posner & Rothbart, 2000), as well as suggesting that cognition and emotion are fully integrated by school age (Blair, 2002). However, the empirical data on this cognition–emotion developmental process are sparse, and existing work tends to focus on cross-sectional samples of preschool children (e.g., Kerr & Zelazo, 2004; Rothbart, Ellis, Rueda, & Posner, 2003). To date, there have been no longitudinal studies on emerging cognition–emotion relations across very early development, despite speculations that this integration may have its beginnings in infancy (e.g., Bell & Wolfe, 2004; Calkins & Fox, 2002). Nevertheless, pieces of the developmental puzzle can be assembled from existing research examining some basic emotion and cognition processes, and researchers who traditionally focus on one domain or the other have begun to address the likely behavioral and biological processes that link the two domains. This volume represents an attempt to present these first efforts by examining—systematically—hypotheses about the codevelopment of basic emotional and cognitive processes across childhood and by integrating research that has taken some first steps toward studying both emotion and cognition processes.

Our rationale for examining emotion and cognition together in this volume emanates from multiple conceptual and empirical literatures. First, recent work in the area of self-regulation in children and adults has noted that both emotion and cognition processes are clearly implicated in the successful regulation of thought and behavior (Baumeister & Vohs, 2004; Gray, 2004; Lewis & Stieben, 2004). A second literature focusing on early childhood psychopathology has emphasized that among children with early adjustment difficulties, deficits in both emotion and cognitive processing are often observed (Cicchetti & Posner, 2005; Nigg & Huang-Pollock, 2003). A third relevant literature has examined these processes from a neuroscientific framework that links emotion and cognition processes in the developing brain (Bell & Wolfe, 2004; Nigg & Huang-Pollock, 2003; Posner & Rothbart, 1994, 2000). Such an approach offers a functional explanation for the dynamic processes that direct the interaction between emotion and cognition during early childhood. It is surprising that despite the considerable theoretical work describing this functional relation, there has been relatively little empirical work in developmental psychology focusing on emerging emotion–cognition relations in early development and how these links may affect child outcomes. Our goal for this volume was to bring together prominent scientists whose work is beginning to address these relations.

This edited volume is organized around three areas of work that explicitly or implicitly address the relations between emotional and cognitive processes and the implications of such functioning for social relationships, school performance, and mental health. Part I addresses basic behavioral and biobehavioral developmental processes associated with emotion and emotion control and with cognition and cognitive control, as well as attentional control. Part II focuses on the application of developmental neuroscience and genetics to these basic behavioral processes, thus providing a functional brain–behavior link for conceptualizing cognition-emotion interactions. Part III highlights research on atypical emotion and cognitive processing and the implications for early adjustment problems and for functioning in the typical academic and social setting of school. Implications for clinical and education research and interventions are the focus of this final section. The afterword synthesizes the theory and research presented in the volume, with speculations on the likely developmental pathways that may be implicated in normative development, as well as suggestions for future research to further elucidate both the connections among these processes and to better understand how individual differences in child functioning may emerge. Each of these research areas is crucial for conceptualizing the integrative nature of emotion and cognition across development.

PART I: BASIC DEVELOPMENTAL PROCESSES

Fundamental to any effort to describe and explain development is a clear need to examine these emotion and cognition processes at a behavioral and biobehavioral level early in development, when differential growth will provide a window on their emerging relations (Blair, 2002). A first important step in examining the relations between emotion and cognition at this level involves specification of the component processes within each domain (Blair, 2002; Gray, 2004). The discrete processes to be examined in this endeavor are described in these six chapters.

From a developmental point of view, it is especially useful to describe explicit types of emotional and cognitive processes, their biological foundation, and how they emerge. Such specificity may provide insight into successful developmental adaptation to the peer and school environment as well as nonnormative developments and problems that emerge as a result of deficits in specific components of emotion and cognition at particular points in development (Calkins, 2007; Calkins, Graziano, & Keane, 2007). All of the authors in Part I focus on developing emotion–cognition relations at the biobehavioral level and discuss various contextual factors that may affect this developing association.

Clancy Blair and Tracy Dennis (chap. 2) present a developmental psychobiological approach to cognition–emotion relations over early development. The chapter focuses on ways in which a number of aspects of early experience may shape the development of relations between cognition and emotion, emphasizing the ways in which emotional and physiological arousal may facilitate goal-directed activity, which has clear implications for school readiness, developmental disabilities, and mood/anxiety problems.

Susan Calkins and Stuart Marcovitch (chap. 3) describe emotion regulation and executive functioning in early development both from a normative "what happens when" perspective and with special attention to the predictive implications of the development of these controls. Calkins and Marcovitch note the shared biological and psychological foundations of these processes, as well as their common predictive utility, in arguing that integration emerges early. The chapter addresses the development of the ability to control emotional arousal, an ability that allows children to engage in challenging tasks that provide opportunities for using and practicing cognitive function skills (Calkins & Dedmon, 2000), as fundamental to some of the more sophisticated and later developing cognitive control skills.

Pamela Cole, Laura Marie Armstrong, and Caroline K. Pemberton (chap. 4) examine the role of language in the development of emotion regulation. Although this role is well acknowledged, this chapter highlights how specific interactions between children and adults predict specific regulatory outcomes.

Ross Thompson (chap. 5) profiles the means by which relational processes influence young children's developing representations of emotion, their feelings about their emotions, and their capacities to manage emotions in academic and social contexts. Relational processes include a caregiver's sensitivity and support, conversational prompts to emotion understanding, and the broader warmth and security of the parent-child relationship. Thompson notes that each of these dimensions relates in particular ways to children's ability to independently regulate emotion.

Philip D. Zelazo, Li Qu, and Amanda Kesek (chap. 6) discuss how emotion influences the development of cognitive control. They contrast *hot* (highly emotional) and *cool* (not emotional) executive function tasks. Hot tasks rely on the affective aspects of executive function and are associated with orbitofrontal cortex, whereas cool tasks rely on more purely cognitive aspects and are associated with dorsolateral prefrontal cortex. Zelazo and colleagues present a model for the regulation of affect and motivation based on their research on hot and cool executive function tasks.

Research on basic biobehavioral developmental processes is essential to fill an important gap in our understanding of the complex interactions between emotion and cognition at the behavioral level. Brain-based research has highlighted how these basic developmental processes operate at the neurological level, shedding further light on developing emotion–cognition interactions. Much of this neurophysiological research has also highlighted individual differences in brain–behavior relations, which may also reflect genetic contributions to emotion and cognition interactions.

PART II: NEUROSCIENTIFIC AND GENETIC CONTRIBUTIONS

The authors of the chapters in Part II focus on developing emotion–cognition relations at the cortical or genetic level. Recent work in developmental neuroscience has identified specific brain regions that may play a functional role in the deployment of attention and in the processing and regulation of emotion and cognition, suggesting that these processes are controlled by closely related areas in the brain (Davis, Bruce, & Gunnar, 2002; Davidson, Putnam & Larson, 2000) and may become integrated very early in development (Posner & Rothbart, 1994, 1998). This work has identified areas of the prefrontal cortex as central to the effortful regulation of behavior via the executive attention system. This system is guided by the anterior cingulate cortex (ACC), which includes two major subdivisions. One subdivision governs cognitive and attentional processes and has connections to the prefrontal cortex. The second subdivision governs emotional processes and has connections with the limbic system and peripheral autonomic, visceromotor, and endocrine systems (Lane & McRae, 2004; Luu & Tucker, 2004).

Recent research has suggested that these subdivisions have a reciprocal relation (Davidson et al., 2000; Davis et al., 2002). Moreover, the functional relation between these two areas of the cortex provides a biological mechanism for the developmental integration of specific types of knowledge and control processes in childhood. The functioning of this biological mechanism may be the source of individual differences in the process of emotion–cognition integration in early development. Such individual differences likely reflect basic genetic, as well as experiential, processes. Both types of process are addressed in the four chapters of this section of the volume.

Martha Ann Bell, Denise Green, and Christy Wolfe (chap. 7) discuss their longitudinal work regarding psychobiological mechanisms of cognition–emotion integration in early development. Using frontal electroencephalogram measures during infancy, early childhood, and middle childhood, they highlight individual differences in the developing relations between a specific aspect of executive functioning (i.e., working memory and inhibitory control) and emotion and attention.

Kirby Deater-Deckard and Paula Mullineaux (chap. 8) discuss several of the predominant theories (e.g., temperament, social cognition) regarding the development of individual differences in emotion expression and regulation and in cognitive skills and performance. They also review evidence from behavioral genetic studies pertaining to the independence of, and connections between, emotion and cognition, and suggest some next steps for more fully integrating genetic studies of these two domains of development.

Mark H. Johnson (chap. 9) shows that infants are born attuned to stimuli that have social importance. In the first part of the chapter, he reviews literature and recent findings suggesting that there are cognitive processes associated with the specialized processing of faces, particularly gaze, in the infant brain. The second part of the chapter focuses on infant processing of another important aspect of the infant's social world: the human body and the actions that it will produce.

Marc D. Lewis (chap. 10) reflects on day-to-day infant behavior during emotion-eliciting situations. Lewis links this behavior to brain motivation systems. In particular, he argues that motivation influences concept formation.

Findings from basic biobehavioral studies and from brain-based research can be combined to provide a framework for studying the integration of emotion and cognition with respect to developmental outcome. Implications of emerging emotion–cognition relations for both mental health and school achievement are discussed in Part III of this volume.

PART III: IMPLICATIONS FOR CLINICAL AND EDUCATIONAL RESEARCH

To date, most of the work that examines developmental predictors of child mental health and school performance has examined very specific emotional or cognitive predictors of particular types of disorders or specific academic skills. For example, in the realm of emotional development, problems characterized by poor or undercontrolled emotion regulation may be broadly related to externalizing behavior problems characterized by aggression (Calkins, Gill, & Williford, 1999). In addition, the overcontrol of emotion may characterize children with anxiety and depression, which are indicators of internalizing spectrum problems (Eisenberg, Smith, Sadovsky, & Spinrad, 2004). Thus, much past research has indicated that patterns of emotion expression and emotion regulation that children acquire early in development influence the nature of their subsequent psychological functioning in important ways (Fox & Calkins, 2003). Similarly, work in cognitive development has focused on predictors of specific types of performance deficits that hinder children's school performance. For example, immature executive functioning is common in children with attention problems (Nigg, Hinshaw, Carte, & Treuting, 1998; Hinshaw, 1994), but executive function deficits have also been linked to conduct problems and learning style differences (Moffitt, 1993, Pennington & Ozonoff, 1996). However, the development of childhood psychopathology and academic performance difficulties may be of greater concern when there are deficits in both emotion and cognition processing. Clearly, then, emerging emotion–cognition relations and possible atypical development have implications for both clinical and education research. Those implications are highlighted in the chapters of this part of the book.

Frederick Morrison, Claire Cameron Ponitz, and Megan M. McClelland (chap. 11) discuss the importance of self-regulation for school success and highlight the origins of variability in the preschool years. They also focus on the measurement of behavioral and cognitive self-regulation, the sources of growth in self-regulation (e.g., family, preschool, school, child gender) and larger sociocultural factors, and the impact of self-regulation on school achievement and adaptation.

Joel Nigg, Michelle M. Martel, Molly Nikolas, and B. J. Casey (chap. 12) highlight the intersection of emotion and cognition in developmental psychopathology by focusing on attention-deficit/hyperactivity disorder (ADHD), impulsivity, and types of externalizing behavior. Specifically, they outline the potential intersecting influences of cognitive and emotional dysregulation in ADHD in children, along with potential mechanism distinctions between types of externalizing behavior based on relatively greater involvement of cognitive versus emotional dysregulatory processes.

To date, the foundational research on emotion–cognition integration has operated within behavioral, psychobiological, or intervention research literatures. The merging of these three research areas is essential for an integrative investigation of emotion and cognition.

The volume concludes with a brief afterword by Martha Ann Bell and Susan D. Calkins that summarizes the promise of the integration of emotion and cognition for future developmental research on basic and neurological processes, as well as implications for applied work and intervention research. We also note some of the conceptual and empirical challenges to such a direction and acknowledge that this kind of work should be approached as a necessary complement to, rather than a replacement for, research addressing emotion and cognition processes independently of one another, as each has a clear contribution to make to an understanding of psychological development.

In summary, the chapters in this volume highlight the foundations of developing relations between emotion and cognition by focusing on basic behavioral processes and on brain mechanisms of emotion and cognition. The focus on both behavior and brain mechanisms of emotion–cognition integration make this volume unique in the developmental literature. Adding to the distinctive content of this volume is the translational research highlighting emotion–cognition impact on mental health and school performance. The contributors to this volume are doing some of the field's most innovative research, and it is our hope that this volume will influence future work in this rapidly evolving area.

REFERENCES

Baumeister, R. F., & Vohs, K. D. (2004). *Handbook of self-regulation: Research, theory, and applications*. New York: Guilford.

Bell, M. A., & Deater-Deckard, K. (2007). Biological systems and the development of self-regulation: Integrating behavior, genetics, and psychophysiology. *Journal of Developmental & Behavioral Pediatrics, 28*, 409–420.

Bell, M. A., & Wolfe, C. D. (2004). Emotion and cognition: An intricately bound developmental process. *Child Development, 75*, 366–370.

Bjorklund, D. F. (1987). How age changes in knowledge base contribute to the development of children's memory: An interpretive review. *Developmental Review, 7,* 93–130.

Blair, C. (2002). School readiness: Integrating cognition and emotion in a neurobiological conceptualization of children's functioning at school entry. *American Psychologist, 57,* 111–127.

Brainerd, C. J. (1977). Cognitive development and concept learning: An interpretative review. Psychological Bulletin, 84, 919-939.

Bransford, J. D., Brown, A. L., & Cocking, R. R. (Eds.). (1999). *How people learn: Brain, mind, experience, and school.* National Research Council, Washington, DC: National Academic Press.

Cacioppo, J. T. & Berntson, G. G. (1999). The affect system: Architecture and operating characteristics. *Current Directions in Psychological Science, 8,* 133–137.

Calkins, S. D. (2007). The emergence of self-regulation: Biological and behavioral control mechanisms supporting toddler competencies. In C. Brownell & C. Kopp (Eds.),*Transitions in early socioemotional development: The toddler years* (pp. 261–284). New York: Guilford.

Calkins, S. D., & Dedmon, S. E. (2000). Physiological and behavioral regulation in two-year-old children with aggressive/destructive behavior problems. *Journal of Abnormal Child Psychology, 28,* 103–118.

Calkins, S. D., & Fox, N. A. (2002). Self-regulatory processes in early personality development: A multilevel approach to the study of childhood social withdrawal and aggression. *Development and Psychopathology, 14,* 477–498.

Calkins, S. D., Gill, K., & Williford, A.P. (1999). Externalizing problems in two-year-olds: Implications for patterns of social behavior and peers' responses to aggression. *Early Education and Development, 10,* 267–288.

Calkins, S. D., Graziano, P. & Keane, S. P. (2007), Cardiac vagal regulation differentiates among behavior problem subtypes. *Biological Psychology, 74.* 144–153.

Cicchetti, D., & Posner, M. I. (2005). Cognitive and affective neuroscience and developmental psychopathology [Editorial]. *Development and Psychopathology, 17,* 569–575.

Cole, P. M., Martin, S. E., & Dennis, T. A. (2004). Emotion regulation as a scientific construct: Methodological challenges and directions for child development research. *Child Development, 75,* 317–333.

Davidson, R. J., Putnam, K. M., & Larson, C. L. (2000, July 28). Dysfunction in the neural circuitry of emotion regulation—a possible prelude to violence. *Science, 289,* 591–594.

Davis, E. P., Bruce, J., & Gunnar, M. R. (2002). The anterior attention network: Associations with temperament and neuroendocrine activity in 6-year-old children. *Developmental Psychobiology, 40,* 43–56.

Eisenberg, N., Smith, C. L., Sadovsky, A., Spinrad, T. L. (2004). Effortful control: Relations with emotion regulation, adjustment, and socialization in childhood. In R. R. Baumeister & K. D. Vohs (Eds.), *Handbook of self-regulation: Research, theory & applications* (pp. 259–282). New York: Guilford.

Eisenberg, N., Fabes, R. A., & Murphy, B. (1995). The relations of shyness and low sociability to regulation and emotionality. *Journal of Personality and Social Psychology, 68,* 505–517.

Fabes, R. A. & Eisenberg, N. (1992). Young children's coping with interpersonal anger. *Child Development, 63,* 116–128.

Fox, N. A., & Calkins, S. D. (2003). The development of self-control of emotion: Intrinsic and extrinsic influences. *Motivation and Emotion, 27,* 7–26.

Gaskins, I. W. (1994). Classroom applications of cognitive science: Teaching poor readers how to learn, think, and problem solve. In K. McGilly (Ed.), *Classroom lessons: Integrating cognitive theory and classroom practice* (pp. 129–154). Cambridge, MA: MIT Press.

Gray, J. R. (2004). Integration of emotion and cognitive control. *Current Directions in Psychological Science, 13,* 46–48.

Griffin, S. A., Case, R., & Siegler, R. S. (1994). Rightstart: Providing the central conceptual prerequisites for first formal learning of arithmetic to students at risk for school failure. In K. McGilly (Ed.), *Classroom lessons: Integrating cognitive theory and classroom practice* (pp. 25–49). Cambridge, MA: MIT Press.

Hinshaw, S. P. (1994). *Attention deficits and hyperactivity in children.* Thousand Oaks, CA: Sage.

Izard, C. E., & Malatesta, C. Z. (1987). Perspectives on emotional development: Differential emotions theory of early emotional development. In J. D. Osofsky (Ed.), *Handbook of infant development* (2nd ed.; pp. 494–554). Oxford, England: Wiley.

Kerr, A., & Zelazo, P. D. (2004). Development of "hot" executive function: The children's gambling task. *Brain and Cognition, 55,* 148–157.

Ladd, G., Birch, S., & Buhs, E. (1999). Children's social and scholastic lives in kindergarten: Related spheres of influence? *Child Development, 70,* 1373–1400.

Lewis, M. D. & Stieben, J. (2004). Emotion regulation in the brain: Conceptual issues and directions for developmental research. *Child Development, 75,* 371–376.

Lane, R. D., & McRae, K. (2004). Neural substrates of conscious emotional experience. In M. Beauregard (Ed.), *Consciousness, emotional self-regulation and the brain* (pp. 87–122). Philadelphia: John Benjamins.

Luu, P. & Tucker, D. M. (2004). Self-regulation by the medial frontal cortex: Limbic representation of motive set-points. In M. Beauregard (Ed.), *Consciousness, emotional self-regulation and the brain* (pp. 123–162). Philadelphia: John Benjamins.

Moffitt, T. E. (1993). Adolescence-limited and life-course-persistent antisocial behavior: A developmental taxonomy. *Psychological Review, 100,* 674–701.

Nigg, J. T., Hinshaw, S. P., Carte, E. T., & Treuting, J. J. (1998). Neuropsychological correlates of childhood attention-deficit/hyperactivity disorder: Explainable by comorbid disruptive behavior or reading problems? *Journal of Abnormal Psychology, 107,* 468–480.

Nigg, J. T., & Huang-Pollock, C. L. (2003). An early-onset model of the role of executive functions and intelligence in conduct disorder/delinquency. In

L. Benjamin, T. Moffitt, & A. Caspi (Eds.), *Causes of conduct disorder and juvenile delinquency* (pp. 227–253). New York: Guilford Press.

Pennington, B. F. & Ozonoff, S. (1996). Executive functions and developmental psychopathology. *Journal of Child Psychology and Psychiatry and Allied Disciplines, 37*, 51–87.

Posner, M. I., & Rothbart, M. K. (1994). Attentional regulation: From mechanism to culture. In P. Bertelson & P. Eelen (Eds.), *International perspectives on psychological science: Vol. 1. Leading themes* (pp. 41–55). Hillsdale, NJ: Erlbaum.

Posner, M. I., & Rothbart, M. K. (2000). Developing mechanisms of self-regulation. *Development and Psychopathology, 12*, 427–441.

Rothbart, M. K. (2004). Temperament and the pursuit of an integrated developmental psychology. *Merrill-Palmer Quarterly, 50*, 492–505.

Rothbart, M. K., Ellis, L. K., Rueda. M. R., & Posner, M. I. (2003). Development mechanisms of temperamental effortful control. *Journal of Personality, 71*, 1113–1143.

Schacter, S., & Singer, J. E. (1962). Cognitive, social, and physiological determinants of emotional state. *Psychological Review, 69*, 379–399.

Stipek, D. J., & Ryan, R. H. (1997). Economically disadvantaged preschoolers: Ready to learn but further to go. *Developmental Psychology, 33*, 711–723.

Zajonc, R. B. (1980). Feeling and thinking: Preferences need no inferences. *American Psychologist, 35*, 151–175.

I

BASIC DEVELOPMENTAL PROCESSES

2

AN OPTIMAL BALANCE: THE INTEGRATION OF EMOTION AND COGNITION IN CONTEXT

CLANCY BLAIR AND TRACY DENNIS

Models of relations between emotion and cognition suggest that the two aspects of experience are closely integrated, sometimes working in unison and at other times working in opposition. Consequently, a richer understanding of both domains of psychological development requires that they be studied simultaneously within context. Unfortunately, much of the research on emotion and cognition tends to focus on one or the other aspect of experience, and relatively few studies have directly examined relations between the constructs developmentally. Furthermore, the research that does examine relations between them has tended to focus on negative emotion, with the implicit and at times explicit assumption that emotion is the nemesis of reason and that appropriate self-regulation emerges from cognitive dominance of emotional reactivity (cf. Bechara & Damasio, 2005; J. R. Gray, 2004). This taming of the raging emotional beast through cool, collected cognition, however, is only one example of relations between emotion and cognition. A more accurate depiction of optimal relations between these general aspects of the self, we believe, is one in which they are balanced and mutually supportive.

FOCUS OF THIS CHAPTER

To illustrate the optimal balance hypothesis, in this chapter we focus on contexts in which development is occurring and apply an organizational approach to specific topics in child development. We are interested in (a) the development of emotional reactivity (generally grouped into broad domains of approach and withdrawal) and the ways in which reactivity is expressed and regulated; (b) the relation of this reactivity and regulation to the development of indicators of cognitive control referred to as *executive functions* (EFs); and (c) the ways in which interrelations between emotional reactivity and EFs can reach or fail to reach an optimal balance (Blair, 2002; Dennis, 2006).

Approach and Withdrawal Motivation

We take as our starting point the idea that emotions by definition are rooted in neural affective signaling systems that are both consciously and nonconsciously represented. Emotional responses rapidly signal potential harm or benefit in relation to well-being and thus serve to prioritize certain cognitions and actions. The general motivating function of emotion has historically been classified into the two broad categories of approach and withdrawal motivation (Schneirla, 1957). Experiences that evoke specific emotions (e.g., disgust, fear) activate components of physiological and motor systems that promote withdrawal, referred to as the *behavioral inhibition system* (BIS); those that occasion other emotions (e.g., joy, interest) result in the activation of physiological and motor systems that promote approach, referred to as the *behavioral activation system* (BAS; Carver & White, 1994; J. A. Gray, 1987).

An important focus for psychological research concerns the assessment of approach and withdrawal tendencies (sensitivity to appetitive or aversive stimulation) distinct from personality and felt emotion, and the relation of these tendencies to specific neural circuitry and behaviors (Carver & Scheier, 1998; Sutton & Davidson, 1997). In this research, a key point is that emotions and associated approach–withdrawal action tendencies occur automatically, prior to or outside of conscious awareness (Bargh & Chartrand, 1999), but are also the product of perceptual and cognitive appraisals that are under conscious control (Ochsner & Gross, 2005). Here, the give give-and and-take between bottom-up emotion eliciting approach–withdrawal tendencies and top-down executive cognitive control capacities reflects the hierarchical and integrated nature of brain structure and function. A relatively rapid and automatic information processing stream, composed of medial and orbital structures of prefrontal cortex (PFC) and limbic and brainstem structures associated with autonomic arousal and the stress response, provides the neural substrate for approach-withdrawal and the generation and interpretation of emotional responses to stimulation (Barbas, 1995; Critchley, 2005). An important aspect of vertebrate neural evolution, however, has been the development of frontal cortical networks that allow for internally controlled regulation of automatic and reflexive responses to aversive and appetitive stimuli (Luu, Tucker, & Derryberry, 1998). This internal mediation manages arousal within acceptable levels and makes use of information in the limbic networks to promote attention and memory in order to anticipate experience and to plan actions and responses (Barbas, 2000; Dolan, 2002).

In the primate brain, a key structure in the give-and-take between emotional and cognitive information processing is the anterior cingulate cortex (ACC; Allman, Hakeem, Erwin, Nimchimsky, & Hof, 2001). Anatomically this area is a transitional one that is active in response to tasks that make high demands on the control of attention due to the presence of conflicting information and the detection of errors, which are more likely to occur in the course of tasks with high conflict and to be associated with heightened anxiety and vigilance. Thus, the ACC can be considered as an intermediary between emotional arousal and higher order executive cognition (Paus, 2001).

In its role as an intermediary, the ACC can be understood to function cybernetically to establish homeostatic set points for reciprocal activity between emotional reactive and cognitive control areas of the brain (Luu & Tucker, 2004; Pribram, 1960). These set points are understood to be flexibly altered over time in response to experience through a process of biased homeostasis, or *allostasis* (for a general description of allostasis, see McEwen, 2000,). The resulting reactive or regulatory behaviors then reflect both internal as well as external constraints and incorporate learning, adaptation, and anticipation of future contingencies and goals.

Relations Between Emotion and Cognition

From the perspective of allostasis, affective states modify set points at which higher order cognition is called upon. The notion of optimal balance therefore provides for facilitating emotion as well as inhibiting cognitive control. Evidence in support of this point at the behavioral and neural levels in adults indicates specificity in relations between emotional arousal and cognitive control. In the examination of the relation of emotional arousal to performance on a quintessential EF task, the generic n-back (which requires the individual to maintain information in working memory and to execute a rule-based response in the face of distracting information), task performance was preferentially influenced by emotional state. Positive emotion-facilitated performance was observed when the information to be held in mind was verbal (i.e., words), but impaired performance was observed when the information to be maintained in working memory was nonverbal (i.e., faces). The opposite pattern was obtained when negative emotion was induced. Fear arousal was associated with enhanced nonverbal performance but impaired verbal performance (J. R. Gray, Braver, & Raichle, 2002). These differences in performance were mirrored in differences in levels of brain activity observed using functional magnetic resonance imaging, with increased activation in left dorsal lateral PFC associated with positive emotional enhancement of verbal working memory and increased activation in right dorsal lateral PFC associated with negative emotional enhancement of nonverbal working memory for faces.

In children, the balance between cognition and emotion has been examined in a number of ways. One way has been through the examination of approach–withdrawal tendencies. Specifically, children with increased sensitivity to aversive stimulation (i.e., high BIS) have been shown to exhibit higher concurrent levels of cognitive control and executive attention (Blair, Peters, & Granger, 2004; Dennis & Chen, 2007a). The point here is that at resting levels of arousal, children with a higher level of withdrawal sensitivity may be more likely to exhibit cognitive control on relatively mundane tasks because of a homeostatic set point for arousal that facilitates the utilization of cognitive control abilities in a resting state. It is necessary, however, to consider both development and the intensity of emotional arousal. Developmentally, heterotypic continuity in early childhood is seen in a positive correlation between high temperamental approach in infancy (referred to as *surgency*) and the aspect of temperamental self-regulation referred to as *effortful control*. In contrast, however, high surgency in the toddler period (24 months of age) is negatively correlated with effortful control in early childhood (Putnam, Rothbart, & Gartstein, 2008). Furthermore, in terms of the intensity of arousal, relations between high relative BIS and EF task performance are consistent with a quadratic, inverse U relation between arousal and performance as outlined by Yerkes and Dodson (1908). In this relation, high levels of arousal impair performance on complex tasks, such as EF tasks, whereas, at intermediate levels of arousal, performance on complex tasks reaches optimal levels. In contrast to performance on complex tasks, however, performance on simple reaction time and attention focusing tasks is positively linearly related to arousal (Diamond, Campbell, Park, Halonen, & Zoladz, 2007). Consideration of relations between EFs and arousal from the perspective of Yerkes and Dodson is consistent with the idea of an allostatic motivational set point (Luu & Tucker, 2004) through which rapid and automatic emotional reactions to experience either call on and engage processes of executive cognitive control or shut them down in favor of more automatized and reactive aspects of cognition and behavior.

From the perspective of emotion–cognition balance, it is also necessary to consider the extent to which the association between approach and withdrawal tendencies, as indicators of arousal, and cognitive control may depend on the type of control capacity being considered (Dennis, 2006). For example, in a study of typically developing preschoolers, increased inhibitory control predicted greater compliance in children low in approach but no changes in compliance in children high in approach. In contrast, increased affective soothability predicted greater compliance but reduced persistence in children high in approach. This would seem to indicate that for children with higher BAS, the ability to down-regulate emotion is associated with greater behavior regulation but with a negative consequence of decreased engagement.

Similarly, the notion of optimal balance between emotion and cognition suggests that for children high in behavioral inhibition, EFs could lead to overregulation, reduced attentional flexibility, and increased inhibition leading to internalizing types of behavior problems and decreased persistence (e.g., Murray & Kochanska, 2002). For example, in a study of children at risk of emotional and conduct problems, temperamental effortful control was related to a lower level of internalizing problems at age 4 but to no change or even slight increases in internalizing problems at age 6 (Dennis, Brotman, Huang, & Gouley, 2007).

The literature on anxiety and attention provides a further example of characteristic relations between emotion and cognition, particularly in terms of the imbalance that can result from increases in the level of anxious arousal. Many studies have documented the disruptive influence of clinical or elevated anxiety on attentional flexibility and other aspects of cognition such as EFs (Compton, 2003) and have shown that anxiety narrows attentional focus and biases attention toward threat and fear-related stimuli (Bishop, Duncan, Brett, & Lawrence, 2004). Elevated anxiety increases the negative impact of threat-related emotional stimuli on EFs (Jazbec, McClure, Hardin, Pine, & Ernst, 2005), as seen in conflict interference tasks (Fenske & Eastwood, 2003). As well, EF deficits are observed in introverts relative to extroverts but only in a multitasking context in which arousal interferes with performance (Lieberman & Rosenthal, 2001). Similarly, neural responses related to cognitive control also indicate relations between arousal and performance. The error-related negativity (ERN) and the anterior N2 are event-related brain potentials reflecting error and conflict monitoring functions of the ACC. These neural responses are enhanced among individuals showing trait and clinical levels of anxiety (Hajcak, McDonald, & Simons, 2003). In many cases, these enhanced ERP responses are correlated with reduced attention performance (Dennis & Chen, 2007a) but may, in other cases, bolster attentional focus and enhance cognitive performance when levels of arousal are within a normative range (Dennis & Chen, 2007b; Ladouceur et al., 2006).

DEVELOPMENT OF EMOTION–COGNITION INTEGRATION AND BALANCE IN CHILDREN

Like the clinical and neuroimaging research literatures, developmental research indicates that emotion and cognition frequently work together to activate specific brain systems and behaviors that provide for adaptive responses to experience. For the study of child development, an important question concerns how systems contributing to emotional arousal and to cognitive control develop in tandem. How does a child arrive at a given set point or allostatic relation between emotional arousal and cognitive control? Of pressing interest are the ways in which the development of the emotion–cognition balance influences adaptive behavior in various contexts, particularly under conditions of early psychosocial disadvantage.

A central emphasis in the developmental approach to emotion–cognition interaction is on context as a constituent influence on individual development (Magnusson & Cairns, 1996). Consideration of context and the timing of experience help to determine the ways in which emotional arousal and cognitive control combine to produce specific behavioral and psychological outcomes. The most influential and encompassing context for children is that of early caregiving. Research on the development of emotional arousal and cognitive control in the context of the parent–child relationship is a mainstay of the child study literature. The influence of the behavior of primary caregivers, usually mothers, on multiple aspects of emotional arousal and regulation has been extensively studied (Calkins, 2004; Calkins, Smith, Gill, & Johnson, 1998). As this research indicates, one primary way in which early disadvantage affects child development is through disruption of the parent–child relationship, with attendant consequences for socioemotional development (McLoyd, 1990).

Caregivers and teachers in preschool and early school contexts are a second source of meaningful relationships in children's lives. Again, it may be that one aspect of the relation of early psychosocial disadvantage to poor academic outcomes for children is that children from low-SES homes have difficulty regulating emotion within school environments. Problems with emotion regulation and with relationships with teachers and peers are associated with learning delays and poor academic achievement (Mashburn & Pianta, 2006). One important goal in the promotion of academic achievement for children facing early disadvantage is to further understand the practical implications of emerging emotion–cognition balance within the specific contexts of classrooms and schools.

Readiness for School

In the promotion of academic achievement, children's readiness for school is a topic of ongoing concern to parents, educators, and social policymakers. The number of children perceived by their teachers to be unready for kindergarten is substantial. At the turn of the 20th century, approximately one half to one quarter of a nationally representative sample of kindergarten teachers stated that more than one half of the students in their classes were exhibiting problems with self-regulation indicative of poor school readiness (Rimm-Kaufman, Pianta, & Cox, 2001).

In many ways the task of adjustment to and success in early school environments can be characterized in terms of emotion–cognition balance (Blair, 2002). That is, to meet the expectations of early schooling, children must exhibit an appropriate level of emotional and motivational arousal that facilitates rather than impedes the application of EFs to tasks important for learning and for the development of a sense of self as one who does well both academically and socially at school. The age at which children begin formal schooling, age 6 on average, is one at which children are expected to begin to strike an effective balance between cognition and emotion and to manage emotion and arousal appropriately to function effectively within that environment (Raver, 2002). To manage the expectations of the classroom, children need to be able to appropriately increase and decrease emotional arousal, to accurately interpret social-emotional cues and signals, and to focus and sustain attention even in the face of emotional challenges. As a result, children begin to develop positive and meaningful interactions with teachers and classmates. The context of schooling requires this, and of course schools, classrooms, and teachers vary in the extent to which they provide conditions that facilitate such a process for children.

A developmental model of influences on school adaptation from the perspective of emotion–cognition balance is outlined in Figure 2.1. In the figure, context is defined by expectations for levels of children's psychological and behavioral development before and during the early school years, particularly as seen in the teacher–child relationship and levels of instructional support, both of which are important determinants of children's successful adaptation to school (Hamre & Pianta, 2005). As shown in the figure, however, individual child differences in set points for emotional reactivity and cognitive control combine with contextual factors to determine adjustment to school. Children's self-regulation abilities and agency in school both determine and are determined by the underlying emotion–cognition balance and by context, as defined by the quality of relationships with teachers and peers. What constitutes an appropriate or optimal regulatory balance between emotion and cognition varies among children and is assumed to be determined as much by context as by biology. The biological level of the model, including genetic, neural, and physiological influences, can be considered as representing an endophenotype (Gottesman & Gould, 2003) relevant to successful adaptation to school environments. That is, it provides for preliminary tendencies that may increase the probability of behaviors that are adaptive or consistent with the demands of the specific context of school. The extent to which the underlying endophenotype is associated with behaviors relevant to regulation and developing agency and school adaptation is dependent upon the environment of school and the degree to which it supports or thwarts adaptive behaviors.

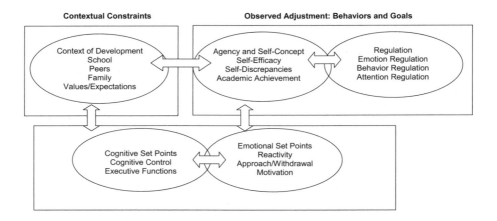

Contextual Constraints

Observed Adjustment: Behaviors and Goals

Context of Development
School
Peers
Family
Values/Expectations

Agency and Self-Concept
Self-Efficacy
Self-Discrepancies
Academic Achievement

Regulation
Emotion Regulation
Behavior Regulation
Attention Regulation

Cognitive Set Points
Cognitive Control
Executive Functions

Emotional Set Points
Reactivity
Approach/Withdrawal
Motivation

Figure 2.1. Genetic and endophenotypic constraint.

In research on school readiness, assessment of child approach–withdrawal sensitivity at the level of the emotional set point as outlined in the model, using parent-report on the Behavioral Inhibition System/Behavioral Activation System (BIS/BAS) scales (Carver & White, 1994), indicated as expected that BIS/BAS sensitivity was related to physiological arousal associated with limbic and autonomic reactivity to mild stress (Blair, 2003; Blair, Peters, & Granger, 2004). Specifically, relatively higher BIS, indicating increased withdrawal sensitivity, was associated with increased autonomic arousal, as assessed by cardiac vagal tone, an indicator of the influence of the parasympathetic branch of the autonomic nervous system on the heart, and also with increased salivary cortisol, an indicator of the reactivity of the limbic hypothalamic–pituitary–adrenal (HPA) axis stress response system.

Furthermore, BIS and, most important, HPA reactivity as indicated by salivary cortisol were both positively correlated with teacher report of social competence and behavior regulation in the classroom and also with cognitive control abilities as indicated by measures of EF (Blair, Granger, & Razza, 2005). Relations of BIS and HPA reactivity with EFs are of particular interest given the close association of these aspects of cognition with the control of behavior and with the coordination of PFC cortical networks (Wolfe & Bell, 2007). In particular, EF is closely associated with PFC, and both EF and PFC undergo rapid development in the preschool period (Diamond, 2002; Zelazo, Muller, Frye, & Marcovitch, 2003).

Also, consistent with the focus on self-regulation in the process of early schooling, measures of EF were better predictors of early learning outcomes in children than were measures of general cognitive ability. Specifically, for both mathematics and early reading ability, associations with EF were present over and above those for measures of general intelligence (Blair & Razza, 2007). Of course, the measures of EF were moderately correlated with these general cognitive ability measures, but it was EF specifically, rather than cognitive ability generally, that was most indicative of how children were doing in math and reading at the end of the kindergarten year.

With respect to Figure 2.1, these findings are consistent with a process in which systems associated with emotional arousal and cognitive control are working in a balanced, integrated, and organized fashion to promote behaviors associated with school readiness. Aspects of emotional and cognitive well-being are positively related to teachers' perceptions of children's behavior and to observed indicators of academic ability. As such, they have important implications for early education policy. Ostensibly, schooling is about the acquisition of knowledge, of learning the alphabet, the times tables, and other essential pieces of information. In the rush to characterize and evaluate the efficacy of early schooling, however, a focus on knowledge acquisition, including learning how to read, without a concomitant and perhaps superordinate emphasis on the processes through which children acquire knowledge, is inappropriate. A focus on early schooling as the process through which children "learn how to learn" helps to reorient the emphasis from one of knowledge acquisition to one of self-regulation and emotion–cognition balance, of the motivated ability to recognize and organize important pieces of information and to engage interpersonally with teachers and others in the process of acquiring skills and knowledge.

Overall, developmental study of school readiness helps to highlight the dynamic relation between emotion and cognition. When the PFC corticolimbic system is functioning at an optimal level, it promotes motivation and engagement that support cognitive control, engagement, and early learning. Such motivation and engagement then foster a developing sense of purpose and efficacy in school-related endeavors that in turn promotes learning and increased ability to regulate emotion and cognition in the service of academic learning. In contrast, factors that interfere with integrated PFC corticolimbic functioning, whether constitutional or environmental, disrupt the emotion-cognition balance, with resulting difficulties in learning and behavior.

Emotion–Cognition Balance in Developmental Disability

The context of developmental delay provides a useful further illustration of emotion–cognition balance and integration in context. Deficits in social competence indicative of problems with emotional reactivity and arousal, as defined by behavioral expectations for healthy mental development versus early developing psychopathology, as well as deficits in mental development, particularly in the instance of idiopathic mental retardation, indicate that neither cognition nor emotion is preeminent in development. When one domain of functioning is impaired, the other will be affected, and processes of compensation are needed. For example, an individual can have extensive cognitive control, but without emotional processes intact, proper engagement with and interpretation of the environment are compromised. Processes of compensation and contextual support, however, can allow for the imbalance to be remediated to some extent as a means of optimizing cognitive and social functioning. We illustrate this point by considering the ways in which delays in social interaction and in mental development impact and are impacted by the developing balance between cognition and emotion.

An important forerunner of the work on emotion–cognition integration described in this chapter is found in research on the quality of life and adaptive functioning in individuals for whom mental development is delayed. Whether in individuals with idiopathic mental retardation (MR) occurring in the absence of any established pathology or in individuals with established disability, as in Down syndrome (DS), research on the development of personality and emotion–cognition integration, independent of overall level of general intellectual functioning, provides unique insight. In particular, the application of the developmental science approach to the study of behavior in individuals with MR and DS (Bennett-Gates & Zigler, 1999) provides an important example of the idea that investigation of any one domain of functioning in the absence of others leads to an inaccurate view of development. For that reason, any instance of developmental delay in an aspect of either cognition or emotion broadens understanding not only of developmental disability but also of typical development.

In foundational research on the development of children with DS, Cicchetti and colleagues explored relations between emotional and cognitive development and found that the level of emotional development parallels that of cognitive development (Cicchetti & Schneider-Rosen, 1984). For example, research on smiling and laughter in infants with DS indicated that children who exhibited lower levels of developmentally appropriate laughter also showed exhibited information processing deficits and hypotonia (Cicchetti & Sroufe, 1976). Earlier and more prolonged laughter in response to relatively complex social and visual items was associated with a higher level of cognitive development, and earlier laughter (prior to 10 months of age) was associated with a higher level of mental development at the age of 2 years. Remarkably, early laughter was a better predictor of later cognitive development than was early cognitive development. Rapidly processing incongruity, along with sufficient emotional arousal and neuromuscular capacity, is a necessary component for laughter. In the case of infants with DS, therefore, the balance between emotion and cognition in relation to socially appropriate emotional communication (smiling and laughter) would appear to rely equally on cognitive and affective factors.

The results of studying the relations between emotional and cognitive development in young children with DS suggest a further point relevant to early development: Increases in cognition and emotion provide for increases in the type and quality of interaction with others that in turn provide for further cognitive advances. Research supporting this point makes clear, however, that early cognitive impairments can interfere with processes of emotional development and negatively impact early relations with caregivers. Disrupted early care relations can then lead to delays in the development of the autonomous self and in the shift to internal sources of emotional and behavioral regulation; a further result could be an increased reliance on external support from caregivers. As a consequence of disorganized relations between early cognitive and emotional development, children with DS are more likely to experience delays in the development of internal state language and experience deficits in self–other differentiation and theory of mind. Targeted interventions to enhance aspects of caregiving designed to promote the transition from external to internal support can perhaps reduce negative sequelae of emotion–cognition imbalance.

Similar to the study of the development of affect in DS, the motivational approach to the study of MR (Zigler, 1969) and the characterization of MR as a disorder of self-regulation (Whitman, 1990) provide further instances of the intertwined nature of cognitive and emotional development. Zigler and coworkers' (e.g., Bybee & Zigler 1998; Zigler & Hodapp, 1986) research on personality development in MR yielded an invaluable example of the ways in which development in the cognitive domain and development in the emotional domain are mutually reinforcing. Focusing on the individual with MR as a whole person, not only a person with delayed mental development, Zigler (1999) described the motivational deficit that the individual with MR is likely to experience through repeated failure on cognitive tasks. This experience of repeated failure is then thought to accentuate specific personality characteristics of dependence on or withdrawal from others and to lead to a lowered expectancy of success (Bybee & Zigler, 1998). In Zigler's theory, constructs such as *outerdirectedness*, a tendency to become overly reliant on external information to guide behavior, and *positive and negative reaction tendencies*, that is, to react either very positively or very negatively to interactions with others, are central to a model in which performance on cognitive tasks is understood to reflect a combination of atypical motivation tendencies as well as deficits in intellectual abilities. As originally proposed by Zigler (1969), these personality characteristics of children with MR result at least partially from social deprivation, particularly in the instance of institutional rearing. Individuals who exhibit outerdirectedness imitate the answers of others, even in the instance of knowing a given answer to be incorrect, rather than independently generate possible unique solutions. Similarly, positive and negative reaction tendencies describe temperamental inclinations in individuals with MR relating to an overdependence on others or to a general wariness of others that impede the development of self-efficacy and intrinsic motivation (Hodapp, Burack, & Zigler, 1990).

The characterization of MR in terms of self-regulation emphasizes the role that problems with the regulation of emotion may play in the etiology of

MR as opposed to viewing problems with emotional development in individuals with MR only as sequelae of intellectual deficits (Whitman, 1990). For example, it is well established that children with idiopathic MR exhibit a level of intellectual functioning across a range of cognitive abilities that is expected at a given developmental age and that the developmental progression of cognitive abilities is essentially the same as that in typically developing individuals, albeit at a slower rate (Bennett-Gates & Zigler, 1999). This developmental perspective is distinct from a difference perspective, in which cognitive deficits in persons with MR are hypothesized to result from a core cognitive deficit that is present in persons with MR but not in typically developing individuals. Although this "development versus difference" debate in the MR literature has been definitively settled in favor of the developmental perspective, it is interesting to note that executive cognitive functions constitute the one area of cognitive ability in which there is some evidence for levels of performance in persons with MR below that expected for mental age. Given that EFs are perhaps unique indicators of emotion–cognition integration and balance, these cognitive deficits are consistent with a motivational and self-regulatory approach to MR and likely represent an important individual differences factor that may relate to quality of life and adaptive behavior in persons with MR (Blair & Patrick, 2007).

Mood and Behavioral Problems

As with the study of emotion–cognition relations in DS and MR, problems with mood and anxiety may be characterized by unique *characteristic imbalances* in emotion–cognition integration. In contrast to DS and MR, cognition in developing psychopathology is relatively intact, but the presence of increased negative emotional arousal may cause changes in cognition, which in part may be a compensatory response to problems with the regulation of emotional arousal. There is a small but growing body of research demonstrating processes of cognitive compensation for disordered emotional reactivity. For example, in one study (Ladouceur et al., 2006), children ages 8 and 16 years of age completed an emotional Go/NoGo task in which they were presented with specific facial expressions (angry, fearful, sad, happy, neutral) indicating the need to respond (Go trials) or not respond (NoGo trials). Children showing depression had significantly faster reaction times to sad face Go trials, whereas anxious children had significantly slower reaction times to neutral face Go trials. These results suggest that emotional processing influences performance on a cognitive control task and that this performance varies with mood problems. Further research has shown low positive emotionality to interact with cognitive capacities in the development of risk of depression (Hayden, Klein, Durbin, & Olino, 2006). For example, children showing low positive emotionality at age 3, a potential risk factor for depression, showed greater helplessness and decreased positive information processing biases. These results suggest that some aspect of cognitive vulnerability to depression may be related to early differences in positive emotionality.

In several recent electrophysiological studies of emotion–attention interactions in children, associations between emotional processing and cognitive performance differed between children showing externalizing and internalizing behavior problems (Lewis, Lamm, Segalowitz, Stieben, & Zelazo, 2006; Stieben et al., 2007). In school-age children showing predominantly externalizing (aggressive) symptoms versus both externalizing and internalizing (mood) symptoms, cognitive control performance in a mood induction context resulted in larger ERN responses, reflecting greater recruitment of cognitive control resources. In contrast, in the non-mood induction context alone, nondisordered children showed increased ERN compared with externalizing children. These findings suggest that in contexts requiring mood regulation, cortical activity is enhanced in children showing mood and behavioral symptoms and that children with externalizing problems may require negative emotion to recruit typical and adaptive levels of prefrontal activity, especially following errors. Consistent with this, in subsequent source analyses on the ERN response, typically developing children showed neural sources in the region of the dorsal ACC, whereas externalizing children showed little frontal activity and instead showed neural source waveforms in the area of the PCC. Children showing both internalizing and externalizing symptoms showed a similar posterior source but also showed sources in the right orbital frontal cortex and right ventral ACC. It is important to note that these source analysis results suggest problem-specific patterns of emotion–cognition integration and neural mechanisms of emotion regulation.

These suggestive early findings in this field of research point to the need for future studies examining the degree to which affective tendencies and cognitive control together influence the specific strategies children use to regulate emotions. For example, it may be that children with specific temperament characteristics, such as enhanced BAS, tend to use discrepancy-reducing strategies such as problem solving in approach contexts (e.g., when trying to obtain a reward or desired goal). If the goal is unobtainable, these strategies may prove inadequate, and individuals may instead regulate by disengaging from tasks and redirecting toward a new activity (Carver, 2004). In children with high enough cognitive control to "put the brakes" on the approach drive, blocked goals might create a specific susceptibility to giving up rather than tolerating frustrations and disappointments. On the other hand, if children with high approach have relatively low control, they may use more disruptive regulatory strategies such as opposition and venting and may evidence frustration rigidly across multiple contexts (stable and context inappropriate). These patterns are associated with susceptibility to impulsivity and externalizing problems (Cole, Michel, & Teti, 1994).

In contrast, children with greater BIS may tend to use discrepancy-enlarging strategies in avoidance contexts, such as withdrawal from threatening or undesired outcomes. If these strategies are inadequate, individuals may instead avoid their negative emotions through strategies such as self-soothing and distraction, particularly if they have higher levels of cognitive control. Yet, high levels of control may exacerbate behavioral inhibition associated with avoidance and lead to problems of overcontrol of emotion and social inhibition. If highly avoidant children have poor control, they may instead become agitated and use more extreme avoidant regulatory strategies, such as physical avoidance, freezing, and withdrawal, and do so rigidly across contexts, even those posing little threat (Buss, Davidson, Kalin, & Goldsmith, 2004). If such avoidant strategies are used chronically, it may put children at risk of problems with anxious arousal (Heller & Nitschke, 1997). These hypotheses have only rarely been tested in relation to emotion regulation (Dennis, 2006), although they have been applied to the study of other processes, such as effortful control, conscience, and social skills (Fowles & Kochanska, 2000).

CONCLUSIONS

In this chapter, we have reviewed research and theory focusing on emotion–cognition balance and integration in development. Whereas there has been a tendency in work on emotion–cognition relations to view the domains of functioning as reciprocal, largely emphasizing the disorganizing influence of emotion and the organizing role of cognitive control, the optimal balance view considers how both cognitive control and emotional reactivity constrain and organize regulatory behavior and how context must be considered when describing what constitutes appropriate self-regulation. In this way, the term *emotion–cognition balance* not only refers to the processes by which cognition "controls" emotions, or emotions "control" cognitions but also reflects how feedback-driven interactions solve the fundamental challenge of effectively adapting to and shaping environments.

Several bodies of research and theoretical perspectives have informed this chapter, including temperament theory (Posner & Rothbart, 2000) and control theory (Carver, 2004). In the future, it may be that neurophysiological measurement of responses related to the activity of neural areas central to cognition–emotion integration, such as cingulate cortex and limbic and dorsal prefrontal information processing streams, can greatly enhance researchers' ability to examine these processes at an extremely rapid temporal resolution. In addition, research examining both fast and slow stress response systems, including the HPA axis, will continue to provide a neurobiological view on the give-and-take between emotion and cognition and the ways in which the two achieve patterns of balance or imbalance in relation to developmental processes of both short- and long-term adjustment and adaptation. In particular, we propose that considering the notion of an optimal balance, rather than limiting views to reciprocal relations between emotion and cognition, can expand understanding of how individual differences and developmental contexts work together in the development of psychopathology as well as positive adjustment. The optimal balance approach has the potential to refine the application of cognitive and affective neuroscience to theories of development and in turn to direct future hypotheses in neuroscientific investigations. By emphasizing the notion of integration and allostasis rather than control of one domain over the other, the tenets of organizational and organismic perspectives on the study of development can be realized.

REFERENCES

Allman, J. M., Hakeem, A, Erwin, J. M., Nimchimsky, E., & Hof, P. (2001). The anterior cingulate: The evolution of an interface between emotion and cognition. In A. R. Damasio, A. Harrington, J. Kagan, B. McEwen, H. Moss, & R. Shaikh (Eds.), *Annals of the New York Academy of Sciences: Vol. 935. Unity of knowledge: The convergence of natural and human science* (pp. 107–117). New York: New York Academy of Sciences.

Barbas, H. (1995). Anatomic basis of cognitive-emotional interactions in the primate prefrontal cortex. *Neuroscience and Biobehavioral Reviews, 19,* 499–510.

Barbas, H. (2000). Connections underlying the synthesis of cognition, memory, and emotion in primate prefrontal cortices. *Brain Research Bulletin, 52,* 319–330.

Bargh, J. A., & Chartrand, T. L. (1999). The unbearable automaticity of being. *American Psychologist, 54,* 462–479.

Bechara, A., & Damasio, A. R. (2005). The somatic marker hypothesis: A neural theory of economic decision. *Games and Economic Behavior, 52,* 336–372.

Bennett-Gates, D. & Zigler, E. (1999). Motivation for social reinforcement: Positive- and negative-reaction tendencies. In D. Bennett-Gates & E. Zigler (Eds.), *Personality development in individuals with mental retardation* (pp. 107–129). Cambridge, England: Cambridge University Press.

Bishop, S., Duncan, J., Brett, M., & Lawrence, A. D. (2004). Prefrontal cortical function and anxiety: Controlling attention to threat-related stimuli. *Nature Neuroscience, 7,* 184–188.

Blair, C. (2002). School readiness. *American Psychologist, 57,* 111–127.

Blair, C. (2003). Behavioral inhibition and behavioral activation in young children: Relations with self-regulation and adaptation to preschool in children attending Head Start. *Developmental Psychobiology, 42,* 301–311.

Blair, C., Granger, D., & Razza, R. P. (2005). Cortisol reactivity is positively related to executive function in preschool children attending Head Start. *Child Development, 76,* 554–567.

Blair, C., & Patrick, M. (2006). Fluid cognitive ability: A neglected aspect of cognition in research on mental retardation. *International Review of Research on Mental Retardation, 32,* 131–158.

Blair, C., Peters, R., & Granger, D. (2004). Physiological and neuropsychological correlates of approach/withdrawal behavior in preschool. *Developmental Psychobiology, 45,* 113–124.

Blair, C., & Razza, R. P. (2007). Relating effortful control, executive function, and false-belief understanding to emerging math and literacy ability in kindergarten. *Child Development, 78,* 647–663.

Buss, K. A., Davidson, R. J., Kalin, N. H., & Goldsmith, H. H. (2004). Context-specific freezing and associated physiological reactivity as a dysregulated fear response. *Developmental Psychology, 40,* 583–594.

Bybee J., & Zigler, E. (1998). Outerdirectedness in individuals with and without mental retardation: A review. In R. Hodapp & J. Burack (Eds.), *Handbook of mental retardation and development* (pp. 434–461). Cambridge, England: Cambridge University Press.

Calkins, S. (2004). Early attachment processes and the development of emotional self-regulation. In R. Baumeister & K. Vohs (Eds.), *Handbook of self-regulation: Research, theory, and applications* (pp. 324–339). New York: Guilford Press.

Calkins, S., Smith, C. Gill, K., & Johnson, M. (1998). Maternal interactive style across contexts: Relations to emotional, behavioral, and physiological regulation during toddlerhood. *Social Development, 7,* 350–369.

Carver, C. S. (2004). Negative affects deriving from behavioral approach. *Emotion, 4,* 3–22.

Carver, C., & Scheier, M. (1998). *On the self-regulation of behavior.* Cambridge, England: Cambridge University Press.

Carver, C. S., & White, T. L. (1994). Behavioral inhibition, behavioral activation, and affective responses to reward and punishment: The BIS/BAS scales. *Journal of Personality and Social Psychology, 67,* 319–333.

Cicchetti, D. & Schneider-Rosen, K. (1984). Theoretical and empirical considerations in the investigation of the relationship between affect and cognition in atypical populations of infants. In C. Izard, J. Kagan, & R. Zajonc (Eds.), *Emotions, cognition, and behavior* (pp. 366–406). Cambridge, England: Cambridge University Press.

Cicchetti, D., & Sroufe, L. A. (1976). The relationship between affective and cognitive development in Down's syndrome infants. *Child Development, 47,* 920–929.

Cole, P. M., Michel, M. K., & Teti, L. O. (1994). The development of emotion regulation and dysregulation: A clinical perspective. In N. A. Fox (Ed.), The development of emotion regulation: Biological and behavioral considerations. *Monographs of the Society for Research in Child Development, 59*(2–3, Serial No. 240), 273–100.

Compton, R. (2003). The interface between emotion and attention: A review of evidence. *Behavioral and Cognitive Neuroscience Reviews, 2,* 115–129.

Critchley, H. (2005). Neural mechanisms of autonomic, affective, and cognitive integration. *Journal of Comparative Neurology, 493*, 154–166.

Dennis, T. (2006). Emotional self-regulation in preschoolers: The interplay of child approach reactivity, parenting, and control capacities. *Developmental Psychology, 42*, 84–97.

Dennis, T. A., Brotman, L. M., Huang, K., & Gouley, K. K. (2007). Effortful control, social competence, and adjustment problems in children at risk for psychopathology. *Journal of Clinical Child and Adolescent Psychology, 36*, 442–454.

Dennis, T. A., Chen, C. C. (2007a) Emotional face processing and attention performance in three domains: Neurophysiological mechanisms and moderating effects of trait anxiety. *International Journal of Psychophysiology, 65*, 10–19.

Dennis, T.A., Chen, C. C. (2007b). Neurophysiological mechanisms in the emotional modulation of attention :The interplay between threat sensitivity and attentional control. *Biological Psychology, 76*, 1–10.

Derryberry, D., & Rothbart, M. K. (1997). Reactive and effortful processes in the organization of temperament. *Development and Psychopathology, 9*, 633–652.

Diamond, A. (2002). Normal development of the prefrontal cortex from birth to young adulthood: Cognitive functions, anatomy, and biochemistry. In D. T. Stuss & R. T. Knight (Eds.), *Principles of frontal lobe function* (pp. 466–503). New York: Oxford University Press.

Diamond, D. M., Campbell, A. M., Park, C. R., Halonen, J., & Zoladz, P. R. (2007). The temporal dynamics model of emotional memory processing: A synthesis on the neurobiological basis of stress-induced amnesia, flashbulb and traumatic memories, and the Yerkes-Dodson law. *Neural Plasticity*. Article 60803. Available at http://www.hindawi.com/journals/np/

Dolan, R. J., (2002, November 8). Emotion, cognition, and behavior. *Science, 298*, 1191–1194.

Fenske, M. J. & Eastwood, J. D. (2003). Modulation of focused attention by faces expressing emotion: Evidence from flanker tasks. *Emotion, 3*, 327–343.

Fowles, D. C., & Kochanska, G. (2000). Temperament as a moderator of pathways to conscience in children: The contribution of electrodermal activity. *Psychophysiology, 37*, 788–795.

Gottesman, I. & Gould, T. (2003). The endophenotype concept in psychiatry: Etymology and strategic intentions. *American Journal of Psychiatry, 160*, 636–645.

Gray, J. A. (1987). *The psychology of fear and stress*. Cambridge, England: Cambridge University Press.

Gray, J. R. (2004). Integration of emotion and cognitive control. *Current Directions in Psychological Science, 13*, 46–48.

Gray, J. R., Braver, T. S., & Raichle, M. E. (2002). Integration of emotion and cognition in the lateral prefrontal cortex. *Proceedings of the National Academy of Sciences USA, 99*, 4115–4120.

Hajcak, G., McDonald, N., & Simons, R. F. (2003). Anxiety and error-related brain activity. *Biological Psychology, 64*, 77–90.

Hamre, B., & Pianta, R. (2005). Can instructional and emotional support in the first-grade classroom make a difference for children at risk of school failure? *Child Development, 76,* 949–967.

Hayden, E. P., Klein, D. N., Durbin, C. E., & Olino, T. M. (2006). Positive emotionality at age 3 predicts cognitive styles in 7-year-old children. *Development and Psychopathology, 18,* 409–423.

Heller, W., & Nitschke, J. B. (1997). Regional brain activity in emotion: A framework for understanding cognition in depression. *Cognition & Emotion, 11,* 637–661.

Hodapp, R., Burack, J., & Zigler, E. (1990). The developmental perspective in the field of mental retardation. In J. Burack & R. Hodapp (Eds.), *Issues in the developmental approach to mental retardation* (pp. 3–26). Cambridge, England: Cambridge University Press.

Jazbec, S., McClure, E., Hardin, M., Pine, D. S., & Ernst, M. (2005). Cognitive control under contingencies in anxious and depressed adolescents: An antisaccade task. *Biological Psychiatry, 58,* 632–639.

Ladouceur, C. D., Dahl, R. E., Williamson, D. E., Birmaher, B., Axelson, D. A., Ryan, N. D., et al. (2006). Processing emotional facial expressions influences performance on a Go/NoGo task in pediatric anxiety and depression. *Journal of Child Psychology and Psychiatry, and Allied Disciplines, 47,* 1107–1115.

Lewis, M. D., Lamm, C., Segalowitz, S. J., Stieben, J., & Zelazo, P. D. (2006). Neurophysiological correlates of emotion regulation in children and adolescents. *Journal of Cognitive Neuroscience, 18,* 430–443.

Lieberman, M. D., & Rosenthal, R. (2001). Why introverts can't always tell who likes them: Multitasking and nonverbal decoding. *Journal of Personality and Social Psychology, 80,* 294–310.

Luu, P., & Tucker, D. M. (2004). Self-regulation by the medial frontal cortex: Limbic representation of motive set-points. In M. Beauregard (Ed.), *Consciousness, emotional self-regulation and the brain* (pp. 123–161). Amsterdam: John Benjamins.

Luu, P., Tucker, D. M., & Derryberry, D. (1998). Anxiety and the motivational basis of working memory. *Cognitive Therapy and Research, 22,* 577–594.

Magnusson, D. & Cairns, R. (1996). Developmental science: Toward a unified framework. In R. Cairns, G. Elder, & J. Costello (Eds.), *Developmental science* (pp. 7–30). Cambridge, England: Cambridge University Press.

Mashburn, A.J. & Pianta, R. C. (2006). Social relationships and school readiness. *Early Education and Development, 17,* 157–176.

McEwen, B. S. (2000). The neurobiology of stress: From serendipity to clinical relevance. *Brain Research, 886,* 172–189.

McLoyd, V. (1990). The impact of economic hardship on black families and children: Psychological distress, parenting, and socioemotional development. *Child Development, 61,* 311–346.

Murray, K. T., & Kochanska, G. (2002). Effortful control: Factor structure and relation to externalizing and internalizing behaviors. *Journal of Abnormal Child Psychology, 30,* 503–514.

Ochsner, K. N., & Gross, J. J. (2005). The cognitive control of emotion. *Trends in Cognitive Sciences, 9*, 242–249.

Paus, T. (2001). Primate anterior cingulate cortex: Where motor control, drive, and cognition interface. *Nature Reviews: Neuroscience, 2*, 417–424.

Posner, M., & Rothbart, M. (2000). Developing mechanisms of self-regulation. *Development and Psychopathology, 12*, 427–441.

Pribram, K. H. (1960). A review of theory in physiological psychology. *Annual Review of Psychology, 11*, 1–40.

Putnam, S. P. Rothbart, M. K., & Gartstein, M. A. (2008). Homotypic and heterotypic continuity of fine-grained temperament during infancy, toddlerhood, and early childhood. *Infant and Child Development, 17*, 387–405.

Raver, C. (2002), Emotions matter: Making the case for the role of young children's emotional development for early school readiness. *Society for Research in Child Development Social Policy Report, 16*, 1–19.

Rimm-Kaufman, S., Pianta, R. C., & Cox, M. (2001). Teachers' judgments of problems in the transition to school. *Early Childhood Research Quarterly, 15*, 147–166.

Schneirla, T. C. (1957). The concept of development in comparative psychology. In D. Harris (Ed.), *The concept of development: An issue in the study of human behavior* (pp. 78–108). Minneapolis: University of Minnesota Press.

Stieben, J., Lewis, M. D., Granic, I., Zelazo, P. D., Segalowitz, S., & Pepler, D. (2007). Neurophysiological mechanisms of emotion regulation for subtypes of externalizing children. *Development and Psychopathology, 19*, 455–480.

Sutton, S. & Davidson, R. (1997). Prefrontal brain asymmetry: A biological substrate of the behavioral approach and inhibition systems. *Psychological Science, 8*, 204–210.

Whitman, T. L. (1990). Self-regulation and mental retardation. *American Journal on Mental Retardation, 94*, 347–362.

Wolfe, C. D., & Bell, M. A. (2007). The integration of cognition and emotion during infancy and early childhood: Regulatory processes associated with the development of working memory. *Brain and Cognition, 65*, 3–13.

Yerkes, R. M., & Dodson, J. D. (1908). The relation of strength of stimulation to rapidity of habit-information. *Journal of Comparative Neurology and Psychology, 18*, 459–482.

Zelazo, P. D., Muller, U., Frye, D., & Marcovitch, S. (2003). The development of executive function in early childhood. *Monographs of the Society for Research on Child Development, 68*(3), vii–137.

Zigler, E. (1969). Developmental versus difference theories of mental retardation and the problem of motivation. *American Journal on Mental Deficiency, 73*, 536–556.

Zigler, E. (1999). The individual with mental retardation as a whole person. In E. Zigler & D. Bennett-Gates (Eds.), *Personality development in individuals with mental retardation* (pp. 1–16). New York: Cambridge University Press.

Zigler, E., & Hodapp, R. M. (Eds.) (1986). *Understanding mental retardation*. New York: Cambridge University Press.

3

EMOTION REGULATION AND EXECUTIVE FUNCTIONING IN EARLY DEVELOPMENT: INTEGRATED MECHANISMS OF CONTROL SUPPORTING ADAPTIVE FUNCTIONING

SUSAN D. CALKINS AND STUART MARCOVITCH

Of long-standing interest to the field of developmental psychology has been the significance of early emotional and cognitive skills for later socioemotional functioning, academic achievement, and mental health. Implicit in such interest is the notion that early skills, abilities, and tendencies may forecast a child's success or failure in the larger worlds of school and peers. In this chapter we consider the early emergence of two hallmarks of emotional and cognitive development, emotion regulation and executive functioning, each of which appears to be fundamental to later adaptive behavior. Given the functional characterization of both of these processes as

The writing of this chapter was supported in part by a National Institutes of Health Research Scientist Career Development Award (K02) to Susan D. Calkins (MH 74077).

control mechanisms, we examine the degree to which their emergence is a consequence of shared foundational biological and psychological mechanisms, and we suggest a framework for integrating them that may be informative of the developmental processes through which they emerge. Within this framework we examine evidence for differential growth in these domains and suggest possible mechanisms through which these processes influence one another mutually and transactionally over the course of early development. Finally, we pose unresolved questions and offer directions for future research.

EMOTION REGULATION IN EARLY CHILDHOOD

Numerous definitions have been offered for the construct of *emotion regulation*, in both child and adult emotion literatures (Gross & Thompson, 2007). Our definition reflects recent theoretical and empirical work in both developmental (Cole, Martin, & Dennis, 2004; Fox & Calkins, 2003) and clinical psychology (Keenan, 2000) that highlights the fundamental role played by emotion processes in both child development and child functioning (Eisenberg et al., 2000) and that is anchored in the measurement of such processes during emotionally evocative situations (Calkins & Hill, 2007). Consistent with many of our colleagues (e.g., Eisenberg, Hofer, & Vaughn, 2007; Gross & Thompson, 2007), we view emotion regulation processes as those behaviors, skills, and strategies, whether conscious or unconscious, automatic or effortful, that modulate, inhibit, and enhance emotional experiences and expressions (Calkins & Hill, 2007). We also view the dimension of emotional reactivity as part of the emotion regulation process, although we, like some of our colleagues (Gross & Thompson, 2007), see a value in examining this element of the process as distinct from the efforts to manage it (these efforts being what we refer to as the *control dimension*; Fox & Calkins, 2003). The emotion regulation process is clearly a dynamic one in which reactive and control dimensions alter one another across time. Moreover, in our view, the reactive dimension, as opposed to the control dimension, is present and functional early in neonatal life, as it is strongly influenced by genetic and biological factors (Fox & Calkins, 2003). Finally, we note that the display of emotional reactivity and emotion control is implicated in both interpersonal relationships and socioemotional adjustment across the life span (Calkins & Dedmon, 2000; Eisenberg et al., 2007; Thompson & Meyer, 2007).

The broad construct of emotion regulation has been studied using different methodologies across early development (Cole et al., 2004), including through the use of parent reports, psychophysiological measures, and direct observation. Our approach entails the examination of the child's use of specific strategies in emotionally demanding contexts and the effects of these strategies on emotion experience and expression (Calkins & Dedmon, 2000).

We also measure the physiological response of the child to the emotional challenge, assuming that behavioral strategies to deal with emotional arousal are, at least in part, dependent on biological efforts to control arousal (Calkins, 1997). So, for example, we have observed that specific emotion regulation strategies such as self-comforting, help seeking, and self-distraction may assist the young child in managing early temperament-driven frustration and fear responses; that such reactions are observable in laboratory assessments using standard assessment batteries (Calkins & Dedmon, 2000); that a physiological change is observed under such conditions (Calkins & Keane, 2004); and that such behavioral and physiological strategies may also be observed in real-world situations in which the control of negative emotions may be necessary, such as with peers or in school (Calkins, Smith, Gill, & Johnson, 1998; Graziano, Keane, & Calkins, 2007).

Although some children appear to be quite proficient in the use of basic emotion regulation skills at a relatively early age, it is clear that early in development dramatic growth occurs in the acquisition and display of emotion regulation skills and abilities. The process may be described broadly as one in which the relatively passive and reactive neonate becomes a child capable of self-initiated behaviors that serve an emotion regulatory function. The infant moves from near complete reliance on caregivers for regulation (e.g., via physical soothing provided when the infant is held) to independent emotion regulation (e.g., choosing to find another toy to play with, rather than throwing a tantrum, when the desired toy is taken by a companion), although the variability in such regulation across children, in terms of both style and efficacy, is considerable (Buss & Goldsmith, 1998; Calkins, 2009). As the infant makes this transition to greater independence, the caregiver's use of specific strategies and behaviors within dyadic interactions becomes integrated into the infant's repertoire of emotion regulation skills, presumably across both biological and behavioral levels of functioning (Calkins & Dedmon, 2000; Calkins & Hill, 2007). The child may then draw on this repertoire in a variety of contexts, in both conscious, effortful ways (e.g., walking away from a confrontation with a peer) and nonconscious, automatic ways (e.g., averting his or her gaze when confronted by a frightening movie scene or reducing vagal regulation of the heart to facilitate behavior coping; Calkins, Graziano, Berdan, Keane, & Degnan, 2008).

The practice of these newly emerging skills leads to greater automaticity, so that by the time the child is ready to enter the arena of formal schooling, greater effort may be directed toward more demanding academic and social challenges. These expanding interactional contexts, it is important to note, will place demands on the child to integrate emotional and cognitive skills in the service of achieving diverse academic and social goals.

Next, we turn to the domain of executive functioning, which represents a set of cognitive skills that is likely to be as important as emotion regulation in the attainment of these new goals.

EXECUTIVE FUNCTIONING IN EARLY CHILDHOOD

Broadly construed, executive functioning involves a number of higher order cognitive skills, including goal-directed behavior, representational capacity, planning, memory, and inhibition (Carlson, Moses, & Claxton, 2004). These abilities appear to develop somewhat interdependently (Bjorklund & Harnishfeger, 1995) and enhance children's ability to engage in effective goal-directed behavior by reducing their attention to nonessential stimuli and allowing them to consider multiple solutions to a problem. In work with young children, the focus has been primarily on the ability to use working memory and inhibitory control. Young children's abilities to attend to salient aspects of a task, inhibit prepotent responses, and follow rules are often the indicators of early executive function skills. Moreover, these basic cognitive skills are considered foundational to later academic functioning. For example, executive function skills have been linked to literacy and mathematical reasoning in young children (Espy et al., 2004; Gathercole, Brown, & Pickering, 2003).

Assessment of executive function in children and adults typically involves laboratory tasks that require planning, monitoring, and inhibiting. For example, in the Wisconsin Card Sorting Task (WCST; Grant & Berg, 1948), a standard for measuring executive function in adults, participants must use trial and error to match cards on the basis of one of three possible dimensions (e.g., color). After a number of consecutive correct responses, the matching dimension is switched (e.g., to shape) without informing the participant. Perseverative responding occurs when the participant continues to match cards according to the original dimension despite repeated feedback that the response is now incorrect. Correct performance requires several components of executive function: remembering the new sorting dimension, inhibiting responding by the old sorting dimension, and executing the response appropriately.

The development of executive functioning in children has been linked to the development of the frontal lobes and associated neural connections. Consequently, dramatic changes in executive functioning during childhood have been reported, especially between 3 and 5 years of age (e.g., Carlson, Davis, & Leach, 2005; Zelazo, Müller, Frye, & Marcovitch, 2003). For example, Zelazo and colleagues (e.g., Zelazo, Frye, & Rapus, 1996) have used the Dimensional Change Card Sort (DCCS), an age-appropriate version of the WCST in which the rules are explicitly provided to the children. In this task, children as young as 3 years old are capable of sorting cards according to a single dimension (e.g., color), but not until 5 years of age can children reliably inhibit the old rule and sort correctly according to a second dimension (e.g., shape). Despite the growing body of research that focuses on executive functioning in preschoolers, relatively little work has been conducted on its development in the first 3 years of life.

Given the difficulty 3-year-olds have with executive function tasks, it is tempting to claim that processes associated with executive function are immature and undeveloped in infancy and toddlerhood. Some evidence, however, suggests that these processes emerge, at least in a primitive form, early and develop rapidly in the first 3 years of life. Because there is no standard assessment of executive function in the first 3 years of life, researchers have relied on a variety of abilities over a wide range of tasks to infer executive function abilities. One strategy is to examine contexts in which infants and young children display intentional, or cognitively controlled, behavior. Several studies suggest that cognitive control exists, albeit primitively, in younger infants. For example, Meltzoff and Moore (1977) provided compelling evidence that 12- to 21-day-old infants are capable of facial imitation (e.g., tongue protrusion), even after the actor has returned to a neutral state. This can be considered a remarkable indicator of cognitive control because successful imitation requires that infants mentally represent the act over a delay and then use that representation to guide their own unseen behavior. Although this interpretation (and perhaps even the existence of the phenomenon) has been challenged (e.g., Anisfeld et al., 2001), neonatal imitation may be the earliest demonstration of cognitively controlled behavior.

Another potential marker for cognitive control in the first few months of life is the shift from exogenous to endogenous eye movements. From birth, infants move their eyes in response to movement in the visual field (Banks & Salapatek, 1983), but it is not until 2 months of age that they move their eyes for the purpose of scanning a particular form for details. Indeed, some researchers have noted that at around 2 to 3 months of age, infants become more active in seeking out stimulation (Emde, Gaensbauer, & Harmon, 1976). The ability to control eye movements in an active effort to abstract information from the environment is the basis for visual habituation and preference studies, which account for a significant amount of what is now known about infant cognition (Kellman & Spelke, 1983). Thus, fundamental skills that may serve as the foundation for executive functioning appear in the first 3 years of life, although most research in this area suggests that dramatic developments in inhibitory control, working memory, and attention skills are only observable between the ages of 3 and 6 years (Carlson, Mandell, & Williams, 2004; Carlson & Wang, 2007). As children approach the formal schooling period, variations in each of these dimensions of cognitive control become increasingly central in accounting for individual differences in children's self-regulation of learning and problem-solving activities in both the social and academic domains.

EVIDENCE FOR THE DEVELOPMENTAL INTEGRATION OF EMOTIONAL AND COGNITIVE CONTROL

Observation of young children as they function in the world of school and peers makes it clear that cognitive processes are operating within the larger context of control mechanisms that function in emotionally evocative situations as well. An integrative framework for such cognitive and emotion processes has intuitive appeal and considerable theoretical support (Bell & Deater-Deckard, 2007; Calkins & Fox, 2002), but it does not rest on a large empirical literature. Here we explore the support for such an integrated view of emerging emotional and cognitive control in early development.

Biological Processes Linking Emotion and Cognition

The notion that emotion and cognition processes such as emotion regulation and executive functioning are linked developmentally and are functionally interdependent has some support from conceptual and empirical work from a range of biological perspectives, including both development neuroscience and psychophysiology. Such work highlights the linkages between specific central and peripheral processes that govern affective and cognitive processes and suggests shared neural pathways that support both.

For example, one important piece of support for an integrated model of emotion regulation and executive functioning comes from recent work in the area of developmental neuroscience that has identified specific brain regions that may play a functional role in the deployment of attention and in the processing and regulation of emotion, cognition, and behavior (Posner & Rothbart, 2000). More specifically, this work has identified areas of the prefrontal cortex (PFC) as central to the effortful regulation of a range of behaviors via the anterior attention system. This system is guided by the anterior cingulate cortex (ACC), which includes two major subdivisions. One subdivision governs cognitive and attentional processes and has connections to the PFC. A second subdivision governs emotional processes and has connections with the limbic system and peripheral autonomic, visceromotor, and endocrine systems (Lane & McRae, 2004; Luu & Tucker, 2004). Research suggests that these subdivisions have a reciprocal relation (Davidson, Putnam & Larson, 2000; Davis, Bruce, & Gunnar, 2002). Moreover, the functional relation between these two areas of the cortex provides a biological mechanism for the developmental integration of specific types of self-regulatory processes, particularly those implicated in emotion regulation and executive functioning in childhood (Bell & Wolfe, 2004).

Specificity in how these neural processes regulate thought and affect is provided by models that consider higher order versus lower order cortical regulatory processes (chap. 10, this volume; Lewis, 2005; Thompson, Lewis, & Calkins, 2008). Higher order structures such as the ACC and the PFC are hypothesized to mediate executive processes such as those involved in planning, monitoring, and goal setting, whereas lower order structures such as the amygdala and the hypothalamus are responsive to emotional cues and are thus considered more automatic than higher order effortful processes. Important, though, is that the cortex functions in an integrated fashion to link these processes in a feedback loop that supports ongoing behavior that is at once both cognitive and affective (Thompson et al., 2008).

Although often considered separate biological systems, neural and physiological processes operate as feedback systems and are particularly relevant to understanding dynamic processes such as emotion regulation and executive functioning. For example, recent psychophysiological research highlights the role of the autonomic nervous system in regulating many biobehavioral processes. The autonomic nervous system functions as a complex system of afferent and efferent feedback pathways that are integrated with other neurophysiological and neuroanatomical processes, reciprocally linking cardiac activity with central nervous system processes (Chambers & Allen, 2007). Pathways of the parasympathetic nervous system in particular are implicated in these processes, and consequently they play a key role in the regulation of state, motor activity, attention, emotion, and cognition (Porges, 2003). Specifically, the myelinated vagus nerve, originating in the brainstem nucleus ambiguus, provides input to the sinoatrial node of the heart, producing dynamic changes in cardiac activity that allow the organism to transition between sustaining metabolic processes and generating more complex responses to environmental events (Porges, 2007). Of particular interest to researchers studying emotional and cognitive control has been measurement of vagal regulation of the heart when the organism is challenged. This central-peripheral neural feedback loop is functional relatively early in development (Porges, 2007). Considerable research has suggested that vagal regulation withdrawal is linked to a range of behavioral processes that are regulatory in nature and that are observable quite early in development. Greater vagal withdrawal during challenging situations is related to better state regulation, greater self-soothing and more attentional control in infancy (Huffman et al., 1998), fewer behavior problems and more appropriate emotion regulation in preschool (Calkins & Dedmon, 2000; Calkins & Keane, 2004), and sustained attention and effortful control in school-age children (Calkins, Graziano, & Keane, 2007; Suess, Porges, & Plude, 1994). Thus, there is solid empirical evidence that processes that rely on neural integration between higher and lower order structures are also served by peripheral processes that facilitate multiple types of control. An important remaining question is whether there is evidence that this feedback process is observable on a behavioral level, which would provide stronger evidence of the integration of emotion and cognition processes.

Shared Psychological Processes

The psychological process most likely to underlie both emotion regulation and executive function is attention (Bell & Deater-Deckard, 2007; Rothbart, Posner & Kieras, 2006). Development in attentional orienting, sustained attention, and attention shifting has been linked to a range of both emotional and cognitive processes (Posner & Rothbart, 2007); the emergence of attentional processes across infancy and toddlerhood leads to predictable changes in a range of emotional and cognitive skills and supports more sophisticated behaviors required for social interaction and tasks required for successful school performance.

Early efforts at attentional control, up to the age of about 3 months, are thought to be controlled largely by physiological mechanisms driven by posterior orienting systems that are innate (Posner & Rothbart, 1998). By 3 months of age, primitive and more reactive attentional self-regulatory mechanisms of orienting and attentional persistence assist in simple control of behavioral state and emotional reactivity (Eisenberg et al., 2004). The period between 3 and 6 months of age marks a major transition in infant development generally. First, sleep–wake cycles and eating and elimination processes have become more predictable, signaling an important biological transition. Second, the ability of the infant to control arousal levels voluntarily begins to emerge. This control depends largely on attentional control mechanisms and simple motor skills (Rothbart, Ziaie, & O'Boyle, 1992) and leads to coordinated use of attention engagement and disengagement, particularly in contexts that evoke negative affect. Infants are now capable of engaging in self-initiated distraction and of shifting attention from a source of negative arousal to more neutral nonsocial stimuli.

The emergence of voluntary control of attention occurring during the infant's 1st year coincides with the development of three related but anatomically distinct attentional systems. The first attentional system of importance is the reticular activating system ascending from the brainstem to the cortex and thought to be involved in maintaining and adjusting general alertness. It is believed that this system focuses attention on salient aspects of the environment and prevents distraction, thus facilitating defensive behavior (Derryberry & Rothbart, 1997). The second attentional system maturing during the end of the 1st year of life is the posterior attentional system. Neurologically, this system is distributed across the brain's superior colliculus, the pulvinar nucleus of the thalamus, and the parietal lobe within the cortex. The operations of this system allow attention to move from one location to another through engagement and disengagement of attention. In addition, this system allows for the adjustment of the breadth of attention to focus closely on the details or to give a broader, more general picture of the information to be processed. The third system, which develops later than the other attentional systems and is proposed to be the most important to the development of effortful control, is the anterior attentional system. This system is located within the frontal cortex and is viewed as an executive system that regulates sensory information (Rothbart, Derryberry, & Posner, 1994). Furthermore, Posner and Rothbart (1992) suggested that this system underlies the conscious, willful, or effortful control of behavior through which the individual can regulate more reactive motivational functions. Although aspects of effortful control can be seen at the end of the 1st year, this system is relatively late to develop, with the most rapid maturation occurring during toddlerhood and preschool (Derryberry & Rothbart, 1997).

The development and integration of the three attentional systems provides the young child with the neural mechanisms necessary to regulate emotional reactivity through orienting, redirecting, and maintaining attentional focus. Effortful control of attention also permits the young child to engage in a broader array of cognitive tasks (Eisenberg et al., 2004). By toddlerhood, effortful control of attention plays a key role in delaying behavior and in suppressing and slowing behavior (Kochanska, Murray, & Harlan, 2000), all components of the behavioral regulation that is necessary for successful social and academic functioning.

Predictions to Developmental Outcomes

Considerable research on emotion regulation demonstrates quite convincingly that the display of affect and affect regulation is a powerful mediator of interpersonal relationships and socioemotional adjustment, including behavioral self-control, as early as the first few years of life and continuing throughout childhood (Thompson & Meyer, 2007). In terms of behavioral control, for example, Stifter, Spinard, and Braungart-Rieker (1999) found that emotional regulation in response to frustration in infancy was related to compliance in toddlerhood. Eisenberg, Fabes, and colleagues have reported in several studies (Eisenberg et al., 1993; Eisenberg, Fabes, Nyman, Bernzweig, & Pinuelas, 1994) that individuals who are highly emotional in response to anger-inducing events and low in regulation are likely to be aggressive. Shipman, Schneider, and Brown (2004) hypothesized that although problems with emotion regulation may be broadly related to externalizing behavior problems characterized by aggression, they may differentially predict children who are prone to oppositional defiant disorder. Thus, the degree to which the child can manage negative emotions in a constructive way, rather than acting out toward parents and peers, is a predictor of social success and more positive social outcomes (Howse, Calkins, Anastopoulos, Keane, & Shelton, 2003).

Although there is good evidence that early emotion regulation plays an important role in the development of social skills, positive peer relationships, and mental health and that deficits in emotion regulation are implicated in later social and emotional difficulties, relatively little work has explored the relations between emotion regulation and academic outcomes. Dodge and Pettit (2003) noted the coincidence of emotional and behavioral problems and academic difficulties, but empirical tests of the longitudinal relation among these constructs is limited. In one study, we found that toddler emotion regulation predicted kindergarten academic achievement but was mediated by behavioral self-regulation in the classroom (Howse et al.,

2003). In a follow-up of these children, concurrent emotion regulation predicted academic success as measured by teacher reports of appropriate classroom behavior. In all likelihood, early emotion regulation skills are contributing to well-regulated behavior in the classroom, and it is this profile that predicts academic success (Graziano, Reavis, Keane, & Calkins (2007).

In contrast to the prospective work on emotion regulation, no studies have focused directly on whether executive function skills in infancy and toddlerhood predict positive developmental outcomes later in childhood. However, compelling indirect evidence implicates positive developmental trajectories beginning with advanced executive function skills in toddlers. For example, Carlson et al. (2004) found that executive function skills are relatively stable from 24 to 39 months of age and, importantly, that early executive function predicts later theory of mind abilities (see also Hughes, 1998, for a similar pattern between 3 and 4 years of age). In turn, advances in theory of mind are related to a number of positive outcomes, including improvements in cooperative interactions (Dunn, Brown, Slomkowski, Tesla, & Youngblade, 1991) and important antecedents to the understanding of cognitive states (Bartsch & Estes, 1996). A construct that has been tied to executive function, though defined narrowly in terms of inhibitory process, is effortful control. Effortful control of attention has been linked to socially appropriate behavior in the context of an emotionally challenging situation (Kieras, Tobin, Graziano, & Rothbart, 2005).

Although executive function abilities are implicated in academic success (preschool: Alloway, Gathercole, Adams, & Willis, 2005; Espy et al., 2004; elementary school: Bull & Scerif, 2001; Holmes & Adams, 2006; secondary school: Chinnappan & Lawson, 1996; St. Clair-Thompson & Gathercole, 2006), there has been surprisingly little research on whether executive function skills developed prior to school translate into school readiness. Blair and Razza (2007), for example, reported that inhibitory control and attention shifting abilities in Head Start preschool children predicted their literacy and math scores in kindergarten. Clearly, it would be beneficial to conduct a longitudinal study on the development and stability of executive function and cognitive control that spans from infancy into the school years.

Studies have linked executive functioning deficits in children to a range of early behavioral difficulties. For example, immature executive functioning is common in children with attention problems (Nigg, Hinshaw, Carte, & Treuting, 1998), but executive function deficits have also been linked to conduct problems and learning style differences (Moffitt, 1993, Pennington & Ozonoff, 1996). Moreover, the frequently reported association between executive function and disruptive behavior is independent of IQ (Moffitt, 1993). While the causal role of executive functioning deficits has not been examined in longitudinal studies, Rutter (1987) proposed that executive functions mediate the development of psychopathology in children. However, the majority of research highlighting the relation between executive functioning and behavioral difficulties has been cross-sectional or conducted with clinical versus normative between-groups designs in which the effects of executive functioning, independent of behavioral functioning, are difficult to identify.

Relations Between Emotion Regulation and Executive Function in Early Development

Although the empirical literature examining the relations between emotion regulation and executive processes is modest, the few empirical investigations of these relations suggest important links between the two sets of processes in early childhood. During the 2nd and 3rd years, children also acquire a voluntary attentional system that enables them to use deliberate and effortful attentional strategies (Walden & Smith, 1997); these changes in the planful control of attention undoubtedly contribute to goal-directed behavior in both the emotional and cognitive spheres, skills that translate into successful social and academic outcomes. However, little research has examined the extent to which the dimensions of negative emotionality and regulation are linked to the display and development of early cognitive skills such as working memory and planning. In one recent study of preschool children examining emotion regulation and understanding and metacognition and executive functioning, a four-factor model specifying four separate domains of functioning was the best fit for the data (Leerkes, Paradise, O'Brien, Calkins, & Lange, 2008). However, significant relations between the domains of emotion regulation and executive functioning were observed in this sample of 3-year-olds. These data lend support to the notion that emotion regulation and executive functioning are distinct but related sets of process as early as early childhood.

Although there is little empirical work examining these emotion and cognitive processes within the same group of children, work on childhood psychopathology has tangentially addressed this issue. For example, there has there been some work investigating the role of executive functioning in children with behavior problems characterized by emotion dysregulation. Specifically, Riggs, Blair and Greenberg (2003) demonstrated that deficits in executive functioning are linked to externalizing behavior problems in young children. Also, patterns of stable versus declining externalizing behavior problems have been linked to early attentional control (Hill, Degnan, Calkins, & Keane, 2006).

Research to date suggests that children who have difficulty regulating emotions may also have difficulty regulating their behavior in a variety of settings and as a consequence may have difficulty learning and acquiring some of the fundamental social and cognitive skills necessary for academic achievement. Difficulty regulating behavior may occur through different pathways. For example, the ability to control emotional arousal allows children to engage in challenging tasks that provide opportunities for using and practicing executive function skills (Calkins & Dedmon, 2000). Blair (2002) suggested that poor emotion regulation may exert its influence on children through a biological mechanism that inhibits the child's use of higher order cognitive processes. Moreover, children who are skilled at maintaining a positive mood should be more capable of completing difficult school-related tasks, which often require executive function such as inhibition, working memory, and planning. To date, there has been no comprehensive study of how these processes emerge and become integrated over the course of early childhood.

A SELF-REGULATION FRAMEWORK FOR THE DEVELOPMENTAL INTEGRATION OF EMOTION REGULATION AND EXECUTIVE FUNCTIONING

Disparate literatures representing the study of emotion regulation and executive functioning in early development provide solid preliminary support for the interdependence of these two sets of skills. A reasonable next step is to provide a comprehensive theoretical account of this interdependence. Because we believe that emotion regulation and executive functioning are both control processes that are linked in fundamental ways to more basic physiological and attentional processes and have consequences for later-developing and more sophisticated social and cognitive skills, we, like some of our colleagues (Bell & Deater-Deckard, 2007; Blair & Razza, 2007; Eisenberg et al., 2007; Rothbart & Sheese, 2007), embed these processes within the larger construct of self-regulation. So, one way to conceptualize the self-regulatory system is to describe it as adaptive control that may be observed at the level of physiological, attentional, emotional, behavioral, cognitive, and interpersonal or social processes (Calkins & Fox, 2002). Control at these various levels emerges, at least in primitive form, across the prenatal, infancy, toddler, and early childhood periods of development. Fundamental to this developmental process is the maturation of different neural systems and processes that provide a functional mechanism for the behavioral integration we ultimately observe as children mature (Lewis & Todd, 2007). Noteworthy, though, is that the mastery of earlier regulatory tasks becomes an important component of later competencies, and, by extension, the level of mastery of these early skills may constrain the development of later skills. Thus, understanding the development of specific control processes, such as emotional regulation or executive functions, becomes integral to understanding the emergence of other childhood skills and adaptive functioning across developmental domains (Calkins & Fox, 2002).

Developmentalists are charged with the task of understanding the ways in which rudimentary control processes become integrated into more sophisticated functioning. For example, a putatively emotional task of early child-hood, the management of frustration, may be parsed into many smaller chal-lenges for the child, involving processes that are observable in different ways and across different levels of functioning. However, many of these same com-ponent processes might also be involved in the successful negotiation of other childhood challenges that may not have an obvious emotion regulation de-mand, such as a math test, a soccer game, or a plea to a parent to attend a social event. Because it is difficult to determine whether similar processes that are activated in such different contexts are components of the same or different biological and behavioral systems, it may be more useful to adopt an approach that considers multiple levels of analysis of self-regulation, rather than isolating emotion regulation and executive functioning from related, or even integrated, control processes (Calkins, 2009; Calkins & Fox, 2002; Posner & Rothbart, 2000). From this perspective, emotion and cognitive control skills emerge during infancy and toddlerhood as a function of more basic or rudimentary biological and attentional control processes, and they subsequently assume a central role in the development of the more complex self-regulation of behavior and cognition characteristic of early and middle childhood.

We acknowledge that these discrete self-regulatory processes are likely to be so intertwined that once integration across levels occurs in support of more complex skills and behaviors, it is difficult to parse these complex behavioral responses into separate or independent types of control. Never-theless, from a developmental point of view, it is useful to describe explicit types of control and how they emerge, as this specification may provide insight into nonnormative developments and problems that emerge as a result of deficits in specific components of self-regulation at particular points in development.

For example, one hypothesis that we have been exploring (Howse et al., 2003; Leerkes et al., 2008) is that emotion control processes moderate trajectories of development of the other more sophisticated control processes. Our rationale for this hypothesis is derived from recent work in the area of self-regulation more broadly construed and from research in the area of at-tention development. First, at both a neural level and a behavioral level, emotion regulation processes recruit and integrate multiple psychological functions (attention, appraisal, affective experience, and motor responding; Lewis & Stieben, 2004). Thus, it is clear that emotions have the capacity to organize and facilitate, or disorganize and disrupt, other psychological pro-cesses (Cole, Martin, & Dennis, 2004; Gray, 2004), both "in the moment" and at the level of the emergence of these skills over the course of early development (Bell & Wolfe, 2004). Second, emotion control processes ap-pear to emerge earlier in development than do cognitive control processes (Blair, 2002). To the extent that children understand and control emotions successfully, they have a greater opportunity to attend to, assimilate, and process events in the world around them, thus enhancing both social and academic competence. Finally, beyond these in-the-moment effects of emotion, there is emerging empirical evidence that early affective experience influences the acquisition of cognitive control skills of attention and working memory (Bell & Wolfe, 2004).

A final rationale for the primacy of emotional control skills is the development of the neural architecture that underlies such skills. First, recent research on pre- and perinatal risk demonstrates that very early brainstem functioning affects fundamental arousal and attentional processes critical to early emotion expression and control. These brainstem systems mature earlier than the cortical systems that support higher order executive processes (Geva & Feldman, 2008). Early attention processes are clearly recruited for the regulation of emotion. However, the effortful control of attention, in the service of cognitive activity, develops later. Although aspects of effortful control can be seen at the end of the 1st year, this system is relatively late to develop, with the most rapid maturation occurring during preschool (Derryberry & Rothbart, 1997). In addition, the ventral part of the anterior cingulate cortex, hypothesized to link cognitive and emotional control processes, is connected to the limbic system, which supports emotional processing (Bush, Luu, & Posner, 2000). Limbic system processes are considered more primitive and earlier developing, suggesting a neural mechanism for how emotional control may affect the development and deployment of higher order executive control processes. Thus, from both a behavioral and a neuroscience perspective, there appears to be support for the developmental model we have proposed.

IMPLICATIONS AND FUTURE DIRECTIONS

Our model is consistent with recent work in cognitive and emotional development and is supported by both neural and behavioral evidence from a range of studies examining both normal and abnormal development in children and adults. Nevertheless, significant gaps remain in our understanding of how these processes emerge and become integrated over the course of early development.

A primary set of questions about the relations between emotional and cognitive control processes concerns the empirical support for their transactional emergence during infancy and toddlerhood and the primacy of emotion over cognition. Methodological challenges to resolving this issue are significant. Nevertheless, it is necessary to document the fundamental attention processes underlying emotion regulation and executive function, in order to understand their independent emergence. To some extent the methodological challenges may require us to consider the core and/or component processes that underlie these cognitive and emotion skills. It is well recognized that executive functions consist of a loosely allied set of cognitive processes; clearer articulation of the set of processes integral to emotion regulation is needed as well.

A secondary set of questions about the development of important control processes has to do with the potential genetic and environmental factors that may play a role in the development of control. Recent analyses of the genetic component of self-regulation suggest commonalities between emotional and cognitive measures at the level of gene influence (Bell & Deater-Deckard, 2007). Empirical tests of these relations are still quite preliminary. Environmental correlates of the development of emotion regulation have been well documented at both the behavioral and biological level (for a summary of this work, see Calkins & Hill, 2007); similar studies of the environmental factors that affect executive functioning are lacking. Shared biological and psychological processes are at the core of emotion–cognition associations, and similar environmental effects on elements of executive function processes should be studied to the same extent.

A final set of questions yet to be adequately addressed concerns the developmental unfolding of these processes and the precise nature of this unfolding on indices of child functioning. Studies of the trajectories of these processes, predictors of such trajectories, and the implications of individual differences in growth are lacking. The value of a self-regulatory framework is that it orients our thinking toward the significance of control mechanisms for adaptive functioning across a range of contexts and using a variety of indicators (Baumeister & Vohs, 2004). However, studies that adopt a longitudinal approach that considers multiple pathways to adaptation and maladaptation are still needed in this area of research.

REFERENCES

Alloway, T. P., Gathercole, S. E., Adams, A. M., & Willis, C. (2005). Working memory and other cognitive skills as predictors of progress towards early learning goals at school entry. *British Journal of Developmental Psychology, 23,* 417–426.

Anisfeld, M., Turkewitz, G, Rose, S. A., Rosenberg, F. R., Shelber, F. J., Couturier-Fagan, D. A., et al. (2001). No compelling evidence that newborns imitate oral gestures. *Infancy, 2,* 111–122.

Banks, M. S., & Salapatek, P. (1983). Infant visual perception. In M. M. Haith & J. J. Campos (Eds.), *Handbook of child psychology: Vol. 2. Infancy and developmental psychobiology* (4th ed., pp. 436–571). New York: Wiley.

Bartsch, K., & Estes, D. (1996). Individual differences in children's developing theory of mind and implications for metacognition. *Learning and Individual Differences, 8,* 281–304.

Baumeister, R. & Vohs, K. (Eds.). (2004). *Handbook of self-regulation.* New York: Guilford Press.

Bell, M. A., & Wolfe, C. D. (2004). Emotion and cognition: An intricately bound developmental process. *Child Development, 75,* 366–370.

Bell, M. A., & Deater-Deckard, K. (2007). Biological systems and the development of self-regulation: Integrating behavior, genetics, and psychophysiology. Journal of Developmental & Behavioral Pediatrics, 28, 409-420.

Bjorklund, D. F., & Harnishfeger, K. K. (1995). The evolution of inhibition mechanisms and their role in human cognition and behavior. In F. Dempster & C. Brainerd (Eds.), *Interference and inhibition in cognition* (pp. 141–173). San Diego, CA: Academic Press.

Blair, C. (2002). School readiness: Integrating cognition and emotion in a neurobiological conceptualization of children's functioning at school entry. *American Psychologist, 57,* 111–127.

Blair, C., & Razza, R. P. (2007). Relating effortful control, executive function, and false belief understanding to emerging math and literacy ability in kindergarten. *Child Development, 78,* 647–663.

Bull, R., & Scerif, G. (2001). Executive functioning as a predictor of children's mathematics ability. Shifting, inhibition, and working memory. *Developmental Neuropsychology, 19,* 273–293.

Bush, G., Luu, P., & Posner, M. I. (2000). Cognitive and emotional influences in anterior cingulated cortex. *Trends in Cognitive Science, 4,* 215–222.

Buss, K. A., & Goldsmith, H. H. (1998). Fear and anger regulation in infancy: Effects on the temporal dynamics of affective expression. *Child Development, 69,* 359–374.

Calkins, S. D. (1997). Cardiac vagal tone indices of temperamental reactivity and behavioral regulation in young children. *Developmental Psychobiology, 31,* 125–135.

Calkins, S. D. (2009). Regulatory competence and early disruptive behavior problems: The role of physiological regulation. In S. Olson & A. Sameroff (Eds.), *Regulatory processes in the development of behavior problems: Biological, behavioral, and social–ecological interactions* (pp. 86–115). New York: Cambridge University Press.

Calkins, S. D., & Dedmon, S. A. (2000). Physiological and behavioral regulation in two-year-old children with aggressive/destructive behavior problems. *Journal of Abnormal Child Psychology, 2,* 103–118.

Calkins, S. D., & Fox, N. A. (2002). Self-regulatory processes in early personality development: A multilevel approach to the study of childhood social withdrawal and aggression. *Development and Psychopathology, 14,* 477–498.

Calkins, S. D., Gill, K., & Williford, A. P. (1999). Externalizing problems in two-year-olds: Implications for patterns of social behavior and peers' responses to aggression. *Early Education and Development, 10,* 267–288.

Calkins, S. D., Graziano, P., Berdan, L., Keane, S. P., & Degnan, K. (2008). Predicting cardiac vagal regulation in early childhood from maternal–child relationship quality during toddlerhood. *Developmental Psychobiology, 50,* 751–766.

Calkins, S. D., Graziano, P. A., & Keane, S. P. (2007). Cardiac vagal regulation differentiates among children at risk for behavior problems. *Biological Psychology, 74,* 144–153.

Calkins, S. D., & Hill, A. (2007). Caregiver influences on emerging emotion regulation: biological and environmental transactions in early development. In J. Gross (Ed.), *Handbook of emotion regulation* (pp. 229–248). New York: Guilford Press.

Calkins, S. D., & Keane, S. P. (2004). Cardiac vagal regulation across the preschool period: Stability, continuity, and implications for childhood adjustment. *Developmental Psychobiology, 45,* 101–112.

Calkins, S. D., Smith, C. L., Gill, K. L., & Johnson, M. C. (1998). Maternal interactive style across contexts: Relations to emotional, behavioral and physiological regulation during toddlerhood. *Social Development, 7,* 350–369.

Carlson, S. M., Davis, A. C., & Leach, J. G. (2005). Less is more: Executive function and symbolic representation in young children. *Psychological Science, 16,* 609–616.

Carlson, S. M., Mandell, D. J., & Williams, L. (2004). Executive function and theory of mind: Stability and prediction from age 2 to 3. *Developmental Psychology, 40,* 1105–1122.

Carlson, S. M., Moses, L. J., & Claxton, L. J. (2004). Individual differences in executive functioning and theory of mind: An investigation of inhibitory control and planning ability. *Journal of Experimental Child Psychology, 87,* 299–319.

Carlson, S. M., & Wang, T. S. (2007). Inhibitory control and emotion regulation in preschool children. *Cognitive Development, 22,* 489–510.

Chambers, A., & Allen, J. J. B. (2007). Cardiac vagal control, emotion, psychopathology, and health. *Biological Psychology, 74,* 113–115.

Chinnappan, M., & Lawson, M. J. (1996). The effects of training in the use of executive strategies in geometry problem solving. *Learning and Instruction, 6,* 1–17.

Cole, P. M., Martin, S. E., & Dennis, T. A. (2004). Emotion regulation as a scientific construct: Methodological challenges and directions for child development research. *Child Development, 75,* 317–333.

Davidson, R. J., Putnam K. M., & Larson, C. L. (2000, July 28). Dysfunction in the neural circuitry of emotion regulation: a possible prelude to violence. *Science, 289,* 591–594.

Davis, E. P., Bruce, J., & Gunnar, M. R. (2002). The anterior attention network: Associations with temperament and neuroendocrine activity on 6-year-old children. *Developmental Psychobiology, 40,* 43–56.

Derryberry, D., & Rothbart, M. K. (1997). Reactive and effortful processes in the organization of temperament. *Development and Psychopathology, 9,* 633–652.

Dodge, K. A., & Pettit, G. S. (2003). A biopsychosocial model of the development of chronic conduct problems in adolescence. *Developmental Psychology, 39,* 349–371.

Dunn, J., Brown, J., Slomkowski, C., Tesla, C., & Youngblade, L. (1991). Young children's understanding of other people's feelings and beliefs: Individual differences and their antecedents. *Child Development, 62,* 1352–1366.

Eisenberg, N., Fabes, R. A., Bernzweig, J., Karbon, M., Poulin, R., & Hanish, L. (1993). The relations of emotionality and regulation to preschoolers' social skills and sociometric status. *Child Development, 64*, 1418–1438.

Eisenberg, N., Fabes, R. A., Nyman, M., Bernzweig, J., & Pinuelas, A. (1994). The relations of emotionality and regulation to children's anger-related reactions. *Child Development, 65*, 109–128.

Eisenberg, N., Guthrie, I. K., Fabes, R. A., Shepard, S., Losoya, S., Murphy, B. C., et al. (2000). Prediction of elementary school children's externalizing problem behaviors from attention and behavioral regulation and negative emotionality. *Child Development, 71*, 1367–1382.

Eisenberg, N., Hofer, C., & Vaughan, J. (2007). Effortful control and its socioemotional consequences. In J. Gross (Ed.), *Handbook of emotion regulation* (pp. 287–306). New York: Guilford Press.

Eisenberg, N., Spinrad, T. L., Fabes, R. A., Reiser, M., Cumberland, A., Shepard, S. A., et al. (2004). The relations of effortful control and impulsivity to children's resiliency and adjustment. *Child Development, 75*, 25–46.

Emde, R. N., Gaensbauer, T. J., & Harmon, R. J. (1976). Emotional expression in infancy: A biobehavioral study. *Psychological Issues, 10*(1, No. 34).

Espy, K. A., McDiarmid, M. M., Cwik, M. F., Stalets, M. M., Hamby, A., & Senn, T. E. (2004). The contribution of executive functions to emergent mathematic skills in preschool children. *Developmental Neuropsychology, 26*, 465–486.

Fox, N. A., & Calkins, S. D. (2003). The development of self-control of emotion: Intrinsic and extrinsic influences. *Motivation and Emotion, 27*, 7–26.

Gathercole, S. E., Brown, L., & Pickering, S. J. (2003). Working memory assessments at school entry as longitudinal predictors of National Curriculum attainment levels. *Educational and Child Psychology, 20* (3), 109–122.

Geva, R. & Feldman, R. (2008). A neurobiological model for the effects of early brainstem functioning on the development of behavior and emotion regulation in infants: implications for prenatal and perinatal risk. *Journal of Child Psychology and Psychiatry, 49*, 1031–1041.

Grant, D. A., & Berg, E. A. (1948). A behavioral analysis of degree of reinforcement and ease of shifting to new responses in a Weigl-type card-sorting problem. *Journal of Experimental Psychology, 38*, 404–411.

Gray, J. R. (2004). Integration of emotion and cognitive control. *Current Directions in Psychological Science, 13*, 46–48.

Graziano, P. Keane, S. & Calkins, S. D. (2007). Cardiac vagal regulation and early peer status. *Child Development, 78*, 264–278.

Graziano, P. A., Reavis, R. D., Keane, S. P., & Calkins, S. D. (2007). The role of emotion regulation and the student teacher relationship in children's academic success. *Journal of School Psychology, 45*, 3–19.

Gross, J., & Thompson, R. A. (2007). Emotion regulation: Conceptual foundations. In J. Gross (Ed.), *Handbook of emotion regulation* (pp. 3–24). New York: Guilford Press.

Hill, A. L., Degnan, K. A., Calkins, S. D., & Keane, S. P. (2006). Profiles of external-izing behavior problems for boys and girls across preschool: The roles of emo-tion regulation and inattention. *Developmental Psychology, 42*, 913–928.

Holmes, J., & Adams, J. W. (2006). Working memory and children's mathematical skills: Implications for mathematical development and mathematics curricula. *Educational Psychology, 26*, 339–366.

Howse, R. B., Calkins, S. D., Anastopoulos, A. D., Keane, S. P., & Shelton, T. L. (2003). Regulatory contributors to children's kindergarten achievement. *Early Education and Development, 14*, 101–119.

Huffman, L. C., Bryan, Y. E., del Carmen, R., Pedersen, F. A., Doussard-Roosevelt, J. A., & Porges, S. W. (1998). Infant temperament and cardiac vagal tone: Assessments at twelve weeks of age. *Child Development, 69*, 624–635.

Hughes, C. (1998). Executive function in preschoolers: Links with theory of mind and verbal ability. *British Journal of Developmental Psychology, 16*, 233–253.

Keenan, K. (2000). Emotion dysregulation as a risk factor for child psychopathology. *Clinical Psychology: Science and Practice, 7*, 418–434.

Kellman, P. J., & Spelke, E. S. (1983). Perception of partly occluded objects in in-fancy. *Cognitive Psychology, 15*, 483–524.

Kieras, J. E., Tobin, R. M., Graziano, W. G., & Rothbart, M. K. (2005). You can't always get what you want: Effortful control and children's responses to undesir-able gifts. *Psychological Science, 16*, 391–396.

Kochanska, G., Murray, K. T., & Harlan, E. T. (2000). Effortful control in early childhood: Continuity and change, antecedents, and implications for social development. *Developmental Psychology, 36*, 220–232.

Lane, R. D., & McRae, K. (2004). Neural substrates of conscious emotional experi-ence: A cognitive–neuroscientific perspective. In M. Beauregard (Ed.), *Con-sciousness, emotional self-regulation and the brain* (pp. 87–122). Amsterdam: John Benjamins.

Leerkes, E. M., Paradise, M., O'Brien, M., Calkins, S.D., & Lange, G. (2008). Emo-tion and cognition processes in preschool children. *Merrill-Palmer Quarterly, 54*, 102–124.

Lewis, M. D. (2005). Bridging emotion theory and neurobiology through dynamic systems modeling. *Behavioral and Brain Sciences, 28*, 169–194.

Lewis, M. D., & Stieben, J. (2004). Emotion regulation in the brain: Conceptual issues and directions for developmental research. *Child Development, 75*, 371–376.

Lewis, M. D., & Todd, R. M. (2007). The self-regulating brain: Cortical–subcortical feedback and the development of intelligent action. *Cognitive Development, 22*, 406–430.

Luu, P., & Tucker, D. M. (2004). Self-regulation by the medial frontal cortex: Lim-bic representation of motive set-points. In M. Beauregard (Ed.), *Consciousness, emotional self-regulation and the brain* (pp. 123–161). Amsterdam: John Benjamins.

Meltzoff, A. N., & Moore, M. K. (1977, October 7). Imitation of facial and manual gestures by human neonates. *Science, 198*, 75–78.

Moffitt, T. E. (1993). The neuropsychology of conduct disorder. *Development and Psychopathology, 5*, 135–151.

Nigg, J. T., Hinshaw, S. P., Carte, E. T., & Treuting, J. J. (1998). Neuropsychological correlates of childhood attention-deficit/hyperactivity disorder: Explainable by comorbid disruptive behavior or reading problems? *Journal of Abnormal Psychology, 107*, 468–480.

Pennington, B. F., & Ozonoff, S. (1996). Executive functions and development of psychopathology. *Journal of Child Psychology and Psychiatry, 37*, 51–87.

Porges, S. W. (2003). The polyvagal theory: Phylogenetic contributions to social behavior. *Physiology & Behavior, 79*, 503–513.

Porges, S. W. (2007). The polyvagal perspective. *Biological Psychology, 74*, 116–143.

Porges, S. W., & Byrne, E. A. (1992). Research methods for measurement of heart rate and respiration. *Biological Psychology, 34*, 93–130.

Posner, M. I., & Rothbart, M. K. (1992). Attention and conscious experience. In A. D. Milner & M. D. Rugg (Eds.), The neuropsychology of consciousness (pp. 91–112). London: Academic.

Posner, M. I., & Rothbart, M. K. (1998). Summary and commentary: Developing attentional skills. In J. E. Richards (Ed.), *Cognitive neuroscience of attention: A developmental perspective* (pp. 317–323). Mahwah, NJ: Lawrence Erlbaum.

Posner, M. I., & Rothbart, M. K. (2000). Developing mechanisms of self-regulation. *Development and Psychopathology, 12*, 427–441.

Posner, M. I., & Rothbart, M. K. (2007). *Educating the human brain*. Washington, DC: American Psychological Association.

Riggs, N. R., Blair, C. B., & Greenberg, M. T. (2003). Concurrent and 2-year longitudinal relations between executive function and the behavior of 1st and 2nd grade children. *Child Neuropsychology, 9*, 267–276.

Rothbart, M. K., Derryberry, D., & Posner, M. I. (1994). A psychobiological approach to the development of temperament. In J. E. Bates & T. D. Wachs (Eds.), *Temperament: Individual differences at the interface of biology and behavior* (pp. 83–116). Washington, DC: American Psychological Association.

Rothbart, M. K., Posner, M. I., & Kieras, J. (2006). Temperament, attention, and the development of self-regulation. In K. McCartney & D. Phillips (Eds.), *Blackwell handbook of early childhood development* (pp. 338–357). Malden, MA: Blackwell Publishing.

Rothbart, M. K., & Sheese, B. E. (2007). Temperament and emotion regulation. In J. J. Gross (Ed.), *Handbook of emotion regulation* (pp. 331–350). New York: Guilford Press.

Rothbart, M. K., Ziaie, H., & O'Boyle, C. G. (1992). Self-regulation and emotion in infancy. In N. Eisenberg, & R. A. Fabes, (Eds.), *Emotion and its regulation in early development: The Jossey-Bass education series. New directions for child development* (No. 55, pp. 7–23). San Francisco: Jossey-Bass.

Rutter, M. (1987). The role of cognition in child development and disorder. *British Journal of Medical Psychology, 60*, 1–16.

Shipman, K., Schneider, R., & Brown, A. (2004). Emotion dysregulation and psychopathology. In M. Beauregard (Ed.), *Consciousness, emotional self-regulation, and the brain* (pp. 61–85). Amsterdam: John Benjamins.

St Clair-Thompson, H. L., & Gathercole, S. E. (2006). Executive functions and achievements on national curriculum tests: Shifting, updating, inhibition, and working memory. *Quarterly Journal of Experimental Psychology, 59*, 745–759.

Stifter, C. A., Spinard, T. L., & Braungart-Rieker, J. M. (1999). Toward a developmental model of child compliance: The role of emotion regulation in infancy. *Child Development, 70*, 21–32.

Suess, P. E., Porges, S. W., & Plude, D. J. (1994). Cardiac vagal tone and sustained attention in school-age children. *Psychophysiology, 31*, 17–22.

Thompson, R. A., Lewis, M. D., & Calkins, S. D. (2008). Reassessing Emotion Regulation. Child Development Perspectives, 3, 124–131.

Thompson, R. A., & Meyer, S. (2007). Socialization of emotion regulation in the family. In J. J. Gross (Ed.), *Handbook of emotion regulation* (pp. 249–268). New York: Guilford Press.

Walden, T. A., & Smith, M. C. (1997). Emotion regulation. *Motivation and Emotion, 21*, 7–25.

Zelazo, P. D., Frye, D., & Rapus, T. (1996). An age-related dissociation between knowing rules and using them. *Cognitive Development, 11*, 37–63.

Zelazo, P. D., Müller, U., Frye, D., & Marcovitch, S. (2003). The development of executive function in early childhood. *Monographs of the Society for Research in Child Development, 68*(3, Serial No. 274).

4

THE ROLE OF LANGUAGE IN THE DEVELOPMENT OF EMOTION REGULATION

PAMELA M. COLE, LAURA MARIE ARMSTRONG,
AND CAROLINE K. PEMBERTON

Four-year-old Keisha is impatiently waiting for her mother to complete some work so that Keisha can finally open the tempting gift on the table. She is very eager to know what is inside the shiny wrapping. Waiting is hard. Keisha has a toy, a plastic toy horse, but its leg is missing. She frequently speaks to her mother, "Are you done, Mom?" . . . "I wonder what's in it." . . . "Can I open it now?" Each time, her mother reminds Keisha to wait, eventually adding, "If you keep interrupting me, I can't finish and if I don't finish . . ." Keisha plops in her chair, frustrated. "I really want it," she laments, aloud but to herself. "I want to talk to Mommy so I won't open it. If I talk, Mommy won't finish. If she doesn't finish, I can't have it." She sighs deeply, folds her arms, and scans the room. Several minutes later the research assistant returns. Keisha looks at her mother with excited anticipation. Her mother says, "OK, now." Keisha tears open the gift.

This scene from our research suggests that a young child can use language to regulate emotion. This 4-year-old implicitly conveys her desire to her mother, incorporates her mother's words into her own articulation of the dilemma, uses conversation to sustain waiting, and talks to herself about the wait. Keisha's language is a resource for communicating needs, understanding situations, and regulating frustration. Keisha is a typical child, who at age 4 has the ability to verbalize her needs, tolerate routine frustration, and generate strategies for coping with ordinary problems that elicit emotions. This is a good developmental sign. This degree of self-regulatory skill is expected of young school-age children. Those who are regarded as having behavior problems have difficulty regulating emotion as well as Keisha does.

This chapter and portions of the research in it were supported by National Institute of Mental Health Research Award RO1-MH61388 to Pamela M. Cole. We thank the many families who gave us such an intimate view of their discourse with their young children, as well as the colleagues in our lab with whom we aired our ideas.

The ability to self-initiate regulatory strategies develops significantly between the toddler and kindergarten years (Kopp, 1989). During this period, children also make enormous gains in language development. They utter their first words, build a vocabulary, combine words to convey meaning, and acquire grammatical rules. Yet language and emotional development are usually studied separately. In this chapter, we focus on one way that these two domains of development converge, focusing on ways that expressive language development contributes to the early development of skillful emotion regulation. Drawing from empirical studies and from speech samples from our research, we suggest that the integration of expressive language and emotion regulation is not automatic and that both child characteristics (e.g., language skill) and parent–child discourse contribute to the development of self-regulation of emotion.

EVIDENCE THAT LANGUAGE IS IMPORTANT TO EMOTION REGULATION

Four distinct lines of research suggest that expressive language and emotion regulation are linked. First, there is evidence of associations between externalizing behavior problems in children, which often involve emotion regulation difficulties (Cole, Zahn-Waxler, & Smith, 1994; Eisenberg et al., 2001; Gilliom, Shaw, Beck, Schonberg, & Lukon, 2002; Hill, Degnan, Calkins, & Keane, 2006), and language delays (Baker & Cantwell, 1992). Although relations between linguistic and self-regulation processes likely involve executive processes (e.g., attention control), difficulty in understanding and producing verbal information may make a unique contribution to emotion regulation.

Second, evidence suggests that the relation between verbal and nonverbal modes of expression develops over time. During first words and the vocabulary spurt, emotion expressions and utterances are not simultaneous (Bloom & Capatides, 1987). Bloom (1993) maintained that word production and emotional expression each recruit cognitive resources and that language learning therefore is disadvantaged if a child is highly emotional because emotion regulation also requires cognitive resources. This hypothesis remains to be fully tested, but new evidence suggests that verbal processing in very young children requires widespread neural processing (Redcay, Haist, & Courchesne, 2008).

Internal state language is a third way that language may influence emotion regulation (Bretherton, Fritz, Zahn-Waxler, & Ridgeway, 1986; Dunn, Bretherton, & Munn, 1987). The use of emotion terms is associated with young children's socioemotional competence (e.g., Denham et al., 2003; Fabes, Eisenberg, Hanish, & Spinrad, 2001). In addition to strengthening relationship bonds through sharing emotional experiences, parent–child discourse about emotions likely scaffolds children's ability to reflect on their own and others' experiences, fostering emotional self-awareness, which should enhance emotion regulation (Saarni, 1999; Shields et al., 2001).

Finally, self-verbalization has been studied as a feature of self-regulation. Vygotsky (1962) held that preschoolers talk aloud to themselves because they cannot inhibit action, which coincidentally influences their behavior; Luria (1961) regarded children's self-verbalizations as regulatory efforts. These interesting views stimulated research on verbal self-instruction as a therapeutic technique for childhood impulsivity (Meichenbaum & Goodman, 1971), contributed to the belief that self-speech influences mood and action (a key element of cognitive behavioral therapies; e.g., Kendall & Treadwell, 2007), and justified the emphasis on using words to convey feelings and needs and to guide behavior choices in prevention programs fostering socioemotional competence (Greenberg, Kusché, Cook, & Quamma, 1995).

In sum, four diverse lines of research suggest that language contributes to the development of self-regulation of emotion. Of the many ways these two domains may intersect, we focus on how expressive language provides

- an alternative, more articulate means than emotion expression for communicating goals for well-being;
- a tool that enhances the understanding of the emotional experiences of self and others; and
- an additional strategy for guiding and regulating emotions and action.

COMMUNICATING GOALS FOR WELL-BEING

One of the primary functions of emotion is communication (Barrett & Campos, 1987). Emotions are coterminous processes of evaluating circumstances relative to one's well-being and preparing to act in particular ways to maintain or regain well-being. For instance, anger signals both appreciation that goals are thwarted and readiness to act with effort to overcome obstacles to goals for well-being. In the 1st year of life, regulatory aspects of emotion communication are clear. Infants coo and cry, smile and frown, guiding caregivers to meet their needs, and they also read and use others' emotional expressions (e.g., Fernald, 1993). By age 2, infants use others' emotional signals to guide behavior (Repacholi & Meltzoff, 2007; Sorce, Emde, Campos, & Klinnert, 1985). Emotional exchanges with caregivers build the infant's sense of security (Ainsworth, 1992) and attentional and linguistic skills (Landry, Smith, & Swank, 2006; Moreno & Robinson, 2005; Mundy et al., 2007) and promote expectations that distress can be relieved (Cassidy, 1994). Therefore, early emotion communication is a foundation for the development of emotion regulation.

As children first begin to speak, their verbal and nonverbal expressions are sequential rather than simultaneous (Bloom & Capatides, 1987), suggesting that (a) their utterances communicate goals for well-being but (b) verbal and nonverbal channels are not automatically coupled. The ability to speak with emotional expression must develop after early word learning; by preschool age socially competent preschoolers animate their verbal exchanges with emotional expressions (e.g., Garner & Lemerise, 2007). In addition, preschoolers are also able to exert some control over emotional expression (e.g., Cole, 1986; Garner & Power, 1996). By middle childhood this skill is refined (Saarni, 1984), and children can state how context influences their choices about when, with whom, and why to communicate emotion (Gnepp & Hess, 1986; Saarni, 1979).

Skillful emotion regulation therefore involves being emotionally expressive and able to modulate expressivity appropriately (Cole & Hall, 2008; Eisenberg & Fabes, 1992). Language likely contributes to skillful emotion regulation, yet clear evidence of how this develops is lacking. The main themes are stated in research on internal state language, which is thought to enhance the ability to maintain enjoyment and interest, to anticipate, avoid, and resolve negative emotions, and to draw on past events and anticipate future events (Dunn & Brown, 1991; Harris, 1989). In terms of general language abilities, evidence is limited. Verbal skills predict young children's positive emotion expressions and social competence (Cassidy, Werner, Rourke, Zubernis, & Balaraman, 2003; Schultz, Izard, Ackerman, & Youngstrom, 2001) but not their naturally occurring use of internal state terms (Cassidy et al., 2003; Hughes, Lecce, & Wilson, 2007). Verbal ability predicts emotion knowledge, which may mediate emotional behavior (Trentacosta, Izard, Mostow, & Fine, 2006), although executive processing skills must also be involved (Hughes, Cutting, & Dunn, 2001).

In our view, maturation and experience contribute to neurodevelopmental changes that underlie the integration of nonverbal and verbal communication as well as the ability to regulate emotion, including the ability to regulate expression (e.g., speak without laughing). Language development facilitates these abilities by providing a more articulated means of expression, through emotion understanding and self-directed strategies, and by permitting the behavioral flexibility to infuse speech with emotional vitality and to modulate nonverbal expression as befits situational constraints. This integration requires environmental input, such as adult scaffolding, that fosters the appropriate integration of emotional and language processes. For example, mothers' references to thinking and knowing when children are 24 months of age predict the children's emotion understanding at 33 months (Taumoepeau & Ruffman, 2008).

In our home visit data, we witness children's use of expressive language and parental scaffolding of emotion understanding and regulatory strategies:

Mother: You can't find it? Here, let me hold you.

Child: [*whimpering*] Hold me. Hold me.

Mother: [*hugging her son*] Why are you wanting so much holding tonight?

As toddlers acquire expressive language, they readily verbalize their wants but often in resistant, noncompliant ways:

Child: [*whining*] I no like those.

Father: It's broccoli. You like broccoli.

Child: [*angrier*] No! I no like those.

Family discourse can help toddlers coordinate their own and others' needs:

Child: [*angrily*] I want! (reaches for parent's plate)

Mother: Mikey, honey, eat your own, please.

Child: [*calmly*] That Daddy's. This my carrots. This Mommy's.

Father: That's right. Eat your own, please, I want mine.

In sum, during the years when children communicate needs through negative emotion expressions, their expressive language begins to develop rapidly. Through interactions with others, they learn to use words to communicate needs and to deal with the social realities of their interpersonal worlds, an exciting topic for future research.

UNDERSTANDING EMOTIONAL EXPERIENCES OF SELF AND OTHERS

The abilities to conceptualize and reflect on our own and others' emotions and to appreciate that these can differ are central to emotional competence (Saarni, 1999). Emotion understanding aids self-awareness and the construction of a coherent self-narrative (Harris, 1989). A 3-year-old in our lab puzzled hard for a few minutes when asked how to stop feeling angry; then he said tentatively, "When I'm cranky, I take a nap." Understanding effective regulatory strategies is linked to preschoolers' ability to persist at a difficult task (Cole, Dennis, Smith-Simon, & Cohen, 2009). Language skills, both receptive and expressive, should enhance emotion knowledge, which in turn should enhance emotion regulation.

Understanding the Emotions of the Self

Autobiographical memory research addresses the role of language in children's understanding of their own emotions. Autobiographical memory develops during the preschool age years, and language abilities aid (a) the representation of experiences, (b) the organization and evaluation of experience, and (c) the appreciation that past experience can be viewed from multiple perspectives (Nelson & Fivush, 2004). A child's language skill at the time of an event predicts the content, coherence, and organization of the child's narrative, all of which facilitate recall of the event (Kleinknecht & Beike, 2004).

Children's accurate, coherent understanding of their own emotions must benefit from parental language input. When parents elaborate about events in emotionally meaningful contexts, children are more engaged in conversation and their narratives are more coherent (Haden, Haine, & Fivush, 1997). Here we see a parent help a child reflect on her needs:

Mother: Don't cry.

Child: [quieter] I go bed.

Mother: You need to go to bed?

Child: Yeah.

Mother: [laughing] Are you tired?

Child: Yeah.

Family discourse about emotional events may be pancultural (Cervantes, 2002; Fivush & Wang, 2005; Miller, Wiley, Fung, & Liang, 1997), although each developmental niche clearly acculturates the degree to and manner in which children reflect on and resolve past experiences and anticipate emotional events, thus acculturating children's emotions (Cole & Tan, 2007). Evidence is needed to show how this contributes to skill at regulating emotion. Preschool-age children who were more stressed by Hurricane Andrew used less positive internal state language than less stressed children; the use of positive terms immediately after the event predicted psychological functioning 6 years later (Sales, Fivush, Parker, & Bahrick, 2005).

Understanding the Emotions of Others

Accuracy in perceiving and interpreting others' emotions is also central to socioemotional competence (Denham, Mason, & Couchoud, 1995). The ability to recognize others' preferences emerges in infancy (Repacholi & Gopnik, 1997). Between 3 and 5 years of age, children come to make accurate inferences about others' internal states, realizing that these states can differ across individuals (e.g., Lagattuta, 2005; Lagattuta, Wellman, & Flavell, 1997; Rieffe, Terwogt, & Cowan, 2005). The abilities to accurately recognize others' emotions, to understand that one's own emotions may conflict or differ with others', and to attribute different desires, beliefs, emotions, and intentions to others (Harwood & Farrar, 2006; Hughes & Dunn, 1998) are all associated with effective emotion regulation (Dunn & Cutting, 1999; Garner & Power, 1996) and prosocial behavior when others are emotionally negative (Denham & Couchoud, 1991; Eisenberg & Fabes, 1998).

Language plays a role in the development of emotion knowledge. Young children's verbal skills predict concurrent and later emotion knowledge (Fine, Izard, & Trentacosta, 2006; Ruffman, Slade, Rowlandson, Rumsey, & Garnham, 2003), and children with language delays are less accurate in identifying others' emotions and less skillful at anticipating and responding to emotional reactions (Brinton, Spackman, Fujiki, & Ricks, 2007). Early discourse about internal states predicts later theory of mind performance (Hughes & Dunn, 1998), and language is generally believed to enhance perspective taking (e.g., Astington & Jenkins, 1999; Cutting & Dunn, 1999; Slade & Ruffman, 2005), whereas language difficulties impair this ability (Baron-Cohen, 2001; Farrant, Fletcher, & Mayberry, 2006).

Family discourse is a major arena for the exchange of differing views, by explaining feelings and actions and using frequent and varied internal state language (Dunn, Brown, & Beardsall, 1991; Harris, de Rosnay, & Pons, 2005; Meins & Fernyhough, 1999). In such exchanges, antecedents can be linked with consequences, and memories of past situations can be used to understand new emotional experiences (Harris et al., 2005). Here a child recognizes his father's emotional state, and his father links it to a cause:

Child: Daddy, you grumpy.

Father: Yeah, Daddy had a kind of a rough day, hon.

Child: Oh, I had a rough day too.

Father: I bet you did.

In sum, language ability contributes to the development of emotion understanding, both of one's own and others' emotions, and family discourse about emotion contributes to child emotion understanding. Expressive language skill, both content and level, should help a child use thought to regulate emotion in actual emotion-eliciting situations, and family discourse likely fosters the integration of language and emotion regulation.

SELF-DIRECTED VERBALIZATION AS A MEANS OF SELF-REGULATION

The ability to self-regulate emotions is a third feature of emotional competence (Saarni, 1999). Children's self-regulatory abilities develop over the course of early childhood (see, e.g., Rothbart, Ziaie, & O'Boyle, 1992). Children use language to self-regulate, as we often observe in our work. They verbalize to themselves to reflect on and guide their own behavior and to occupy themselves when they must distract from emotion-eliciting circumstances.

Private speech is spoken language directed to the self for the purpose of guiding cognitive performance and regulating behavior (Zivin, 1979). Self-speech is also believed to influence mood, both adaptively (e.g., talking oneself through a difficult moment) and maladaptively (e.g., negative self-statements). Private speech is conceptualized as the use of language as an instrument of thought or as a tool to plan, guide, and monitor problem-solving activity (Luria, 1961; Meichenbaum & Goodman, 1969; Schunk & Zimmerman, 1994; Vygotsky, 1962). Indeed, at any age, private speech is more frequent during difficult or goal-directed tasks than during unstructured activities, and it declines with task familiarity (Berk & Garvin, 1984; Winsler, DeLeon, Wallace, Carlton, & Willson-Quayle, 2003). Private speech is first observed in the early preschool years as overt, externalized self-talk that eventually transitions to covert, internalized private speech (Winsler, Carlton, & Barry, 2000), with an interim period in which less audible self-directed verbalizations are characterized by muttering and lip and tongue movements (Winsler et al., 2003). Children come to realize and take advantage of the self-regulatory functions of private speech; 3-year-olds' private speech occurs in all types of activities, but for 4-year-olds it occurs mainly during goal-directed activities (Winsler et al., 2000).

Vocabulary size and grammatical complexity should contribute to the self-regulatory function of speech by providing a complex, precise, and articulate framework for understanding experience (Harris, 1996), expanding the child's repertoire for organizing and guiding action. Even after speech is fully internalized, an internal monologue can help a child deal with a difficult situation. Children with better verbal skills use more internalized than overt private speech (Berk & Landau, 1993; Berk & Spuhl, 1995) and progress more rapidly through the stages of self-speech (Berk & Garvin, 1984). Because children with more mature private speech are more socially and emotionally competent and have fewer externalizing behaviors (Berk & Landau, 1993; Bivens & Berk, 1990; Winsler et al., 2000; Winsler et al., 2003), spontaneous self-directed verbalizations likely contribute to emotion regulation. Private speech in emotionally challenging circumstances may interrupt or slow emotional responses and facilitate the inhibition or delay of actions that are readied as part of emotional responses (Tomasello, Kruger, & Ratner, 1993). Metcalfe and Mischel (1999) asserted that verbally mediated cognitive activity that is reflective and abstract interrupts stimulus-controlled, concrete, automatic emotional responses. Self-directed verbalizations may enhance access to executive processes involved in down-regulating emotion and remembering problem-solving strategies. Consider this 3-year-old girl, alone and frustrated by a box she cannot open:

> Hannah grunts and mutters fairly continuously for several minutes. Finally, looking sad, she says clearly, "I can't get it. I can't open the box." She sighs and sits back, looking around the room. Then she turns back to

the box and says cheerily, "I think I can do it. I know I can!" She resumes her careful efforts to get the box open.

In addition to monitoring and guiding action, language may help children shift attention or distract themselves, one of the main strategies children have for regulating negative emotion when they cannot control circumstances (Derryberry & Rothbart, 1988; Fox, 1989). For instance, we often see children sing to themselves, generate word games, and talk to themselves to tolerate waiting. A 4-year-old boy, playing with a broken toy similar to the one Keisha played with in our opening vignette, sang to himself, "I am a broken horse with no legs—two legs. Let's go to the hospital. Giddyap, giddyap, giddyap."

These adaptive uses of language are not automatic; self-talk can interfere with performance of well-learned tasks (Meichenbaum & Goodman, 1969). Moreover, its content matters. Negative self-statements are the main target of many empirically based therapies (e.g., Kendall & Ingram, 1989). The goal is not to stop self-talk but to modify its content. Furthermore, the ability to verbalize about emotional experiences brings emotions into awareness and allows the reframing of past experience (Greenberg, 2006).

Adult socialization practices likely influence the use and content of self-verbalization. Children of authoritative parents use age-appropriate private speech (Berk & Spuhl, 1995). Children with behavior problems often have more authoritarian parents, who tend to rely on commands and prohibitions to control child behavior, which may explain why these children use less private speech (Winsler, Diaz, McCarthy, Atencio, & Chabay, 1999). There is a need for more research on how a child's language ability influences how others speak to the child and how, in turn, such discourse influences a child's use of self-directed speech to plan, evaluate, and guide his or her actions.

INTEGRATING LANGUAGE INTO COMMUNICATING, UNDERSTANDING, AND REGULATING EMOTIONS

To summarize, a child's developing language skills become integrated into skillful emotion regulation through social transactional processes involving child attributes that influence how others interact with him or her and the attributes of those interactions. Child temperament and various cognitive abilities are likely to actively contribute to this process, although we emphasize language abilities in this chapter. Here a parent teaches her child that there are a number of actions one might take to minimize negative emotions:

Child: [*crying*] Mommy!

Mother: Are you okay?

Mother: You want a tissue?

Mother: Can I kiss it and make it better?

Mother: You want to get your baby and make it better?

Mother: Hug your baby.

Mother: Wanna hug your baby?

From the emotional exchanges of the 1st year, emotion and language converge in social interaction. Young children's receptive language skills should figure in the degree to which they profit from a caregiver's verbal messages. Evidence that children with autism have difficulties in both the language and emotion domains may indicate the importance of early social information processing in multiple channels. In addition, caregivers and others model the fluent integration of nonverbal and verbal emotional messages as well as the modulation of expression according to situational demands.

Around the first birthday, parents worry whether their children will talk. Indeed, parental language input at this time is aimed at stimulating language (Hart & Risley, 1995). As children enter a period of increased negativity, including tantrums, defiance, and noncompliance (Buss & Goldsmith, 2007), they begin to speak. Parents' eagerness to understand the child's meaning may explain the dominance of desire terms in their internal state language with toddlers (Jenkins, Turrell, Kogushi, Lollis, & Ross, 2003). Consider this excerpt from one of our home visits. The mother says to her toddler who is having a tantrum: "What do you want? Do you want a cookie? Do you need a nap? I think you need a nap."

A parent's efforts to verbalize about a child's joys and distresses are another point of convergence between emotion and language for the child. Through modeling and direct and indirect parenting, parents must promote the child's ability to integrate language into emotion regulation. Yet only research on internal state language addresses relations between parents' and children's use of language and child emotional competence. Language input varies widely across households, as does an emphasis on emotions, and variations in language input influence the manner in which language is integrated into a child's skillful emotion regulation. Moreover, the basic nature of parent–child verbal exchanges changes as children master spoken language (Hart & Risley, 1995). Once children are speaking, parents often ignore child verbal bids and cease to engage in language stimulation. Interaction is more typified by children initiating verbal exchanges and persisting at speaking even when parents do not respond. These variations and how they influence emotion regulation warrant research.

Another missing piece of the puzzle is how children's emerging language comes into play in emotional moments. One possibility is that their personal narratives provide them with information they can call on in these moments. We predict that children acquire such knowledge when emotional experiences are discussed in ways that are emotionally engaged but low in intensity. Children's emotion language is processed through their personal experiences (Thompson & Lagattuta, 2006), and the more experience a child has with routine emotions, the more able the child is to verbalize about emotions (Denham & Zoller, 1991). Thus, emotional experiences afford opportunities to learn emotion terms, which in turn promote accuracy in children's understanding of their own and others' emotions and therefore social competence. Discourse, in the home and in the child care setting, creates a linguistic framework for understanding emotions, emotional events, and ways they can be managed (Harris, 1996). This may help the child (a) objectify experience, allowing it to more readily be an object of thought; (b) generate mental activity that suspends or slows the emotional response; and (c) access information that helps deal with the situation.

There is much yet to be understood about the conditions that foster children's ability to recruit language-based information when they are emotionally challenged. Young children's private speech in emotionally challenging lab tasks suggests that they call on such knowledge. When parents observe their children through the two-way mirror in the laboratory, they are often amazed to hear their children repeat things that are frequently said at home but to which youngsters appear unresponsive. Alone with a prize he did not want, a 5-year-old uttered aloud, " . . . when you get a lemon, make lemonade." His mother exclaimed that this was often said at home, but she never realized that her son understood the aphorism.

CONCLUSIONS

Evidence from disparate areas of research converges to suggest that language and emotional development must be studied in terms of their mutual influences. In this chapter, we focused on the role of expressive language in the development of emotion regulation, asserting that expressive language provides children with an additional, socially appropriate means of communicating about their needs, with enhanced ability to understand their own and others' emotional lives, and with an additional tool for regulating action. Better expressive skill is associated with greater socioemotional competence, but this is not an automatic relation. Children with oppositional defiant disorder who are also verbally gifted are skillful in their argumentativeness and verbal defiance. Moreover, verbal abilities support maladaptive self-speech, such as rumination and negative self-statements. Thus, the research agenda is to understand the adaptive integration of language with emotion regulation.

Genetic contributions to temperament and intellectual abilities, including language skills, as well as maturation, must influence how a child's language relates to emerging skill at emotion regulation (Kopp, 1989). It seems likely that environmental factors influence how expressive abilities interface with the development of emotion regulation, a view consistent with most models of emotion socialization (e.g., Eisenberg, Cumberland, & Spinrad, 1998). Given the co-occurrence of heightened negative emotion and rapid language development in the period between ages 12 months and 3 years, environmental input during that period may be especially influential. On the other hand, children may need to achieve a certain level of mastery with language, executive attention, and emotion regulation—as in the preschool years—before integration across these domains of development can occur and facilitate self-regulation.

Socialization experiences with adults and other children in and out of the home are likely to be powerful contributors to the ways in which expressive language ability influences the quality of emotion regulation. The degree to which parents use emotion language and converse with children about their experiences is one way in which language input may contribute to skill at emotion regulation. Parents first use terms to describe their own and others' emotional experiences, later introducing those terms to help a child exert more effortful control over behavior, which may depend on the quality of the parent–child relationship (e.g., Ontai & Thompson, 2008). In addition, the manner in which adults harness a child's emerging language skills to help the child to self-regulate (e.g., asking the child what can be done about a problem rather than simply soothing or fixing a problem) should be investigated. An appreciation of how the separate domains of language and emotional development will help us better understand how children become aware of their emotions and regulatory strategies and develop effective and appropriate emotional self-regulation.

REFERENCES

Ainsworth, M. D. S. (1992). A consideration of social referencing in the context of attachment theory and research. In S. Feinman (Ed.), *Social referencing and the social construction of reality in infancy* (pp. 349–367). New York: Plenum Press.

Astington, J. W., & Jenkins, J. M. (1999). A longitudinal study of the relation between language and theory-of-mind development. *Developmental Psychology, 35*, 1311–1320.

Baker, L., & Cantwell, D. P. (1992). Attention-deficit disorder and speech/language disorders. *Comprehensive Mental Health Care, 2*, 3–16.

Baron-Cohen, S. (2001). Theory of mind and autism: A review. *International Review of Research in Mental Retardation, 23, 169*, 1–35.

Barrett, K. C., & Campos, J. J. (1987). Perspectives on emotional development II: A functionalist approach to emotions. In J. D. Osofsky (Ed.), *Handbook of infant development* (2nd ed., pp. 555–578). Oxford, England: Wiley.

Berk, L. E. & Garvin, R. A. (1984). Development of private speech among low-income Appalachian children. *Developmental Psychology, 20*, 271–286.

Berk, L. E., & Landau, S. (1993). Private speech of learning disabled and normally achieving children in classroom academic and laboratory contexts. *Child Development, 64,* 556–571.

Berk, L. E., & Spuhl, S. T. (1995). Maternal interaction, private speech, and task performance in preschool children. *Early Childhood Research Quarterly, 10,* 145–169.

Bivens, J. A. & Berk, L. E. (1990). A longitudinal study of the development of elementary school children's private speech. *Merrill-Palmer Quarterly, 36,* 443–463.

Bloom, L. (1993). *The transition from infancy to language: Acquiring the power of expression.* New York: Cambridge University Press.

Bloom, L., & Capatides, J. B. (1987). Expression of affect and the emergence of language. *Child Development, 58,* 1513–1522.

Bretherton, I., Fritz, J., Zahn-Waxler, C., & Ridgeway, D. (1986). Learning to talk about emotions: A functionalist perspective. *Child Development, 57,* 529–548.

Brinton, B., Spackman, M. P., Fujiki, M., & Ricks, J. (2007). What should Chris say? The ability of children with specific and language impairment to recognize the need to dissemble emotions in social situations. *Journal of Speech, Language, and Hearing Research, 50,* 798–809.

Buss, K. A., & Goldsmith, H. H. (2007). Biobehavioral approaches to early socioemotional development. In C. A. Brownell & C. B. Kopp (Eds.), *Socioemotional development in the toddler years: Transitions and transformations* (pp. 370–395). New York: Guilford Press.

Cassidy, J. (1994). Emotion regulation: Influences of attachment relationships. *Monographs of the Society for Research in Child Development, 59*(2–3, Serial No. 240).

Cassidy, K. W., Werner, R. S., Rourke, M., & Zubernis, L. S., Balaraman, G. (2003). The relationship between psychological understanding and positive social behaviors. *Social Development, 12,* 198–221.

Cervantes, C. A. (2002). Explanatory emotion talk in Mexican immigrant and Mexican American families. *Hispanic Journal of Behavioral Sciences, 24,* 138–163.

Cole, P. M. (1986). Children's spontaneous control of facial expression. *Child Development, 57,* 1309–1321.

Cole, P. M., Dennis, T. A., Smith-Simon, K. E., & Cohen, L. H. (2009). Preschooler's emotion regulation strategy understanding: Relations with maternal socialization and child behavior. *Social Development, 18,* 324–352

Cole, P. M., & Hall, S. B. (2008). Emotion dysregulation as a risk factor for psychopathology. In T. P. Beauchaine & S. P. Hinshaw (Eds.), *Child and adolescent psychopathology* (pp. 265–298). New York: Wiley.

Cole, P. M., Zahn-Waxler, C., & Smith, K. D. (1994). Expressive control during a disappointment: Variations related to preschoolers' behavior problems. *Developmental Psychology, 30,* 835–846.

Cutting, A. L., & Dunn, J. (1999). Theory of mind, emotion understanding, language, and family background: Individual differences and interrelations. *Child Development, 70,* 853–865.

Denham, S. A., Blair, K. A., DeMulder, E., Levitas, J., Sawyer, K., Auerbach-Major, S., et al. (2003). Preschool emotional competence: Pathway to social competence. *Child Development, 74,* 238–256.

Denham, S. A., & Couchoud, E. A. (1991). Social-emotional predictors of preschoolers' responses to adult negative emotion. *Journal of Child Psychology and Psychiatry, 32,* 595–608.

Denham, S. A., Mason, T., & Couchoud, E. A. (1995). Scaffolding young children's prosocial responsiveness: Preschoolers' responses to adult sadness, anger, and pain. *International Journal of Behavior Development, 18,* 489–504.

Denham, S. A., & Zoller, D. (1991). "When my hamster died, I cried": Preschoolers' attributions of the causes of emotions. *Journal of Genetic Psychology, 152,* 371–373.

Derryberry, D., & Rothbart, M. K. (1988). Arousal, affect, and attention as components of temperament. *Journal of Personality and Social Psychology, 55,* 958–966.

Dunn, J., Bretherton, I., & Munn, P. (1987). Conversations about feeling states between mothers and their young children. *Developmental Psychology, 23,* 132–139.

Dunn, J., & Brown, J. (1991). Relationships, talk about feelings, and the development of affect regulation in early childhood. In J. Garber & K. A. Dodge (Eds.), *The development of emotion regulation and dysregulation: Cambridge studies in social and emotional development* (pp. 89–108). New York: Cambridge University Press.

Dunn, J., Brown, J., & Beardsall, L. (1991). Family talk about feeling states and children's later understanding of others' emotions. *Developmental Psychology, 27,* 448–455.

Dunn, J., & Cutting, A. L. (1999). Understanding others, and individual differences in friendship interactions in young children. *Social Development, 8,* 201–219.

Eisenberg, N., Cumberland, A. & Spinrad, T. L. (1998). Parental socialization of emotion. *Psychological Inquiry, 9,* 241–273.

Eisenberg, N., Cumberland, A., Spinrad, T. L., Fabes, R. A., Shepard, S. A., Reiser, M., et al. (2001). The relations of regulation and emotionality to children's externalizing and internalizing problem behavior. *Child Development, 72,* 1112–1134.

Eisenberg, N., & Fabes, R. A. (1992). Emotion, regulation, and the development of social competence. In M. S. Clark (Ed.), *Review of personality and social psychology: Vol. 14. Emotion and social behavior* (pp. 119–150). Newbury Park, CA: Sage.

Eisenberg, N. & Fabes, R. A. (1998). Prosocial development. In W. Damon (Ed.), *Handbook of child psychology* (Vol. 3, 710–778). Chichester, England: Wiley.

Fabes, R. A., Eisenberg, N., Hanish, L. D., & Spinrad, T. L. (2001). Preschoolers' spontaneous emotion vocabulary: Relations to likeability. *Early Education and Development, 12,* 11–27.

Farrant, B. M., Fletcher, J., & Mayberry, M. T. (2006). Specific language impairment, theory of mind, and visual perspective taking: Evidence for simulation theory and the developmental role of language. *Child Development, 77*, 1842–1853.

Fernald, A. (1993). Approval and disapproval: Infant responsiveness to vocal affect in familiar and unfamiliar languages. *Child Development, 64*, 657–674.

Fine, S. E., Izard, C. E., Trentacosta, C. J. (2006). Emotion situation knowledge in elementary school: Models of longitudinal growth and preschool correlates. *Social Development, 15*, 730–751.

Fivush, R., & Wang, Q. (2005). Emotion talk in mother-child conversations of the shared past: The effects of culture, gender, and event valence. *Journal of Cognition and Development, 6*, 489–506.

Fox, N. (1989). Psychophysiological correlates of emotional reactivity in the first year of life. *Developmental Psychology, 25*, 364–372.

Garner, P. W., & Lemerise, E. A. (2007). The roles of behavioral adjustment and conceptions of peers and emotions in preschool children's peer victimization. *Development and Psychopathology, 19*, 57–71.

Garner, P. W. & Power, T. G. (1996). Preschoolers' emotional control in the disappointment paradigm and its relation to temperament, emotional knowledge, and family expressiveness. *Child Development, 67*, 1406–1419.

Gilliom, M., Shaw, D. S., Beck, J. E., Schonberg, M. A., & Lukon, J. L. (2002). Anger regulation in disadvantaged preschool boys: Strategies, antecedents, and the development of self-control. *Developmental Psychology, 38*, 222–235.

Gnepp, J. & Hess, D. L. (1986). Children's understanding of verbal and facial display rules. *Developmental Psychology, 22*, 103–108.

Greenberg, L. (2006). Emotion-focused therapy: A synopsis. *Journal of Contemporary Psychotherapy, 36*, 87–93.

Greenberg, M. T., Kusché, C. A., Cook, E. T. & Quamma, J. P. (1995). Promoting emotional competence in school-aged children: The effects of the PATHS curriculum. *Development & Psychopathology, 7*, 117–136.

Haden, C. A., Haine, R. A., & Fivush, R. (1997). Developing narrative structure in parent-child reminiscing across the preschool years. *Developmental Psychology, 33*, 293–307.

Harris, P. L. (1989). *Children and emotion: The development of psychological understanding.* Cambridge, MA: Basil Blackwell.

Harris, P. L. (1996). Desires, beliefs and language. In P. Carruthers & P. K. Smith (Eds.), *Theories of theories of mind* (pp. 344–354). Cambridge, England: Cambridge University Press.

Harris, P. L., de Rosnay, M., & Pons, F. (2005). Language and children's understanding of mental states. *Current Directions in Psychological Science, 14*, 69–73.

Hart, B., & Risley, T. R. (1995). *Meaningful differences in the everyday experience of young American children.* Baltimore: Paul H. Brookes.

Hart, B., & Risley, T. R. (1999). *The social world of children learning to talk*. Baltimore: Paul H. Brookes.

Harwood, M. D., & Farrar, J. M. (2006). Conflicting emotions: The connection between affective perspective taking and theory of mind. *British Journal of Developmental Psychology, 24*, 401–418.

Hill, A. L., Degnan, K. A., Calkins, S. D., & Keane, S. P. (2006). Profiles of externalizing behavior problems for boys and girls across preschool: The roles of emotion regulation and inattention. *Developmental Psychology, 42*, 913–928.

Hughes, C., Cutting, A. L. & Dunn, J. (2001). Acting nasty in the face of failure? Longitudinal observations of "hard-to-manage" children playing a rigged competitive game with a friend. *Journal of Abnormal Child Psychology, 29*, 403–416.

Hughes, C., & Dunn, J. (1998). Understanding mind and emotion: Longitudinal associations with mental-state talk between young friends. *Developmental Psychology, 34*, 1026–1037.

Hughes, C., Lecce, S. & Wilson, C. (2007). "Do you know what I want?": Preschoolers' talk about desires, thoughts and feelings in their conversations with sibs and friends. *Cognition and Emotion, 21*, 330–350.

Izard, C. E., Trentacosta, C. J., King, K. A. & Mostow, A. J. (2004). An emotion-based prevention program for Head Start children. *Early Education and Development, 15*, 407–422.

Jenkins, J. M., Turrell, S. L., Kogushi, Y., Lollis, S., & Ross, H. S. (2003). A longitudinal investigation of the dynamics of mental state talk in families. *Child Development, 74*, 905–920.

Kendall, P., & Ingram, R. (1989). Cognitive-behavioral perspectives: Theory and research on depression and anxiety. In P. Kendall & D. Watson (Eds.), *Anxiety and depression: Distinctive and overlapping features* (pp. 27–53). Orlando, FL: Academic Press.

Kendall, P. C., & Treadwell, K. R. H. (2007). The role of self-statements as a mediator in treatment for youth with anxiety disorders. *Journal of Consulting and Clinical Psychology, 75*, 380–389.

Kleinknecht, E., & Beike, D. R. (2004). How knowing and doing inform an autobiography: Relations among preschoolers' theory of mind, narrative, and event memory skills. *Applied Cognitive Psychology, 18*, 745–764.

Kopp, C. B. (1989). Regulation of distress and negative emotions: A developmental view. *Developmental Psychology, 25*, 343–354.

Lagattuta, K. H. (2005). When you shouldn't do what you want to do: Young children's understanding of desires, rules, and emotions. *Child Development, 76*, 713–733.

Lagattuta, K. H., Wellman, H. M., & Flavell, J. H. (1997). Preschoolers' understanding of the link between thinking and feeling: Cognitive cuing and emotional change. *Child Development, 68*, 1081–1104.

Landry, S. H., Smith, K. E., & Swank, P. R. (2006). Responsive parenting: Establishing early foundation for social, communication, and independent problem-solving skills. *Developmental Psychology, 42*, 627–642.

Luria, A. R. (1961). *The role of speech in the regulation of normal and abnormal behavior*. Oxford, England: Liveright.

Meichenbaum, D. & Goodman, J. (1969). Reflection-impulsivity and verbal control of motor behavior. *Child Development, 40*, 785–797.

Meichenbaum, D. H., & Goodman, J. (1971). Training impulsive children to talk to themselves: A means of developing self-control. *Journal of Abnormal Psychology, 77*, 115–126.

Meins, E., & Fernyhough, C. (1999). Linguistic acquisitional style and mentalising development: The role of maternal mind-mindedness. *Cognitive Development, 14*, 363–380.

Metcalfe, J. & Mischel, W. (1999). A hot/cool-system analysis of delay of gratification: Dynamics of willpower. *Psychological Review, 106*, 3–19.

Miller, P. J., Wiley, A. R., Fung, H., & Liang, C. (1997). Personal storytelling as a medium of socialization in Chinese and American families. *Child Development, 68*, 557–568.

Moreno, A. J., & Robinson, J. L. (2005). Emotional vitality in infancy as a predictor of cognitive and language abilities in toddlerhood. *Infant and Child Development, 14*, 383–402.

Mundy, P., Block, J., Delgado, C., Pomares, Y., Van Hecke, A. V., & Parlade, M. V. (2007). Individual differences and the development of joint attention in infancy. *Child Development, 78*, 938–954.

Nelson, K., & Fivush, R. (2004). The emergence of autobiographical memory: A social cultural developmental theory. *Psychological Review, 111*, 486–511.

Ontai, L. L., & Thompson, R. A. (2008). Attachment, parent-child discourse and theory-of-mind development. *Social Development, 17*(1), 47–60.

Redcay, E., Haist, F., & Courchesne, E. (2008). Functional neuroimaging of speech perception during a pivotal period in language acquisition. *Developmental Science, 11*, 237–252.

Repacholi, B. M., & Gopnik, A. (1997). Early reasoning about desires: Evidence from 14- and 18-month-olds. *Developmental Psychology, 33*, 12–21.

Repacholi, B. M., & Meltzoff, A. N. (2007). Emotional eavesdropping: Infants selectively respond to indirect emotional signals. *Child Development, 78*, 503–521.

Rieffe, C., Terwogt, M. M., & Cowan, R. (2005). Children's understanding of mental states as causes of emotions. *Infant and Child Development, 14*, 259–272.

Rothbart, M. K., Ziaie, H., & O'Boyle, C. (1992). Self-regulation and emotion in infancy. In N. Eisenberg & R. A. Fabes (Eds.), *Emotion and self-regulation in early development: New directions in child development* (pp. 7–24). San Francisco: Jossey-Bass.

Ruffman, T., Slade, L., Rowlandson, K., Rumsey, C., & Garnham, A. (2003). How language relates to belief, desire, and emotion. *Cognitive Development, 18*, 139–158.

Saarni, C. (1979). Children's understanding of display rules for expressive behavior. *Developmental Psychology, 15*, 424–429.

Saarni, C. (1984). An observational study of children's attempts to monitor their expressive behavior. *Child Development, 55,* 1504–1513.

Saarni, C. (1999). *The development of emotional competence.* New York: Guilford Press.

Sales, J. D., Fivush, R., Parker, J., & Bahrick, L. (2005). Stressing memory: Long-term relations among children's stress, recall and psychological outcome following Hurricane Andrew. *Journal of Cognition and Development, 6,* 529–545.

Schultz, D., Izard, C. E., Ackerman, B. P. & Youngstrom, E. A. (2001). Emotion knowledge in economically disadvantaged children: Self-regulatory antecedents and relations to social difficulties and withdrawal. *Development & Psychopathology, 13,* 53–67.

Schunk, D. H., & Zimmerman, B. J. (Eds.). (1994). *Self-regulation of learning and performance: Issues and educational applications.* Hillsdale, NJ: Erlbaum.

Shields, A., Dickstein, S., Seifer, R., Giusti, L., Magee, K. D., & Spritz, B. (2001). Emotional competence and early school adjustment: A study of preschoolers at risk. *Early Education and Development, 12,* 73–96.

Slade, L., & Ruffman, T. (2005). How language does (and does not) relate to theory of mind: A longitudinal study of syntax, semantics, working memory and false belief. *British Journal of Developmental Psychology, 117–141.*

Sorce, J. F., Emde, R. N., Campos, J. J., & Klinnert, M. D. (1985). Maternal emotional signaling: Its effect on the visual cliff behavior of 1-year-olds. *Developmental Psychology, 21,* 195–200.

Taumoepeau, M., & Ruffman, T. (2008). Stepping stones to others' minds: Maternal talk relates to child mental state language and emotion understanding at 15, 24, and 33 months. *Child Development, 79,* 284–302.

Thompson, R. A., & Lagattuta, K. (2006). Feeling and understanding: Early emotional development. In K. McCartney & D. Phillips (Ed.), *The Blackwell handbook of early childhood development* (pp. 317–337). Oxford, England: Blackwell.

Tomasello, M., Kruger, A. & Ratner, H. (1993). Cultural learning. *Behavioral & Brain Sciences, 16,* 495–511.

Trentacosta, C. J., Izard, C. E., Mostow, A. J. & Fine, S. E. (2006). Children's emotional competence and attentional competence in early elementary school. *School Psychology Quarterly, 21,* 148–170.

Vygotsky, L. S. (1962). *Thought and language.* Oxford, England: Wiley.

Winsler, A., Carlton, M. P., & Barry, M. J. (2000). Age-related changes in preschool children's systematic use of private speech in a natural setting. *Journal of Child Language, 27,* 665–687.

Winsler, A., DeLeon, J. R., Wallace, B. A., Carlton, M. P., & Willson-Quayle, A. (2003). Private speech in preschool children: Developmental stability and change, across-task consistency, and relations with classroom behavior. *Journal of Child Language, 30,* 583–608.

Winsler, A., Diaz, R. M., McCarthy, E. M., Atencio, D. J., & Chabay, L. A. (1999). Mother-child interaction, private speech, and task performance in preschool children with behavior problems. *Journal of Child Psychology and Psychiatry, 40,* 891–904.

Zivin, G. (1979). *The development of self-regulation through private speech.* New York: Wiley.

5

FEELING AND UNDERSTANDING THROUGH THE PRISM OF RELATIONSHIPS

ROSS A. THOMPSON

Psychology has a long tradition of regarding emotion and cognition as separable and independent, perhaps even in conflict. This tradition has deep roots in ancient and modern Western philosophy and is most visibly manifested in psychology in the ideas of psychoanalytic theory. Freud and his followers devoted unique attention to the importance of emotions in thinking, motivation, and behavior, but they often portrayed emotions as irrational and maladaptive, especially as they functioned in unconscious processes. This psychoanalytic legacy remains influential today, even among scholars of different theoretical orientations, and helps to explain current interest in emotion regulation as a rational, adaptive mechanism to "tame" the impulses of raw emotion, especially through cognitive control.

The contributions to this volume reflect how far psychologists have come in recognizing the intimate connections between emotion and cognition throughout development. Beginning with the young infant's emerging capacity to accurately interpret facial expressions of emotion and with the baby's emotional response to expectations of the caregiver's behavior, it is apparent that cognitive growth and emotional development are mutually influential. Emotion–cognition interrelationships are further evident in the emergence of social referencing, the growth of emotion understanding, the development of self-referential emotions, the emergence of empathy, joint humor, and other forms of shared emotionality, and the variety of influences contributing to the development of emotion self-regulation (see reviews by Saarni, Campos, Camras, & Witherington, 2006; Thompson, 2006a). Research in these areas has also contributed to a change in prevalent portrayals of the influence of emotion in development. Rather than being viewed merely as a primitive, irrational force that must be managed to permit socialized conduct, emotion is increasingly regarded as a biologically adaptive, constructive influence on children's developing social transactions, self-awareness, interpersonal sensitivity—and thinking.

Contemporary psychologists have not entirely abandoned their traditional approaches to emotion, however, and in one important respect they should not. The psychoanalytic emphasis on the influence of early, close relationships on emotional growth and understanding can be a significant contribution to contemporary thinking about cognition–emotion interrelationships. The Freudian view—expanded by Rene Spitz, Margaret Mahler, Erik Erikson, and many others—that young children perceive their own emotions and those of others through the prism of how caregivers nurture, evaluate, communicate about, and otherwise respond to their feelings offers a potentially valuable window into how emotion representations are colored by early relational experience. It is a view that has been more recently advanced by the contemporary inheritors of the developmental psychoanalytic legacy, attachment theorists.

This chapter is devoted to examining and advancing the contributions of attachment theory to contemporary research on the developmental association of emotion and cognition. Through its emphasis on broad and narrow features of relational experience that influence the growth of representations of the self and others, attachment theory offers provocative ideas about how young children represent and interpret emotional experience. What is particularly important about the contemporary climate of developmental research, however, is how the ideas of attachment theorists intersect with those of others who study developing representations of psychological experience from alternative theoretical approaches. One of my purposes, therefore, is to show how the formulations of attachment theory can be elucidated and clarified by contemporary research on young children's conceptual growth while also providing important insights into the relational construction of early emotional understanding. I profile relevant research from my own laboratory group and others, and I also offer suggestions for future research directions concerning the developmental interaction of emotional experience, representation, and relationships.

INTERNAL WORKING MODELS AND
COGNITION–EMOTION INTERACTION

Drawing from their psychoanalytic forebears, attachment theorists believe that early caregiving experience is important to psychological development for several reasons (Ainsworth, 1973; Bowlby, 1969/1982; see also Thompson, 2006a). The caregiver's sensitivity provides a foundation for a secure or insecure relationship with the caregiver that, in turn, fosters other developing competencies through the effects of security on exploratory play, social skills, and self-confidence. As a rudimentary index of the early harmony of the relationship between parent and child, moreover, security of attachment is an avenue by which other socialization processes occur, including the child's acceptance of the adult's guidance, identification with the parent and internalization of the parent's values, and other benefits of a mutually responsive relationship (Maccoby, 1984; Waters, Kondo-Ikemura, Posada, & Richters, 1991).

Internal Working Models

The most provocative explanation for the influence of security of attachment on psychological growth is through the mental representations of people and relationships that are believed to be inspired by attachment relationships. According to attachment theorists, these mental representations—known as *internal working models* (IWMs)—influence how infants conceptualize their caregivers, their attachment relationships, and themselves. IWMs begin with the simple affective–perceptual schemas and rudimentary social expectations that enable infants to forecast the immediate behavior of their attachment figures. In the months and years that follow, these IWMs are thought to develop into broader dynamic representational systems that, among other things, provide guidance about how to interact with others, expectations for close relationships, and self-perceptions that influence other developing belief systems (see Bretherton & Munholland, 1999). As a consequence, IWMs constitute interpretive filters through which children and adults organize their understanding of new experiences and relationships in ways that are consistent with past experiences and expectations. IWMs influence, for example, how people choose new partners and interact with them in ways that are based on, and thus help to confirm, the biases created from earlier attachment relationships. In a sense, attachment security contributes to the development of affective–cognitive representations that influence how young children feel and think about themselves and the social world.

Such a view is consistent with the findings of other research literatures. Studies of the development of early social expectations (Lamb & Lewis, 2005) indicate, for example, that young infants develop salient expectations that affect their responsiveness to caregivers. Research on the development of episodic memory (Hudson, 1993) and autobiographical memory (Nelson & Fivush, 2004) indicates that relational processes influence how young children construct memories of events of personal significance.

Research based on script theory (describing the development of generalized event representations) shows that young children develop hierarchically organized representations of familiar experiences that vary (and change developmentally) in their generalization across contexts and people (Fivush, 2006). Studies of social information–processing biases (Lemerise & Arsenio, 2000) show the influence of attribution biases and other expectations on peer behavior, although the origins of these biases are not well understood. Much more research is needed on the association of these and other representational processes with early relational influences as suggested by attachment theory. The potential contribution of the IWM concept is that it offers a portrayal of developing mental representations that is integrative, affectively colored, and relationally based. The problem with the IWM concept, however, is its inclusiveness and vague definition. Critics from within and outside attachment theory have noted, for example, that as it is presently conceptualized, the concept of IWMs can be flexibly enlisted to explain the association between attachment security and a vast array of correlates because the defining features, development, and sequelae of IWMs are not well defined by attachment theorists (Belsky & Cassidy, 1994; Thompson & Raikes, 2003b). This is because the IWM is, in Bowlby's (1973) theory, a conceptual metaphor, not a well-articulated theoretical construct.

Despite this, an expanding research literature documents the association between the security of attachment and a broad variety of social–cognitive outcomes that are consistent with theoretical portrayals of a security-based network of mental representations like the IWM. Secure children are not only more socially competent with friends and exhibit more positive personality qualities, they are also more advanced in emotion understanding, exhibit more positive expectations for peer behavior, show greater compliance, cooperation, and other indicators of emergent conscience, have a more positive self-concept, and exhibit enhanced emotion regulation when compared with insecurely attached children (see reviews by Thompson, 2006a, 2008). In a recent report from the National Institute of Child Health and Human Development Study of Early Child Care, Raikes and Thompson (2008a) found that the security of attachment at 24 and 36 months predicted social–cognitive abilities at 54 months and first grade, even with measures of maternal sensitivity controlled. Securely attached children were more likely to identify socially competent and relevant solutions to social problem-solving tasks, were less likely to make negative motivational attributions to peers, and were less lonely than insecurely attached children.

Constructing Mental Working Models

It seems apparent that attachment security is relevant not only to developing behavioral tendencies but also to how young children think about themselves and the social world. In what ways, therefore, could the security of attachment lead to these kinds of mental representations of relationships, self, and other people? Attachment theorists have proposed that, in addition to the positive social expectations and self-esteem fostered by sensitive care, the content and quality of parent–child discourse may also influence young children's developing social and emotional representations. According to Bretherton (1993), for example, parents and children in secure relationships are likely to engage in more candid, open, and fluid communication that enables greater personal disclosure, particularly of disturbing experiences or negative emotions that are troubling or confusing to young children. When this occurs, security is fostered not only by the parent's behavioral responsiveness but also by his or her understanding and reassurance conveyed in conversation. By contrast, when parents are critical or dismissive of the fears or anxieties of their young children, emotional communication is impaired and reassurance may not be forthcoming. Children may come to believe that their own negative emotions are less manageable, more overwhelming, and less comprehensible compared with children in secure attachments.

Parent–child conversations—whether about disturbing experiences or ordinary daily events—are also likely to contribute to young children's understanding of the behavior of other people as parents clarify others' feelings, motives, goals, expectations, and other psychological influences. These mentalistic and motivational explanations in discussions of shared experiences are almost inevitable as adults interpret the social behavior they observe in light of their own psychological inferences and judgments. In parent–child conversation, therefore, young children are likely to achieve insight into the features of social and emotional understanding, as well as self-awareness, that have been associated with attachment security (see also Thompson, 2000, 2006a).

This view is consistent with research literatures describing the significance of parent-child discourse for early conceptual growth (see Thompson, 2006b; Wareham & Salmon, 2006). Discourse about mental states in the context of shared social activity is, along with the young child's inductive inferences, an important influence on developing theory of mind and other aspects of psychological understanding (Astington & Baird, 2005; Carpendale & Lewis, 2004). Emotion understanding is associated with how often parents discuss feelings with their children and the elaborativeness of their conversational prompts (Dunn, 2002). The content and richness of parent–child conversation influence event representation and episodic memory (Ornstein, Haden, & Hedrick, 2004), the quality of autobiographical memory (Nelson

& Fivush, 2004), and even young children's anticipatory event representations (Hudson, 2002). These conclusions are consistent with the view that young children rely on the claims of the adults they trust on a wide variety of issues of importance to them, especially on matters that they cannot independently confirm (Harris, 2007). Young children have an early and intense interest in understanding the thoughts, feelings, and intentions of others, but because these are invisible and often confusing mental states, they would naturally rely on what they learn from conversations with parents.

There is also evidence that parents in secure relationships talk differently with their young children about these psychological phenomena compared with parents who have insecurely attached children. Although evidence is limited, a number of studies have shown that the mothers of secure children are more elaborative and evaluative in their style of conversation with their offspring (for a review, see Reese, 2002). An elaborative style elicits relatively detailed conversations about the child's experiences, typically because mothers ask more open-ended who-what-when-where-why questions, expand on their young child's contributions to the conversation, ask follow-up questions, and provide evaluations of the child's responses that may confirm or correct what the child has said. Studies of event representation and autobiographical memory have found elaborative discourse by mothers to be important because it contributes to richer, more detailed representations of and deeper memory for events by young children (Hudson, 1993, 2002; Nelson & Fivush, 2004).

Although little is known about why some mothers speak in a more elaborative, evaluative manner with their young offspring, one recent study found that mothers who are more secure in their attachment representations spoke more elaboratively with their preschoolers when reminiscing about past events than did nonsecure mothers (Reese, 2007). Another study found that secure mothers provided more frequent references to emotion in their reminiscing about shared experiences (Bost et al., 2006). It is possible that their own security provides mothers with more confidence to explore the diverse features of personal experiences, including both positive and negative aspects of those experiences. In so doing, they may also be contributing to greater depth and richness in the psychological representations (or IWMs) of their young children.

Taken together, attachment research has suggested that the multifaceted relational experiences associated with a secure attachment contribute to more constructive behavioral tendencies and more positive representations of others and the self. These representations emerge because the parental sensitivity that initially led to a secure attachment is likely to be maintained in styles of parent–child conversation that provide support, reassurance, and enhanced understanding of the psychological processes underlying interpersonal interaction. This conjecture is supported not only by attachment research but also by other research literatures that have described how the content and quality of discourse influences the growth of young children's representations of the social world, understanding of self, and constructive memory (see also chap. 4, this volume). It may also be true that parent–child conversations help young children to derive the implicit rules for getting along with others and broader expectations for the characteristics of people that are also incorporated into the IWM concept, but much more research on these issues is needed. In a manner that is consistent with attachment formulations and also with neo-Vygotskian perspectives (e.g., Rogoff, 1990) and sociocultural cognitive developmental formulations (Nelson, 1996), parent–child conversational discourse may be a foundational relational influence on children's developing capacities for representing the inner psychological experience that they share with other human beings. In this manner, relational experience bridges emotional growth and the cognitive representations of emotion and other facets of psychological understanding.

As this research review indicates, however, much more remains to be learned. What are the characteristics of elaborative discourse, and does it contribute to emotional understanding as it does to event representation and autobiographical memory? How do the security of attachment and the quality of parent–child conversation jointly contribute to young children's developing understanding of themselves and the psychological world? What other influences on the parent–child relationship might also be influential? If it is not only what is said but also who says it that influences the development of psychological understanding, how does this inform understanding of the development of children's emotion understanding?

DEVELOPING MENTAL MODELS OF EMOTION THROUGH SOCIAL INTERACTION

My colleagues and I became interested in these questions in our efforts to understand how attachment security contributes to young children's social competence with peers and other close partners. We sought to explore the hypothesis that a secure attachment contributes to enhanced emotion understanding of others, which can facilitate social competence. This would be consistent with the general formulations of a security-based IWM, but this approach would enable us to study the functioning of IWMs in a more specific, refined manner.

We used two measures of emotion understanding with a sample of 4-year-olds (Laible & Thompson, 1998). The first measure was adapted from a procedure by Fabes, Eisenberg, McCormick, and Wilson (1988) in which research assistants at the child's preschool or child care program watched for spontaneous emotional outbursts from any other child that could be observed by the target child. After noting the emotion and its cause, the assistant then approached the target child to ask what the other child was feeling, and why, and the accuracy of the response was later coded on the basis of the concordance of the child's response with the research assistant's observation of the situation.

The second measure was an affective perspective–taking task developed by Denham (1986) in which children were presented with short stories enacted by a research assistant using puppets and narration. At the conclusion of each story, the children were asked to show how the story character felt at the conclusion by attaching to the puppet a felt face that the child had earlier identified as representing a sad, happy, angry, or fearful emotion. Nearly half the stories that children heard described emotional responses that were different from those the child would experience in the same situation, according to maternal report (e.g., feeling excited rather than frightened at the approach of a large dog), and these stories are typically more challenging for young children. Summary scores for these two measures of emotion understanding were highly correlated, contributing to the validity of each, so they were combined for further analysis.

Securely attached children scored higher on this composite measure of emotion understanding than did insecurely attached children. They were also higher on the portion of the first measure that specifically assessed children's understanding of the causes of their peers' emotions in child care or preschool settings. Of particular interest was that the conceptual advantage of secure children was in understanding negative emotions. When scores for each measure were decomposed to distinguish responses to positive and negative emotion-eliciting circumstances, securely attached children scored higher on the index of negative emotion understanding, but there were no differences on the derived index of positive emotion understanding. Their relatively greater proficiency in understanding and explaining the causes of others' negative feelings is consistent with theoretical portrayals of the benefits of a secure attachment to emotion understanding (Bretherton, 1993).

The greater proficiency in emotion understanding by secure children has been replicated in our lab (Ontai & Thompson, 2002; Raikes & Thompson, 2006) and by others (Steele, Steele, Croft, & Fonagy, 1999). Moreover, Denham, Blair, Schmidt, and DeMulder (2002) showed how, in a preschool sample, the security of attachment was predictive of later social competence through the effects of security on enhanced emotional competence. Although more research is needed, it appears that the relational experiences associated with a secure attachment enhance young children's understanding of others' emotions—especially their negative emotions—in ways that may be relevant to their capacities for social interaction.

Parent–Child Conversation and Developing Emotion Understanding

What relational experiences associated with a secure attachment enhance emotion understanding? In particular, does the quality of mother–child conversation foster comprehension of others' feelings?

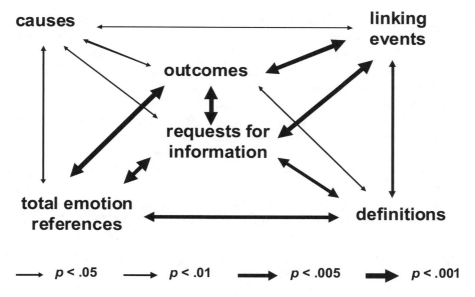

Figure 5.1. Correlational associations between maternal discourse variables. From "Early Understanding of Emotion, Morality, and the Self: Developing a Working Model," by R. A. Thompson, D. Laible, and L. Ontai, in *Advances in Child Development and Behavior* (Vol. 31, p. 156), by R. V. Kail (Ed.), 2003, San Diego, CA: Academic Press. Copyright 2003 by Elsevier. Reprinted with permission.

These questions guided our follow-up study (Ontai & Thompson, 2002). We observed a sample of 3-year-olds with their mothers as they conversed about emotion-relevant topics, and we also assessed the security of attachment. Two mother–child conversation tasks were used. First, we asked mothers to recall with the child a recent event in which the child had displayed negative emotion. We focused on negative emotional experiences because of the findings of the preceding study and theoretical expectations that securely attached children would exhibit better comprehension of negative feelings. Second, we asked mothers to talk with their children about a series of one-page pictorial stories involving emotional themes (e.g., a girl is afraid about her first day in a new class). We chose this storytelling format because the minimal narrative structure would, we thought, better exhibit mothers' preferences for discussing emotions with their offspring.

From these transcribed mother–child conversations about emotion, we coded many aspects of the mother's discourse. These included (a) the *frequency* of her references to emotion, (b) her description of the *causes* of emotion, (c) portrayals of the *outcomes* of emotion, (d) *definitions* of emotion (such as explaining an emotion term), (e) *linking events* in the child's life to the situation or story to help the child better understand the emotion, and (f) *requests for information* from the child related to emotion. We found that these elements of maternal emotion-related discourse were highly interrelated, as depicted in the correlational associations presented in Figure 5.1.

We also used a global rating of the mother's overall *elaborative* conversational style and found that each of the discourse features in Figure 5.1 was significantly associated with elaborative style. These findings suggest that there is a strong network of interrelated features of maternal emotion-related discourse associated with elaborative speech that is likely to be provocative of children's developing emotion understanding. This is consistent with the richness and detail of the parent–child conversations in which mothers are elaborative in their conversational prompts.

Two years later, these children returned to the lab with their mothers. In addition to being assessed for the security of attachment, children responded to the Denham affective perspective-taking task as in the earlier study. We found, as we had before, that a secure attachment at age 5 was associated with higher scores on emotion understanding, particularly of negative emotions, even controlling for attachment at age 3. With respect to the measures at age 3, we discovered that the security of attachment interacted with the quality of mother–child conversation in predicting emotion understanding 2 years later. More specifically, securely attached children whose mothers had used a more elaborative style of discourse at age 3 were more advanced in their understanding of positive emotions at age 5.

These findings were the first to indicate that early elaborative conversations with attachment figures are provocative not only of better event representation and autobiographical memory but also of emotion understanding, especially for securely attached children. They were not, however, the last; Laible (2004) found that emotion understanding in 4-year-olds was significantly predicted by both attachment security and the mother's use of elaborative discourse and discussion of emotion in the context of reminiscing about events in the recent past. In an independent sample, Laible and Song (2006) found that maternal elaboration in reminiscing predicted preschoolers' emotion understanding. These findings are important for characterizing the elements of mother–child conversation that are important to developing emotion understanding in young children. Beyond the frequency of emotion references in maternal speech, in other words, it is the overall discourse context of these references that is important: specifically, elaborative and evaluative speech that unfolds emotion incidents within a broader explanatory context by posing questions about emotion causes and outcomes, linking events to the child's experience, defining emotional terms, and soliciting information from the child about emotion concepts. In this manner, emotion and cognition are both fostered by the quality of conversations young children share with their caregivers.

The understanding fostered by this style of maternal discourse extends beyond comprehension of emotion. Laible and Thompson (2000) found that maternal references to feelings in conversations about the recent past predicted 4-year-olds' conscience development: More frequent maternal descriptions of emotions were associated with greater behavioral cooperation and compliance. In a prospective study, furthermore, Laible and Thompson (2002) found that maternal references to feelings during conflict episodes with children at age 2½ predicted children's conscience at age 3. In neither study did maternal references to rules and the consequences of breaking them predict children's conscience development. Taken together, these findings suggest that one of the consequences of maternal elaborative discussion of feelings is that it sensitizes preschoolers to others' needs and to the human consequences of wrongdoing. This portrayal of the humanistic origins of an early moral consciousness is in stark contrast to the punishment-and-obedience portrayal of young children in classic Kohlbergian theory, and it suggests that the conceptual catalysts of mother–child conversation extend beyond emotion understanding to other dimensions of social competence and psychological understanding.

Constructing Understanding in Challenging Circumstances

In middle-class families, discussion of emotion might focus on relatively benign encounters with mean siblings or scraped knees. In families at sociodemographic risk, the circumstances in which young children experience and observe emotion can be much less benign and might include domestic violence, a depressed caregiver, or threats to the child. Our next study focused on the development of emotion understanding in young children from at-risk families because the relational influences on emotional growth, as well as their impact on children's representations of emotion, are likely to be more complex and challenging.

The sample was recruited from Early Head Start, an early intervention program designed to provide family support and promote child development among families living in poverty (see Raikes & Thompson, 2006, 2008b, for further details and related analyses). When children were age 2, mothers completed inventories concerning depressive symptomatology and emotional risk factors (e.g., alcohol or drug abuse in the family, domestic violence, a family member with anger management problems), and child–mother attachment security was assessed. A year later, children completed Denham's affective perspective-taking task for assessing emotion understanding, and mothers and children were observed discussing recent events when the child felt happy, angry, or sad. From transcriptions of their conversations, we counted the frequency of mothers' references to emotion. We also included two measures of the child's emotion language as an index of developing emotion knowledge: the child's use of negative emotion words and the child's ability to independently generate labels for emotional states. These measures were highly correlated, so they were combined for analysis.

A series of regression analyses revealed both direct and indirect effects of broad family and relational influences at age 2—attachment security, maternal depression, and emotional risks—on maternal and child emotion lan-

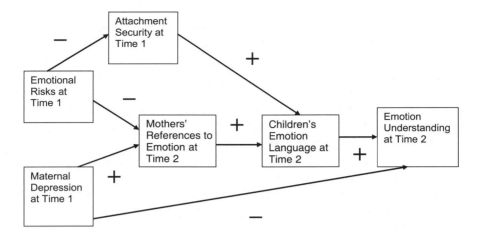

Figure 5.2. Relations between family emotional climate, attachment security, mothers' references to emotion, child emotion language, and child emotion understanding.

guage in relation to children's emotion understanding at age 3 (see Figure 5.2). Maternal depressive symptomatology and family emotional risks were each negatively associated with children's emotion understanding, but in different ways. Mothers who reported greater emotional risks within the family when children were 2 were less likely to talk about emotions when reminiscing with children at age 3. Emotional experiences were, for these mothers, perhaps troubling matters that restricted conversational access with their offspring. Mothers' diminished emotion language was associated, in turn, with children's diminished emotion language that, in turn, predicted poorer emotion understanding.

Maternal depression when children were age 2 was positively associated with mothers' conversational references to emotion at age 3. Depressed mothers may have been more attuned to emotion in themselves and others. Depression also, however, had a direct and unmediated negative prediction of children's emotion understanding at age 3. In this respect, depressive symptomatology seems to have also colored the emotional climate of the mother–child relationship such that children's emotion understanding at the follow-up assessment was lower, perhaps owing to the confused and confusing affective behavior of the caregiver in the hopelessness, self-critical attributions, and hostile behavior characteristic of depressed individuals. It is important that where maternal depression was concerned, the mother's more frequent references to emotion in parent–child conversation do not seem to have enhanced emotion understanding because of the different relational context in which they occurred.

Finally, as other studies have found, a secure attachment was positively predictive of emotion understanding at age 3. However, in this study of an at-risk group, the effects of attachment were not direct but, rather, were mediated by children's emotion language in conversation with their mothers. This raises the intriguing possibility that the benefits of attachment security are in how it enables children more readily to reflect on and identify emotions, particularly negative emotions, which may be one of the benefits of the more open communication shared by securely attached children with their mothers (Bretherton, 1993). Elucidating specifically how a secure attachment promotes emotion understanding in light of these findings is thus is an important future research goal.

Taken together, the findings of this study with an at-risk sample of families confirm both the importance of mother–child conversation to the development of emotion understanding and the broader relational context in which such conversation occurs. Whereas the development of emotion understanding is enhanced when caregivers talk more about people's feelings in middle-class homes, mothers' references to emotion in at-risk families are affected by the emotional climate of the home and, when mothers are depressed, their conversational references to emotion are not associated with greater emotion understanding of offspring. Attachment security—another relational influence—has a positive influence on developing emotion understanding primarily through its effects on children's greater facility with emotion language in parent–child conversation. In this constellation of catalysts to emotion understanding, the emotional climate of the parent–child relationship shapes the influence of conversation on developing emotion understanding.

CONCLUSION

Children's developing representations of emotional experience are among the more significant forms of emotion–cognition interaction. As important as their maturing conceptual skills are, it is becoming increasingly clear that young children also benefit from learning about emotion through conversations with adults. Such conversational catalysts not only provide children with insight into psychological experience but also embed developing emotional understanding in a relational context. In viewing the development of feeling and understanding through a relational prism, it is important not only *what* is said about emotion but also by *whom* and the *quality of the relationship* in which conversation occurs.

This is the idea behind attachment theorists' concept of the "internal working models" that guide understanding of people, relationships, and self from the perspective of the security or insecurity of attachment relationships. Accumulating research evidence on the social–cognitive correlates of attachment security is consistent with this idea of security-based mental representations, and the IWM concept is enlivened and specified by allied research in other conceptual domains, such as social expectations, event representation, social information–processing biases, autobiographical memory, and social scripts. Because IWMs are built on these conceptual constituents related to the encoding, interpretation, and retention of social information, the allied research literatures provide conceptual and methodological tools for elucidating the development and functioning of IWMs within the context of secure and insecure relationships and the broader emotional climate of the home.

Our research has provided one example of how to study security-related IWMs in the context of research on emotion understanding, conscience, and (in other research in our lab) self-awareness, emotion regulation, and other well-defined developmental processes that are elements of IWMs. This research has shown that the content and quality of mother–child conversational discourse are important influences on developing representations of emotion in self and others, that secure and insecure parent–child relationships are characterized by different styles of discourse that are related to developing emotion understanding in young children, and that security interacts with the conversational quality in shaping emotion knowledge. Beyond this, it is also clear that, especially for families in sociodemographic stress, other features of the emotional climate of the home influence the quality of mother–child conversation in ways directly relevant to the development of emotion representations.

This work is the beginning of a productive exploration of children's appropriation of social understanding from the conceptual catalysts of interaction in close relationships. Young children's developing representations of other people are also likely to be affected, for example, by how others' motives and intentions are characterized by caregivers in constructive ways or in a manner likely to inspire greater avoidance or suspicion. As parents convey implicit judgments of admirable or inappropriate conduct, coach offspring in emotion regulation, or explain the reasons for conflict and how to avoid it, they shape the implicit decision rules for relationships and expectations for others that children take with them into new social interactions. As we begin to better understand these relational influences from within and outside the formulations of attachment theory, it becomes possible to better comprehend the social construction of understanding and the relational influences that are central to it.

REFERENCES

Ainsworth, M. D. S. (1973). The development of infant-mother attachment. In B. Caldwell & H. Ricciuti (Eds.), *Review of child development research: Vol. 3* (pp. 1–94). Chicago: University of Chicago Press.

Astington, J. W., & Baird, J. A. (Eds.) (2005). *Why language matters for theory of mind*. New York: Oxford University Press.

Belsky, J., & Cassidy, J. (1994). Attachment: Theory and evidence. In M. Rutter & D. Hay (Eds.), *Development through life* (pp. 373–402). Oxford: Blackwell.

Bost, K. K., Shin, N., McBride, B. A., Brown, G. L., Vaughn, B. E., Coppola, G., et al. (2006). Maternal secure base scripts, children's attachment security, and mother-child narrative styles. *Attachment & Human Development, 8,* 241–260.

Bowlby, J. (1969/1982). *Attachment and loss, Vol. 1. Attachment* (2nd Ed.). New York: Basic.

Bowlby, J. (1973). *Attachment and loss, Vol. 2. Separation: Anxiety and anger.* New York: Basic.

Bretherton, I. (1993). From dialogue to internal working models: The co-construction of self in relationships. In C. A. Nelson (Ed.), *Memory and affect in development. Minnesota Symposia on Child Psychology: Vol. 26* (pp. 237–263). Hillsdale, NJ: Erlbaum.

Bretherton, I., & Munholland, K. (1999). Internal working models in attachment relationships: A construct revisited. In J. Cassidy & P. Shaver (Eds.), *Handbook of attachment* (pp. 89–111). New York: Guilford Press.

Carpendale, J. I. M., & Lewis, C. (2004). Constructing an understanding of mind: The development of children's social understanding within social interaction. *Behavioral and Brain Sciences, 27,* 79–96.

Denham, S. A. (1986). Social cognition, prosocial behavior, and emotion in preschoolers: Contextual validation. *Child Development, 57,* 194–201.

Denham, S., Blair, K., Schmidt, M., & DeMulder, E. (2002). Compromised emotional competence: Seeds of violence sown early? *American Journal of Orthopsychiatry, 72,* 70–82.

Dunn, J. (2002). Mindreading, emotion, and relationships. In W. W. Hartup & R. K. Silbereisen (Eds.), *Growing points in developmental science* (pp. 167–176). New York: Psychology Press.

Fabes, R. A., Eisenberg, N., McCormick, S. E., & Wilson, M. S. (1988). Young children's appraisals of others' spontaneous emotional reactions. *Developmental Psychology, 27,* 858–866.

Fivush, R. (2006). Scripting attachment: Generalized event representations and internal working models. *Attachment & Human Development, 8,* 283–289.

Harris, P. L. (2007). Trust. *Developmental Science, 10,* 135–138.

Hudson, J. A. (1993). Understanding events: The development of script knowledge. In M. Bennett (Ed.), *The child as psychologist* (pp. 142–167). New York: Harvester Wheatsheaf.

Hudson, J. A. (2002). "Do you know what we're going to do this summer?" Mothers' talk to young children about future events. *Journal of Cognition and Development, 3,* 49–71.

Laible, D. (2004). Mother-child discourse in two contexts: Links with child temperament, attachment security, and socioemotional competence. *Developmental Psychology, 40,* 979–992.

Laible, D., & Song, J. (2006). Constructing emotional and relational understanding: The role of affect and mother-child discourse. *Merrill-Palmer Quarterly, 52,* 44–69.

Laible, D. J., & Thompson, R. A. (1998). Attachment and emotional understanding in preschool children. *Developmental Psychology, 34*, 1038–1045.

Laible, D. L., & Thompson, R. A. (2000). Mother-child discourse, attachment security, shared positive affect, and early conscience development. *Child Development, 71*, 1424–1440.

Laible, D. J., & Thompson, R. A. (2002). Mother-child conflict in the toddler years: Lessons in emotion, morality, and relationships. *Child Development, 73*, 1187–1203.

Lamb, M. E., & Lewis, C. (2005). The role of parent-child relationships in child development. In M. H. Bornstein & M. E. Lamb (Eds.), *Developmental science: An advanced textbook* (5th Ed., pp. 429–468). Mahwah, NJ: Erlbaum.

Lemerise, E. A., & Arsenio, W. F. (2000). An integrated model of emotion processes and cognition in social information processing. *Child Development, 71*, 107–118.

Maccoby, E. E. (1984). Socialization and developmental change. *Child Development, 55*, 317–328.

Nelson, K. (1996). *Language in cognitive development: The emergence of the mediated mind.* New York: Cambridge.

Nelson, K., & Fivush, R. (2004). The emergence of autobiographical memory: A social-cultural developmental theory. *Psychological Review, 111*, 486–511.

Ontai, L. L., & Thompson, R. A. (2002). Patterns of attachment and maternal discourse effects on children's emotion understanding from 3 to 5 years of age. *Social Development, 11*, 433–450.

Ornstein, P. A., Haden, C. A., & Hedrick, A. M. (2004). Learning to remember: Social-communicative exchanges and the development of children's memory skills. *Developmental Review, 24*, 374–395.

Raikes, H. A., & Thompson, R. A. (2006). Family emotional climate, attachment security, and young children's emotion understanding in a high-risk sample. *British Journal of Developmental Psychology, 24*, 89–104.

Raikes, H. A., & Thompson, R. A. (2008a). Attachment security and parenting quality predict children's problem-solving, attributions, and loneliness with peers. *Attachment & Human Development, 10*, 319–344

Raikes, H. A., & Thompson, R. A. (2008b). Conversations about emotion in high-risk dyads. *Attachment & Human Development, 10*, 359–377.

Reese, E. (2002). Social factors in the development of autobiographical memory: The state of the art. *Social Development, 11*, 124–142.

Reese, E. (2007). *Maternal coherence in the Adult Attachment Interview is linked to maternal reminiscing and to children's self concept.* Unpublished manuscript, University of Otago, Dunedin, New Zealand.

Rogoff, B. (1990). *Apprenticeship in thinking.* New York: Oxford University Press.

Saarni, C., Campos, J. J., Camras, L. A., & Witherington, D. (2006). Emotional development: Action, communication, and understanding. In W. Damon & R. M. Lerner (Eds.) & N. Eisenberg (Vol. Ed.), *Handbook of child psychology:*

Vol. 3. Social, emotional, and personality development (6th ed., pp. 226–299). New York: Wiley.

Steele, H., Steele, M., Croft, C., & Fonagy, P. (1999). Infant-mother attachment at one year predicts children's understanding of mixed emotions at six years. *Social Development, 8,* 161–178.

Thompson, R. A. (2000). The legacy of early attachments. *Child Development, 71,* 145–152.

Thompson, R. A. (2006a). The development of the person: Social understanding, relationships, self, conscience. In W. Damon & R. M. Lerner (Eds.) & N. Eisenberg (Vol. Ed.), *Handbook of child psychology: Vol. 3. Social, emotional, and personality development* (6th ed., pp. 24–98). New York: Wiley.

Thompson, R. A. (2006b). Conversation and developing understanding: Introduction to the special issue. *Merrill-Palmer Quarterly, 52,* 1–16.

Thompson, R. A. (2008). Early attachment and later development: Familiar questions, new answers. In J. Cassidy & P. R. Shaver (Eds.), *Handbook of attachment: Theory, research, and clinical applications* (2nd ed., pp. 348–365). New York: Guilford Press.

Thompson, R. A., Laible, D., & Ontai, L. (2003a). Early understanding of emotion, morality, and the self: Developing a working model. In R. Kail (Ed.), *Advances in child development and behavior* (Vol. 31, pp.137–171). San Diego, CA: Academic Press.

Thompson, R. A., & Raikes, H. A. (2003b). Toward the next quarter-century: Conceptual and methodological challenges for attachment theory. *Development and Psychopathology, 15,* 691–718.

Wareham, P., & Salmon, K. (2006). Mother-child reminiscing about everyday experiences: Implications for psychological interventions in the preschool years. *Clinical Psychology Review, 26,* 535–554.

Waters, E., Kondo-Ikemura, K., Posada, G., & Richters, J. (1991). Learning to love: Mechanisms and milestones. In M. Gunnar & L. Sroufe (Eds.),. *Minnesota Symposia on Child Psychology: Vol. 23. Self processes and development* (pp. 217–255). Hillsdale, NJ: Erlbaum.

6

HOT EXECUTIVE FUNCTION: EMOTION AND THE DEVELOPMENT OF COGNITIVE CONTROL

PHILIP DAVID ZELAZO, LI QU, AND AMANDA C. KESEK

Young children's ability to act deliberately in light of their knowledge is obviously limited. During the 1st few years of life, however, children change from relatively helpless creatures who must rely on their caregivers to fulfill even their most basic needs into complex intellectual and emotional beings who are able to consider alternative perspectives on a situation, plan ahead, and act in a conscious, goal-directed fashion. These changes in children's behavior are studied under the rubric of *executive function* (EF). EF is an umbrella term for a number of subfunctions, including, but not limited to, working memory, inhibitory control, and task-switching (Miyake, Friedman, Emerson, Witzki, & Howerter, 2000).

Traditionally, research on the development of EF has focused on its relatively *cool*, cognitive aspects, often associated with lateral prefrontal cortex (PFC) and elicited by relatively abstract, decontextualized tasks. One such task is the Dimensional Change Card Sort (DCCS; Frye, Zelazo, &

We thank the editors for their helpful comments on a draft of this chapter.

Palfai, 1995; Zelazo, 2006), in which children are shown two target cards (e.g., a blue rabbit, a red boat) and asked to sort a series of bivalent test cards (e.g., red rabbits, blue boats), first according to one dimension (e.g., color) and then according to the other (e.g., shape). Most 3-year-olds perseverate during the post-switch phase, continuing to sort test cards by the first dimension (e.g., Zelazo, Müller, Frye, & Marcovitch, 2003). Although tasks such as these have been valuable in the study of relatively cool EF, they lack an obvious emotional or motivational component. In contrast, however, real-world problems are often thoroughly imbued with emotion—we try to solve them precisely because we care about their solution.

Recent work on the development of EF reflects this insight, and there has been growing interest in the development of relatively *hot* aspects of EF, seen in situations that are emotionally and motivationally significant because they involve meaningful, self-relevant rewards or punishers (e.g., Carlson, Davis, & Leach, 2005; Happaney, Zelazo, & Stuss, 2004; Hongwanishkul, Happaney, Lee, & Zelazo, 2005; Kerr & Zelazo, 2004; Zelazo & Müller, 2002; Zelazo, & Cunningham, 2007). Just as tasks such as the DCCS have demonstrated a dramatic shift in children's cool EF between the ages of 3 and 5 years, there is evidence that children's ability to make prudent decisions in an affective context also improves considerably during this period. For example, on the Children's Gambling Task (Kerr & Zelazo, 2004), a modified version of the Iowa Gambling Task (Bechara, Damasio, A.R., Damasio, H., & Anderson, 1994), preschool-age children (3- to 5-year-olds) are asked to choose on each trial from either of two decks of cards, one advantageous and one disadvantageous. Cards in the disadvantageous deck offered more rewards (two M&Ms) on every trial but were associated with occasional (unpredictable) large losses (up to six M&Ms). Cards in the advantageous deck offered fewer rewards (one M&M) on every trial but the occasional (unpredictable) losses were also fewer (up to one M&M). All children initially prefer the deck with larger rewards on every trial, but age differences emerge over trials, as children are gradually provided with information indicating which deck is better in the long run: Whereas 4- and 5-year-olds learn to make advantageous decisions, 3-year-olds fail to do so (see also Hongwanishkul et al., 2005; Garon & Moore, 2004, 2007).

We believe that a comprehensive characterization of EF and its development must encompass both hot and cool EF, as demonstrated by the recent work on affective decision making. In this chapter, we first describe a neurodevelopmental model of EF that provides a framework for thinking about how cognitive and emotional aspects of experience interact during the conscious control of thought and behavior, and we then show how this model can be used to make sense of two apparently contradictory effects of emotional context on EF in children: (a) the tendency for motivationally significant rewards to undermine EF and (b) the facilitative effect of positive stimuli on EF.

AN ITERATIVE REPROCESSING MODEL

Cognition and emotion have long been studied as if they were separate entities, but research on neural function makes it increasingly obvious that there is no cognition without emotion, and vice versa. Indeed, cognition and emotion are better conceptualized as two integral aspects (or dimensions) of one thing—human psychological experience—although clearly the emotional aspects of an experience may be more or less salient. Zelazo and Cunningham (2007; Cunningham & Zelazo, 2007) proposed a neural model (see Figure 6.1) that captures this more holistic view of cognition and emotion by positioning hot and cool EF on a continuum of reflective processing and by emphasizing the ways in which relatively hot and relatively cool aspects of EF interact when one is solving a problem.

This model follows the course of information processing involved in EF, beginning with the thalamus and the rapid emotional responses generated in the amygdala. These initial responses are then fed into orbitofrontal cortex (OFC), which furnishes relatively simple approach–avoidance (stimulus–reward) rules and is also involved in learning to reverse these rules. In many situations, these simple rules will suffice to produce an adequate response. If they fail to do so, however, the anterior cingulate cortex (ACC) acts as a performance monitor and signals the need for further, higher level reprocessing of action-oriented rules in hierarchically organized regions of lateral PFC. As individuals engage in reflective reprocessing and generate increasingly elaborate reactions to a stimulus, they recruit an increasingly complex hierarchical network of PFC regions (OFC, ventrolateral PFC, and dorsolateral PFC, with rostrolateral PFC playing a transient role in task set selection—the explicit consideration of contexts). These multiple regions then operate simultaneously and in parallel, with higher levels in the hierarchy supplementing and influencing lower levels (both directly and indirectly) but not replacing them.

Figure 6.2 illustrates the ways in which the hierarchically arranged regions of lateral PFC are hypothesized to correspond to EF at different levels of complexity (Bunge & Zelazo, 2006). The figure shows the rule systems that are believed to underlie conscious goal-directed behavior. According to the model, lateral PFC-mediated reprocessing allows one to reflect on relatively simple rules for acting (i.e., operate at a higher level of consciousness; Zelazo, 2004) and formulate higher order rules that control the application of these simpler rules, resulting in more complex rule systems. More complex rule systems permit more flexible top-down cognitive control of thought and behavior. Reflective reprocessing can be viewed as a shift from hotter aspects of EF more directly concerned with relatively simple approach-avoidance discriminations to cooler aspects of EF that involve the maintenance and manipulation of relatively abstract representations. Note that, according to this model, reprocessing accomplishes the functions of working memory (i.e.,

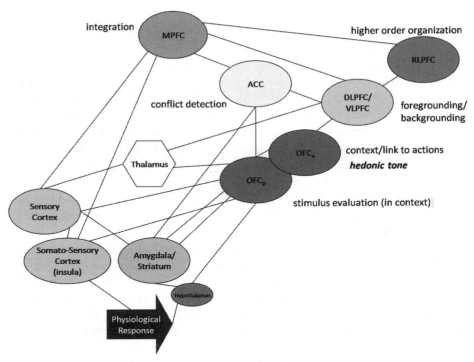

Figure 6.1. The iterative reprocessing model (Cunningham & Zelazo, 2007). Information about a stimulus is processed by the thalamus and projected to the amygdala, leading to an initial motivational tendency to approach or avoid the stimulus, but also initiating further processing of the stimulus by the anterior cingulate cortex (ACC) and orbitofrontal cortex (OFC). OFC and amygdala have outputs to the hypothalamus, which then is involved in generating a physiological response. This response is cortically represented in the insular cortex, which can then serve as in input into the next stage of processing. ACC responds to the motivational significance of the situation (e.g., negative valence) and may recruit additional reprocessing of the stimulus via ventrolateral prefrontal cortex and then dorsolateral prefrontal cortex, with rostrolateral prefrontal cortex playing a transient role in the explicit consideration of contexts. Reprocessing by lateral regions of PFC corresponds to reflection, and it serves to regulate evaluative processing by amplifying or suppressing attention to certain aspects of the situation (thalamic route). Medial prefrontal cortex provides a dynamic model of the relation between reality and one's processing goals, and it influences the extent to which one engages in reprocessing. The iterative reprocessing of information requires complex, interconnected neural networks that allow for the bidirectional flow of information (all connections depicted in the figure are bidirectional). Adapted from "Attitudes and Evaluation: A Social Cognitive Neuroscience Perspective," by W. A. Cunningham and P. D. Zelazo, 2007, *Trends in Cognitive Sciences, 11,* p. 99. Copyright 2007 by Elsevier. Adapted with permission.

keeping rules in mind) and inhibitory control (i.e., more complex rules allow children to select relevant rules for guiding their behavior and avoid relying on outmoded rules, although of course this may be more or less difficult depending on the prepotency of the outmoded rules).

As the model suggests, the motivationally significant aspects of a situation can be processed rapidly (e.g., Anderson, 2005; Cuthbert, Schupp, Bra-

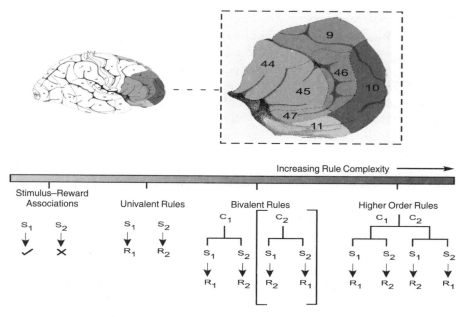

Figure 6.2. A hierarchical model of rule representation in prefrontal cortex (PFC). A lateral view of the human brain is depicted at the top of the figure, with regions of PFC identified by the Brodmann areas (BA) that comprise them: orbitofrontal cortex (BA 11), ventrolateral PFC (BA 44, 45, 47), dorsolateral PFC (BA 9, 46), and rostrolateral PFC (BA 10). The PFC regions are shown in various shades of gray, indicating which types of rules they represent. Rule structures are depicted below, with darker shades of gray indicating increasing levels of rule complexity. The formulation and maintenance in working memory of more complex rules depends on the reprocessing of information through a series of levels of consciousness, which in turn depends on the recruitment of additional regions of PFC into an increasingly complex hierarchy of PFC activation. Note: S = stimulus; check = reward; cross = nonreward; R = response; C = context, or task set. Brackets indicate a bivalent rule that is currently being ignored. From "A Brain-Based Account of the Development of Rule Use in Childhood" by S. Bunge and P. D. Zelazo, 2006, *Current Directions in Psychological Science, 15*, p. 119. Copyright 2006 by Blackwell Publishing. Reprinted with permission.

dley, Birbaumer, & Lang, 2000; Eger, Jedynak, Iwaki, & Skrandies, 2003; Jünghöfer, Bradley, Elbert, & Lang, 2001) and even without full awareness (e.g., Calvo & Lang, 2005; Dimberg & Öhman, 1996; Mack & Rock, 1998; MacLeod & Rutherford, 1992; Mogg, Bradley, Williams, & Mathews, 1993), and they may then demand continued processing—they may capture attention. Indeed, according to the iterative reprocessing model, ventral regions of PFC such as OFC remain more activated in motivationally significant situations even as other regions of PFC are recruited into a hierarchical network of activations. In effect, the simple approach–avoidance tendencies generated in reaction to relatively concrete stimuli are more difficult to ignore in such situations—discriminations at that level become more salient, leading to relatively more ventral PFC (i.e., OFC and perhaps ventrolateral PFC) activation even when higher levels in the hierarchy are also involved. Instead of discrete systems for hot and cool EF, then, hot and cool are viewed as points on a continuum that corresponds to the motivational significance of the problem to be solved. According to this model, it should be easier to engage in reflection and to effect a cognitive separation from the exigencies of the situation, in relatively cool situations. Put differently, manipulations that decrease the salience of aspects of a situation that elicit strong approach or avoidance tendencies will increase the probability of reflection and promote PFC function. At the same time, however, manipulations that promote PFC function (e.g., by increasing levels of neurotransmitters like dopamine, which is related to cognitive flexibility) will allow for more reflective reprocessing and improve EF.

Hot Contexts May Undermine Executive Function

Studies comparing children's EF in an emotional context with their performance in a relatively neutral context have suggested that emotional aspects of a situation may indeed interfere with EF. For example, Carlson et al. (2005) developed the Less Is More Task, in which children are presented with two piles of candies, one large and one small, and must point to the small pile in order to obtain the large pile. Three-year-olds, unlike 4-year-olds, had difficulty inhibiting their desire to point to the preferred, larger reward. When the candy was replaced by abstract symbols, however, 3-year-olds were more likely to indicate the symbol for the small reward in order to obtain the larger reward. The presence of the actual rewards appeared to interfere with children's problem solving, leading to an imprudent, approach-oriented response. In contrast, the use of symbols may allow children to avoid being captured by the simple approach–avoid discrimination and instead engage in the reflective reprocessing required for prudent action in this situation. As Carlson et al. (2005) noted, casting the Less Is More Task in a cooler context via symbols may help children to distance themselves psychologically from the situation (cf. Dewey, 1931/1985; Sigel, 1993).

Another mechanism by which children may achieve psychological distance is labeling (cf. chaps. 4 and 5, this volume). Labeling arguably encourages reflection on whatever is labeled. To assess the effect of labeling on children's hot EF, Müller, Zelazo, Hood, Leone, and Rohrer (2004) developed a task in which children were presented with colored candies on mismatched colored cards and were asked to retrieve a small card that matched the color of the card on which the candy had been placed. Three-year-olds performed poorly unless they were first asked to label the color of the card. In this study, labels apparently helped children divert their attention away from the salient rewards and exert top-down control.

Further evidence of the interfering effect of hot contexts on EF has come from research on children's ability to delay gratification. In a classic delay of the gratification paradigm, developed by Mischel and colleagues (e.g., Mischel & Baker, 1975; Mischel, Ebbesen, & Zeiss, 1972), children are given a choice between a smaller, immediate reward and a larger, delayed reward. They are told that they may summon the experimenter by ringing a bell, which will end their wait but result in the smaller reward. Variations on this paradigm have also been developed. For example, children may be required to hold a candy on their tongue without eating it, or they may be instructed to sit quietly with their back to an experimenter as she conspicuously wraps a gift (Kochanska, Murray, Jacques, Koenig, & Vandegeest, 1996).

Children's performance on delay of gratification tasks has been shown to improve with age during the preschool and early school age years, and a number of studies have demonstrated the impact of reward salience (which should be correlated with subjective assessments of motivational significance) in delay of gratification tasks. Various manipulations of this paradigm have demonstrated that children are willing to wait longer when the rewards are not visible or when distractions are available—whether these be external (e.g., a toy) or internal (e.g., happy thoughts; Mischel & Baker, 1975; Mischel, Ebbesen, & Zeiss, 1972). The way in which rewards are represented cognitively also influences the amount of time children are willing to wait. In general, when children are encouraged to focus on the arousing qualities of the reward, such as taste, the time they are willing to wait is decreased. In contrast, when children are told to focus on the more abstract qualities of the reward, such as its similarities to other objects, they tend to wait longer. For example, Mischel and Baker (1975) found that when the experimenter suggested that children think about the similarities between marshmallows and clouds, or between pretzels and poles, children tended to wait longer than when they were told to focus on the sweet taste of the marshmallows, or the saltiness of the pretzels. Children also tended to wait longer for the rewards when they were told to imagine the rewards as pictures, versus imagining them as real (Moore, Mischel, & Zeiss, 1976). Mischel and colleagues have suggested that children's focusing on the arousing properties of the rewards elicits an approach-oriented, consummatory response. However, children are able to use the abstract qualities of the reward as a reminder of the ultimate goal, without becoming focused on the appetitive aspects of the reward. That is, the emotional salience of the rewards is optimal: Children are motivated to obtain the larger reward, but they are not overwhelmed by the temptation to obtain the treats immediately. In terms of the iterative reprocessing model, manipulations that decrease reward salience improve EF because they help children to disengage attention from simple approach–avoidance discriminations and instead engage in reflective reprocessing.

Prencipe and Zelazo (2005) manipulated motivational significance in a delay of gratification task by asking children either to choose for themselves or to choose on behalf of the experimenter. Results revealed that whereas 3-year-olds typically chose the immediate reward for themselves, they usually told the experimenter that she should wait and take the larger reward. For 4-year-olds, there was no difference between conditions. Again, the younger children—3-year-olds—had difficulty making a prudent decision when the rewards were salient, and they were more likely to make a rational decision in a cooler, less self-relevant context. Arguably, they were better able to engage in reflective processing in the cooler context.

Although several studies have found improvements in hot EF between 3 and 5 years of age, there is evidence that hot EF continues to improve throughout childhood and even adolescence—when it is measured using more complex measures of EF (e.g., Crone & van der Molen, 2004, 2007; Garon & Moore, 2004, 2007). The slow development of hot EF is consistent with the idea that prefrontal cortical networks underlying reflective reprocessing continue to develop beyond childhood (e.g., Giedd et al., 1999; Gogtay et al., 2004). Further work is needed to establish directly the hypothesized connection between the development of hot EF and the elaboration of increasingly complex networks of PFC activation, but the iterative reprocessing model makes clear predictions in this regard. For example, the model predicts that as children develop they will be more likely to engage in reflective processing during challenging measures of hot EF. This should result in increasing reliance on more anterior regions of PFC (i.e., frontalization; cf. Rubia et al., 2000) during performance on these measures. Additionally, both performance on measures of hot EF and activation in PFC should be impaired if participants are prevented from engaging in reflective processing—for example, through response deadlines. Response deadlines should interrupt the cycles of reprocessing involved in reflection and the formulation of higher order rules, resulting in action based on less complex rule systems as well as decreases in activation in anterior regions of lateral PFC. As a final example, the iterative reprocessing model also predicts that manipulations that decrease the salience of those aspects of a situation that elicit strong approach or avoidance tendencies will lead to increases in reflective reprocessing and associated PFC function.

Positive Stimuli May Facilitate Executive Function

Although hot contexts can impair EF when they involve salient aspects of a situation that elicit strong approach or avoidance tendencies, there are other situations in which emotional stimuli appear to facilitate EF—arguably by promoting PFC function and reflective reprocessing. In particular, research has suggested that positive stimuli that do not elicit strong approach or avoidance tendencies inconsistent with goal-directed problem solving may facilitate EF. These stimuli may facilitate EF by inducing a positive mood and increasing dopamine levels in PFC.

Relatively little is known about the effects of mood on young children's cognitive processing, especially on EF (for a review, see Brenner, 2000). Several studies, however, have found that positive mood facilitates performance in ways that may reflect improved EF (see Isen, 2003). For example, Isen (1990) showed that positive mood improved 3-year-old children's ability to perceive relations among a set of nesting cups. Children who received a gift of stickers correctly nested 2.63 cups, whereas children in the control group nested only 1.48 cups. In addition, children in a positive mood were more likely to put cups upside down and stack them as towers, as if they were better able to think about the task in a different way.

In another study, Isen (1990) gave first graders 24 stimuli to sort. Each of these stimuli contained three dimensions: color (blue or white), shape (squares or triangles), and structure (one line or a line with two dots that looked like a smiling face). Children given stickers to induce a positive mood spontaneously sorted the stimuli into more subcategories. Positive mood also improved school-age children's performance on Piagetian class-inclusion problems (e.g., Isen, 1990), Block Design (Rader & Hughes, 2005), and measures of word fluency and creativity (e.g., the Remote Associates Test and Duncker's [1945] Candle Task; e.g., Bryan & Bryan, 1991; Greene & Noice, 1988). Finally, children in a positive mood have been found to wait longer during a delay of gratification test than children in a neutral mood (Seeman & Schwarz, 1974).

In light of findings like these, Ashby, Isen, and Turken (1999) proposed a neuropsychological theory of positive affect according to which positive affect improves the function of PFC and the ACC by increasing the release of dopamine from the ventral tegmental area and the substantia nigra. The role of dopamine in reward has long been established (e.g., Goldman-Rakic, Muly, & Milliams, 2000; Schultz, 2002; Schultz, Dayan, & Montague, 1997; for reviews, see Nieoullon, 2002; Ungless, 2004), and there is now considerable evidence that dopamine plays an important role in the function of the ACC and lateral PFC (for a review, see Arnsten & Robbins, 2002). According to Ashby, Isen, and Turken, (1999), moderately elevated dopamine levels in lateral PFC may facilitate working memory, whereas moderately elevated dopamine levels in the ACC may enhance executive attention and selection of task sets (Ashby, Valentin, & Turken, 2002). In terms of the iterative reprocessing model, transient increases in dopamine should facilitate PFC-mediated reflective reprocessing.

Qu and Zelazo (2007) used the DCCS to investigate the effect of positive stimuli on flexible rule use in 3-year-olds. In the standard version of the DCCS, children were required to sort red and blue boats and rabbits first by shape and then by color (or vice versa). In a new Emotional Faces version, however, children were required to sort happy and sad male and female faces, first by emotion and then by gender (or vice versa). Children performed significantly better on the Emotional Faces version, and the order in which dimensions were presented had no effect—suggesting that the emotional aspects of the stimuli facilitated EF in a relatively general way. A second experiment examined which aspects of the emotional faces were responsible for the facilitation of children's performance. Performance on the standard version was compared with performance on three Contextual Faces versions, in which children were shown happy, sad, or neutral faces and required to sort them by age (child or adult) and then by gender (or in reverse order). Facilitation was only seen in the context of happy faces. This pattern of results is consistent with the suggestion that happy faces induce a mildly positive mood in children and that this improves cognitive flexibility. Further research is required to determine whether the facilitative effect of mildly positive stimuli is mediated by an increase in PFC activation, but so far the results are in line with both the Ashby et al. (1999) model and the iterative reprocessing model.

TIME COURSE OF THE INTERACTION
BETWEEN COGNITION AND EMOTION

Although emotion and cognition always interact, the nature and consequences of this interaction may change over time, and this may be true on many time scales. For example, the influence of emotional contexts on EF may be particularly salient during childhood, when lateral regions of PFC required for reflective reprocessing are still developing. In addition, the impact of emotion on cognitive control may vary as a function of time since the presentation of a motivationally significant stimulus or context, and it may vary across a series of trials. According to the iterative reprocessing model (Cunningham & Zelazo, 2007; Zelazo & Cunningham, 2007), reflective reprocessing takes time to occur, so the effect of relatively unreflective evaluative responses on behavior will be most pronounced if rapid responding is required, and it may be most pronounced early in a series of trials, consistent with the improvement over trials seen in tasks such as the Children's Gambling Task (Kerr & Zelazo, 2004) and the Less Is More Task (Carlson et al., 2005). Finally, the hypothesized effects of dopamine and mood on EF should also vary over time. Kaufmann and Vosburg (2002), for example, analyzed adult participants' solutions to idea production tasks that lasted for a 4-minute period and found that, in general, the participants in a positive mood outperformed other participants. This pattern of results was especially significant during the first minute, however. By the last minute, participants in a positive mood actually produced fewer solutions than those in other types of mood. This reversal may have occurred because people in a positive mood tend to take more initiative in starting and stopping a process, compared with people in other types of mood. For example, people in a negative mood may need to have a clear external signal to stop and switch to a new process, whereas people in a positive mood may initiate such changes on their own (Gasper, 2003). It is possible that after the first 3 minutes during Kaufmann and Vosburg's task, people in a positive mood stopped or reduced processing, whereas people in other mood states kept processing the task. In addition, participants in a positive mood state, compared with those in a neutral mood, tend to generate more task-irrelevant thoughts (Seibert & Ellis, 1991). Interference from irrelevant thoughts may have played an increasingly important role over the time course of the period.

CONCLUSION

The recent interest in hot EF highlights the relevance of bottom-up, motivational processes in cognitive control and undermines overly rational conceptualizations of EF. Indeed, most real-life problems probably elicit cognitive processing in the context of emotional reactions and thus involve interactions among more purely cognitive processes and more purely emotional processes. Relatively little is known about the influence of motivational stimuli on young children's EF, but there is evidence both that young children seem to have more difficulty on hot versions of EF tasks than they do on cool versions (e.g., Carlson et al., 2005; Prencipe & Zelazo, 2005) and that positive aspects of a situation can facilitate cognitive flexibility, a key aspect of EF. In this chapter, we reviewed the iterative reprocessing model, which highlights the role of PFC-mediated reflective reprocessing in EF and emphasizes the way in which relatively hot and relatively cool aspects of EF interact when one is solving a problem. According to this model, hot contexts can impair EF when they elicit strong approach or avoidance tendencies that interfere with reflective reprocessing. At the same time, however, hot contexts may facilitate EF if they increase dopamine levels in PFC. Given the slow development of PFC, and the fact that areas of the brain involved in the rapid processing of emotionally salient stimuli develop earlier than areas of the brain associated with more reflective responding, the effects (both positive and negative) of emotional aspects of a situation on EF may be particularly pronounced in young children, but an interaction between cognition and emotion is likely to underlie EF across the life span. Considerably more work remains to be done to explore the cognitive–affective mechanisms underlying EF, but the iterative reprocessing model provides a neurodevelopmental framework within which this work can be conducted.

REFERENCES

Anderson, A. (2005). Affective influences on the attentional dynamics supporting awareness. *Journal of Experimental Psychology: General, 134,* 258–281.

Arnsten, A. F. T., & Robbins, T. W. (2002). Neurochemical modulation of prefrontal cortical function in humans and animals. In D. T. Stuss & R. T. Knight (Eds.), *Principles of frontal lobe function* (pp. 51–84). New York: Oxford.

Ashby, F. G., Isen, A. M., & Turken, A. U. (1999). A neuropsychological theory of positive affect and its influence on cognition. *Psychological Review, 106,* 529–550.

Ashby, F. G., Valentin, V. V., & Turken, A. U. (2002). The effects of positive affect and arousal and working memory and executive attention: Neurobiology and computational models. In S. C. Moore & M. Oaksford (Eds.), *Emotional cognition: From brain to behaviour. Advances in consciousness research: Vol. 44.* (pp. 245–287). Amsterdam: John Benjamins.

Bechara, A., Damasio, A. R., Damasio, H., & Anderson, S. W. (1994). Insensitivity to future consequences following damage to human prefrontal cortex. *Cognition, 50,* 7–15.

Brenner, E. (2000). Mood induction in children: Methodological issues and clinical implications. *Review of General Psychology, 4,* 264–283.

Bryan, T., & Bryan, J. (1991). Positive mood and math performance. *Journal of Learning Disabilities, 24,* 490–493.

Bunge, S. A., & Zelazo, P. D. (2006). A brain-based account of the development of rule use in childhood. *Current Directions in Psychological Science, 15,* 118–121.

Calvo, M. G., & Lang, P. J. (2005). Parafoveal semantic processing of emotional visual scenes. *Journal of Experimental Psychology: Human perception and Performance, 31,* 502–519.

Carlson, S. M., Davis, A. C., & Leach, J. G. (2005). Less is more: Executive function and symbolic representation in preschool children. *Psychological Science, 16,* 609–616.

Crone, E. A, & van der Molen, M. W. (2004). Developmental changes in real life decision making: Performance on the gambling task previously shown to depend on the vetromedial prefrontal cortex. *Developmental Neuropsychology, 25,* 251–279.

Crone, E. A, & van der Molen, M. W. (2007). Development of decision making in school-aged children and adolescents: Evidence from heart rate and skin conductance analysis. *Child Development, 78,* 1288–1301.

Cunningham, W. A., & Zelazo, P. D. (2007). Attitudes and evaluation: A social cognitive neuroscience perspective. *Trends in Cognitive Sciences, 11,* 97–104.

Cuthbert, B. N., Schupp, H. T., Bradley, M. M., Birbaumer, N., & Lang, P. J. (2000). Brain potentials in affective picture processing: Covariation with autonomic arousal and affective report. *Biological Psychology, 52,* 95–111.

Dewey, J. (1931/1985). Context and thought. In J. A. Boydston & A. Sharpe (Eds.), *John Dewey: The later works, 1925–1953* (Vol. 6, pp. 3–21). Carbondale: Southern Illinois University Press.

Dimberg, U., & Öhman, A. (1996). Behold the wrath: Psychophysiological responses to facial stimuli. *Motivation and Emotion, 20,* 149–182.

Duncker, K. (1945). On problem solving. *Psychological Monographs, 58*(5, Whole No. 270).

Eger, E., Jedynak, A., Iwaki, T., & Skrandies, W. (2003). Rapid extraction of emotional expression: Evidence from evoked potential fields during brief presentation of face stimuli. *Neuropsychologia, 41*, 808–817.

Frye, D., Zelazo, P. D., & Palfai, T. (1995). Theory of mind and rule-based reasoning. *Cognitive Development, 10*, 483–527.

Garon, N., & Moore, C. (2004). Complex decision-making in early childhood. *Brain and Cognition, 55*, 158–170.

Garon, N., & Moore, C. (2007). Awareness and symbol use improves future-oriented decision making in preschoolers. *Developmental Neuropsychology, 31*, 39–59.

Gasper, K. (2003). When necessity is the mother of invention: Mood and problem solving. *Journal of Experimental Social Psychology, 39*, 248–262.

Giedd, J. N., Blumenthal, J., Jeffries, N. O., Castellanos, F. X., Hong, L., Zijdenbos, A., et al. (1999). Brain development during childhood and adolescence: A longitudinal MRI study. *Nature Neuroscience, 2*, 861–863.

Gogtay, N., Giedd, J. N., Lusk, L., Hayashi, K. M., Greenstein, D., Vaituzis, A. C., et al. (2004). Dynamic mapping of human cortical development during childhood through early adulthood. *Proceedings of the National Academy of Sciences, 101*, 8174–8179.

Goldman-Rakic, P. S., Muly, E. C., & Williams, G. V. (2000). D1 receptors in prefrontal cells and circuits. *Brain Research Reviews, 31*, 295–301.

Greene, T. R., & Noice, H. (1988). Influence of positive affect upon creative thinking and problem solving in children. *Psychological Reports, 63*, 895–898.

Happaney, K., Zelazo, P. D., & Stuss, D. T. (2004). Development of orbitofrontal function: Current themes and future directions. *Brain and Cognition, 55*, 1–10.

Hongwanishkul, D., Happaney, K. R., Lee, W., & Zelazo, P. D. (2005). Hot and cool executive function: Age-related changes and individual differences. *Developmental Neuropsychology, 28*, 617–644.

Isen, A. M. (1990). The influence of positive and negative affect on cognitive organization: Some implications for development. In N. L. Stein, B. Leventhal, & T. Trabasso (Eds.), *Psychological and biological approaches to emotion* (pp. 75–94). Hillsdale, NJ: Erlbaum.

Isen, A. M. (2003). Positive affect as a source of human strength. In L. G. Aspinwall & U. M. Staudinger (Eds.), *A psychology of human strengths: Fundamental questions and future directions for a positive psychology* (pp. 179–195). Washington, DC: American Psychological Association.

Jünghöfer, M., Bradley, M. M., Elbert, T., & Lang, P. (2001). Fleeting images: A new look at early emotion discrimination. *Psychophysiology, 38*, 175–178.

Kaufmann, G., & Vosburg, S. K. (2002). The effects of mood on early and late idea production. *Creativity Research Journal, 14*, 317–330.

Kerr, A., & Zelazo, P. D. (2004). Development of "hot" executive function: The Children's Gambling Task. *Brain and Cognition, 55*, 148–157.

Kochanska, G., Murray, K., Jacques, T. Y., Koenig, A., & Vandegeest, K. A. (1996). Inhibitory control in young children and its role in emerging internalization. *Child Development, 67*, 490–507.

Mack, A., & Rock, I. (1998). *Inattentional blindness*. Cambridge, MA: MIT Press.

MacLeod, C., & Rutherford, E. M. (1992). Anxiety and the selective processing of emotional information: Mediating roles of awareness, trait and state variables, and personal relevance of stimulus materials. *Behaviour Research and Therapy, 30*, 479–491.

Mischel, W., & Baker, N. (1975). Cognitive appraisals and transformations in delay behavior. *Journal of Personality and Social Psychology, 31*, 254–261.

Mischel, W., Ebbesen, E. B., & Zeiss, A. R. (1972). Cognitive and attentional mechanisms in delay of gratification. *Journal of Personality and Social Psychology, 21*, 204–218.

Miyake, A., Friedman, N. P., Emerson, M. J., Witzki, A. H., & Howerter, A. (2000). The unity and diversity of executive functions and their contributions to complex "frontal lobe" tasks: A latent variable analysis. *Cognitive Psychology, 41*, 49–100.

Mogg, K., Bradley, B. P., Field, M., & De Houwer, J. (2003). Eye movements to smoking-related pictures in smokers: Relationship between attentional biases and implicit and explicit measures of stimulus valence. *Addiction, 98*, 825–836.

Mogg, K., Bradley, B. P., Williams, R., & Mathews, A. (1993). Subliminal processing emotional information in anxiety and depression. *Journal of Abnormal Psychology, 102*, 304–311.

Moore, B., Mischel, W., & Zeiss, A. (1976). Comparative effects of the reward stimulus and its cognitive representation in voluntary delay. *Journal of Personality and Social Psychology, 34*, 419–424.

Müller, U., Zelazo, P. D., Hood, S., Leone, T., & Rohrer, L. (2004). Interference control in a new rule use task: Age-related changes, labeling, and attention. *Child Development, 75*, 1594–1609.

Nieoullon, A. (2002). Dopamine and the regulation of cognition and attention. *Progress in Neurobiology, 67*, 53–83.

Prencipe, A., & Zelazo, P. D. (2005). Development of affective decision-making for self and other: Evidence for the integration of first- and third-person perspectives. *Psychological Science, 16*, 501–505.

Qu, L., & Zelazo, P. D. (2007). The facilitative effect of positive stimuli on 3-year-olds' flexible rule use. *Cognitive Development, 22*, 456–473.

Rader, N., & Hughes, E. (2005). The influence of affective state on the performance of a block design task in 6- and 7-year-old children. *Cognition and Emotion, 19*, 143–150.

Rubia, K., Overmeyer, S., Taylor, E., Brammer, M., Williams, S. C. R., Simmons, A., et al., (2000). Functional frontalisation with age: Mapping neurodevelopmental trajectories with fMRI. *Neuroscience and Biobehavioral Reviews, 24*, 13–19.

Schultz, W. (2002). Getting formal with dopamine and reward. *Neuron, 36*, 241–263.

Schultz, W., Dayan, P., & Montague, P. R. (1997, March 14). A neural substrate of prediction and reward. *Science, 275*, 1593–1599.

Seeman, G., & Schwarz, J. C. (1974). Affective state and preference for immediate versus delayed reward. *Journal of Research in Personality, 7*, 384–394.

Seibert, P. S., & Ellis, H. C. (1991). Irrelevant thoughts, emotional mood states, and cognitive task performance. *Memory and Cognition, 19*, 507–513.

Sigel, I. (1993). The centrality of a distancing model for the development of representational competence. In R. R. Cocking & K. A. Renninger (Eds.), *The development and meaning of psychological distance* (pp. 91–107). Hillsdale, NJ: Erlbaum.

Ungless, M. A. (2004). Dopamine: The salient issue. *Trends in Neurosciences, 27*, 702–706.

Zelazo, P. D. (2004). The development of conscious control in childhood. *Trends in Cognitive Sciences, 8*, 12–17.

Zelazo, P. D. (2006). The dimensional change card sort (DCCS): A method of assessing executive function in children. *Nature Protocols, 1*, 297–301.

Zelazo, P. D., & Cunningham, W. (2007). Executive function: Mechanisms underlying emotion regulation. In J. Gross (Ed.), *Handbook of emotion regulation* (pp. 135–158). New York: Guilford Press.

Zelazo, P. D., & Müller, U. (2002). Executive functions in typical and atypical development. In U. Goswami (Ed.), *Handbook of childhood cognitive development* (pp. 445–469). Oxford, England: Blackwell.

Zelazo, P. D., Müller, U., Frye, D., & Marcovitch, S. (2003). The development of executive function in early childhood. *Monographs of the Society for Research in Child Development, 68*(3), Serial No. 274.

II

NEUROSCIENTIFIC AND
GENETIC CONTRIBUTIONS

7

PSYCHOBIOLOGICAL MECHANISMS OF COGNITION–EMOTION INTEGRATION IN EARLY DEVELOPMENT

MARTHA ANN BELL, DENISE R. GREENE, AND CHRISTY D. WOLFE

It is traditional in developmental science to use research protocols focused on narrow aspects of development, such as specific social or perceptual processes. This narrow focus allows the research team some level of control in scientific investigations of a process as richly complex as development. Recently, however, there has been growing acknowledgment that this approach results in a fractionated consideration of development (Rothbart, 2004), accompanied by a growing number of conceptual attempts to view development through a more integrative lens. Perhaps the integrative attempt that has drawn the most interest in the developmental literature is one that combines cognitive and emotion processes (e.g., Bell & Wolfe, 2004; Calkins & Fox, 2002; Sokol & Muller, 2007).

Preparation of this chapter was supported in part by National Institutes of Health Grant HD 49878 to Martha Ann Bell. Much of the research reported in this chapter was supported by a Small Grant and a Millennium Grant from the College of Arts and Sciences at Virginia Tech.

The focus of this volume is on the integration of cognition and emotion during development, and our emphasis in this chapter is on early development. Much conceptual work has suggested that the integrative process associated with cognition and emotion may have its foundations in infancy and may demonstrate major development shifts during the 2nd and 3rd years (Bell & Deater-Deckard, 2007; Bell & Wolfe, 2004; Calkins & Fox, 2002; Rothbart, Sheese, & Posner, 2007). Within the developmental field there is the hypothesis that cognitive and emotion processes begin as separate developmental phenomena and become increasingly linked over time, possibly fully integrated by the end of early childhood (Blair, 2002). Empirical data demonstrate this integration with respect to school-related skills (Blair & Razza, 2007).

Expanding knowledge of neuroscience and brain–behavior relations (Sokol & Mueller, 2007) has enhanced the ability to discuss potential mechanisms that may be responsible for interactions between cognitive and emotion processes throughout development (Bell & Deater-Deckard, 2007; Lewis & Todd, 2007; Posner & Rothbart, 2000). We focus on temperament-based attentional control associated with the executive attention system (Posner & Rothbart, 2000) as the psychobiological system associated with developing cognition–emotion relations. Thus, we begin with a brief overview of the early development of attentional control, followed by a discussion of the brain mechanisms associated with attentional control and the measurement of those mechanisms in the developmental literature. Then we highlight specific cognitive control and emotion control behaviors that we propose are regulated by attentional control, and we propose three models by which attentional control is associated with cognition–emotion integration. Our conceptual framework of developing cognition–emotion relations is described in more detail in our recent review (Bell & Deater-Deckard, 2007).

TEMPERAMENT-BASED ATTENTIONAL CONTROL AND THE EXECUTIVE ATTENTION SYSTEM

We consider temperament, and especially temperament-based attentional control, as critical for cognition–emotion integration (Henderson & Wachs, 2007; Posner & Rothbart, 2000; Rothbart et al., 2007). *Temperament* is defined by Rothbart et al. (2007) as biologically based individual differences in emotional reactivity and in the emergence of self-regulation to modulate emotion reactivity beginning late in the 1st year of life. Early regulation of temperament-based emotional distress is facilitated by the development of attentional control associated with the executive attention system (Ruff & Rothbart, 1996). Attentional control is required for resolving conflict among thoughts, feelings, and responses (Rueda, Posner, & Rothbart,

2005). Thus, attentional control is important for the developing regulation of both cognitive and emotion processes (Kopp, 2002).

The executive attention system's influence on the regulation of emotion reactivity by attentional control begins around 10 months of age (Ruff & Rothbart, 1996), when initial developmental changes in cognitive control behaviors, we believe, also begin to be influenced by the executive attention system (Bell & Wolfe, 2004; Diamond, 1985, 2002; Diamond et al, 1997). Attentional control exhibits a rapid course of development during the toddler and preschool years and is the basis of the temperament construct effortful control (Posner & Rothbart, 2000; Rothbart, 2004). *Effortful control* refers to the child's purposeful use of executive attention and involves inhibitory control, detection of errors, and planning. As such, effortful control reflects the influence of temperament on behavior (Posner & Rothbart, 2000). The foundations of effortful control appear around 10 months of age (Rothbart, Derryberry, & Posner, 1994), and a shift in the development of effortful control of behavior seems to occur around 27 to 30 months of age (Kochanska, Murray, & Harlan, 2000). There is great improvement in effortful control at 3 and 4 years of age (Kochanska & Knaack, 2003), with continued development of effortful control through age 7 (Rueda, Posner, & Rothbart, 2004).

NEUROLOGICAL MECHANISMS OF COGNITION–EMOTION INTEGRATION

Our psychobiological framework for the integration of cognition and emotion is dependent on psychophysiology and neuropsychology work on the brain mechanisms of the executive attention system. These mechanisms have been studied using brain imaging measures of the central nervous system and cardiac measures of the autonomic nervous system that have implications for central processes.

Central Nervous System Measures

Bush, Luu, and Posner (2000) proposed that the attentional control skills associated with the executive attention system (encompassing the anterior cingulate cortex [ACC] and other areas of the frontal cortex) regulate both cognitive and emotional processing. The ACC has sections that process cognitive and emotional information separately and that also modulate autonomic nervous system activity (Hajcak, McDonald, & Simons, 2003). The cognitive section is connected with the prefrontal cortex, parietal cortex, and premotor and supplementary motor areas and is activated by tasks that involve choice selection from conflicting information, which may include many working memory tasks (Engle, 2002). The emotion section is connected with the orbitofrontal cortex, amygdala, and hippocampus, among other brain areas, and is activated by tasks with emotion content (Fichtenholtz et al., 2004). It was previously thought that there is always suppression of the affective section during cognitive processing and suppression of the cognitive subdivision during affective processing. However, studies of adults have indicated some level of interaction between the cognition and affective sections of the ACC on emotion conflict tasks (e.g., Bush et al., 2000). It was this particular finding that has focused so much recent attention on the ACC and the executive attention system in the study of cognition–emotion relations.

In research with infants and young children, ACC and other frontal lobe activity usually is inferred using brain electrical activity, such as event-related potentials (ERP) or the ongoing electroencephalogram (EEG). The ERP signal is time-locked to specific repeated stimuli. The EEG is the spontaneous background signal from which ERPs are extracted. The EEG signal has temporal resolution on the order of milliseconds. Thus, postsynaptic changes are reflected immediately in the EEG, making this methodology outstanding for tracking rapid shifts in brain functioning. Furthermore, these brain electrical signals are robust, and the techniques by which they are obtained are relatively simple, noninvasive, and comparatively inexpensive. These characteristics make the EEG one of the more favorable methodologies for studying brain development in infants and children and for relating brain development to changes in behavior (Bell & Wolfe, 2007; Taylor & Baldeweg, 2002).

Because we will be noting some of our EEG findings later in this chapter, we briefly discuss how the ongoing EEG signal is quantified. EEG data typically are analyzed with a Fourier transform, and this analysis results in at least three measures used by EEG researchers: power, coherence, and asymmetry. (We note findings related to EEG power and coherence later in the chapter.) Theoretically, the EEG signal is composed of multiple sine waves cycling at different frequencies. The Fourier transform decomposes the EEG into these different sine waves and estimates the spectral EEG power (in mean square microvolts) at each frequency. The Fourier transform results in information regarding the contribution of each individual frequency to the entire EEG spectrum at a particular electrode site. Increasing power values across age are considered indicative of brain development (Bell, 1998).

EEG power values are usually totaled across frequency bins to form measures of absolute power in a specific frequency band, with power considered a reflection of the excitability of groups of neurons. For adults, alpha activity (8–13 Hz) is the predominant frequency band for adults and "activation" of brain areas underlying specific scalp electrodes is assumed when alpha power values at those electrode sites are lower during cognitive processing than they were during resting baseline. Thus, alpha power and EEG activation are inversely related. EEG power in the adult theta band (4–8 Hz) shows the opposite pattern. That is, activation of brain areas underlying specific scalp electrodes is assumed when theta power values at those electrode sites are higher during cognitive processing than they were during resting baseline.

In the developmental psychophysiology literature there is no standardization of EEG rhythms as found in adult EEG work (Pivik et al., 1993). As a result, little is known regarding the associations of specific frequencies with behaviors during infancy and early childhood. In longitudinal studies examining EEG activity during infancy (Bell & Fox, 1992) or from infancy through early childhood (Marshall et al., 2002), spectral plots revealed a dominant frequency in all scalp leads at all ages at 6 to 9 Hz. Focusing on this particular frequency band during infancy and early childhood is of value only if it can be correlated with behavior, as we discuss later in the chapter.

EEG coherence is the frequency-dependent squared cross-correlation between two scalp electrode sites that reflects the degree of phase synchrony between them (Thatcher, 1994). Coherence values range from 0 to 1, may be related to the strength and number of synaptic connections (Thatcher, 1994), and thus may reflect the level of connectivity between two EEG recording sites. Greater connectivity, however, does not indicate greater brain maturation. Higher coherence values mean that two specific brain regions are working together, which may, or may not, be the most effective use of the cortex at any given age. EEG coherence, unlike EEG power, is not affected by arousal, opening or closing of the eyes, or by state changes. Other than Thatcher's work, little is known about the development of EEG coherence.

During cognitive processing, differences in EEG activity between quiet rest and presentation of stimuli or tasks are assumed to be an indication of cortical functioning at underlying cortical areas. EEG researchers typically are not more specific than to identify global cortical locations when interpreting this form of brain electrical activity. However, it has been shown, using high-density EEG recordings with infants, that attentional control is associated with activity in the ACC (Reynolds & Richards, 2005).

EEG asymmetry has been widely used in research on emotion reactivity and emotion regulation. Typically, asymmetry scores are computed by subtracting left hemisphere power from right hemisphere power in a specific frequency band. The resulting score may be either positive or negative. Based on the adult model that EEG alpha power and activation are inversely related, a positive asymmetry score reflects greater relative right hemisphere power and thus left hemisphere activation (or left asymmetry). A negative asymmetry score reflects greater relative left hemisphere power and thus right hemisphere activation (or right asymmetry). Greater relative left frontal EEG activation has been shown to be associated with approach-related behaviors and emotions. Greater relative right frontal EEG activation has been associated with withdrawal-related behaviors and emotions. Greater relative right frontal activation also is associated with difficulty in regulating negative arousal. Frontal EEG asymmetries are thought to reflect forebrain and limbic sensitivity that is specific to the amygdala (Fox, Henderson, Marshall, Nichols, & Ghera, 2005). The amygdala sends projections to the emotion portion of the ACC and thus is part of the emotion network of the executive attention system.

Autonomic Nervous System Measures

Cardiac measures allow assessment of attentional control via the parasympathetic and sympathetic branches of the autonomic nervous system. The parasympathetic branch is critical to attention regulation (Porges, 1991) via two distinct patterns of cardiac activity. Changes in heart rate (HR) are associated with attention to stimuli, and changes in the variability of the HR are associated with sustained attention.

According to Porges's (1991) polyvagal theory, cardiac vagal tone is a part of parasympathetic control and can be used as an index of physiological self-regulation associated with attention. Vagal tone can be quantified in at least three ways: as HR variability, as the amplitude of respiratory sinus arrhythmia, or as Porges's specific measure of vagal efferents from nucleus ambiguus in the medulla. The vagus nerve to the heart from the nucleus ambiguus serves an inhibitory function of slowing HR and modulating the effects on the heart of the sympathetic branch of the autonomic nervous system. When the environment provides an external demand on the information processing system, the vagal efferents quickly withdraw or suppress vagal tone (termed *withdrawal of the vagal brake* by Porges, 1995) and allow the sympathetic nervous system to increase HR, which is essential for cognitive or emotional responding (Bornstein & Suess, 2000). Thus, cardiac vagal tone can be conceptualized as a measure of the efficiency of central and autonomic neural feedback mechanisms (Thayer & Lane, 2000). Thus, baseline measures are indicative of response potential, and indeed, higher resting baseline measures of vagal tone are associated with more efficient attentional processing (Suess, Porges, & Plude, 1994) and with more reactive emotional responding (Calkins, 1997).

Cardiac measures of autonomic nervous system activity during cognitive processing are widely used in developmental studies. Infants who exhibit decreases in vagal tone during stimulus presentation will habituate more quickly than infants who do not decrease vagal tone during information processing (Bornstein & Suess, 2000). Changes in HR from baseline to task are associated with better performance on working memory tasks in both infants and young children (Bell, 2009). Studies of working memory in adults also show associations among HR, HR variability, and working memory performance (Hansen, Johnsen, & Thayer, 2003). Thus, there may be a link between autonomic nervous system functioning and prefrontal cortical activity.

Measures of vagal tone also have been linked to emotional reactivity and regulation. Infants with higher vagal tone are more emotionally expressive and reactive (Stifter & Corey, 2001). As emotion regulation abilities develop, the reactivity can lead to concentration when attention is critical to the situation or to more expressive reactivity when other circumstances take precedent (Porges, Doussard-Roosevelt, & Maiti, 1994). Vagal tone may be associated with coping behaviors involving attentional control during both infancy and early childhood (Bar-Haim, Fox, van Meenen, & Marshall, 2004).

In sum, current developmental work tends to focus on either brain imaging or cardiac measures of the psychobiology of attentional control and, thus, cognition–emotion integration. A more integrative brain systems approach is essential for appreciating the intricate interconnections between cognitive and emotion processes associated with attentional control. Thayer and Lane (2000) highlighted initial attempts at an integrative brain approach; .these researchers proposed a model incorporating these central and autonomic mechanisms into a neurovisceral model of self-regulation. We have detailed the Thayer and Lane model as essential for a psychobiological approach to developing attentional control and consequent self-regulation (Bell & Deater-Deckard, 2007).

Next we discuss the development of cognitive control and then emotion control and focus on constructs that we consider particularly pertinent to the discussion of cognition–emotion integration. We illustrate our discussion with findings from one of our longitudinal studies (Bell, 2009; Wolfe & Bell, 2004, 2007).

COGNITIVE CONTROL PROCESSES: WORKING MEMORY AND INHIBITORY CONTROL

We conceptualize working memory and inhibitory control as the cognitive control constructs most associated with attentional control (Bell & Deater-Deckard, 2007; Bell & Wolfe, 2004). Working memory and inhibitory control demonstrate great changes during infancy and early childhood (Davidson, Amso, Anderson, & Diamond, 2006; Diamond, 2002; Diamond, Prevor, Callender, & Druin, 1997). Stable individual differences in cognitive regulation measured via working memory and inhibitory control emerge during the preschool years (Bell, Wolfe & Adkins, 2007).

Cognitive control tasks used in developmental research have demonstrated associations with frontal lobe maturation and functioning (Diamond, 2002). The prefrontal cortex has multiple subdivisions, and working memory is a cognitive skill that appears to underlie functioning across all of these prefrontal areas (Levy & Goldman-Rakic, 2000). Of course, like other brain areas, the prefrontal cortex does not work in isolation. This area of the brain serves to moderate the activity of other brain areas, such as superior temporal cortex, posterior parietal cortex, anterior cingulate, and others. Prefrontal cortex also receives information from these other areas and, thus, is modulated by this information (Diamond, 2002). Therefore, although it is widely accepted that prefrontal cortex plays a vital role in working memory, other brain areas are involved as well (Levy & Goldman-Rakic, 2000).

A current conceptualization of working memory highlights a limited-capacity, domain-free controlled attention component that is comparable to the construct of executive attention as defined in Posner's executive attention system (Engle, Kane, & Tuholski, 1999; Posner & Rothbart, 2000). The attentional component is able to maintain short-term memory representations online in the presence of interference or response competition. Thus, this executive attention component is not needed for all cognitive processing but is called into action in circumstances that require inhibition of prepotent responses, error monitoring and correction, and decision making and planning. Engle refers to individual differences in executive attention as *working memory capacity* (Engle et al, 1999). Researchers have demonstrated relations between attentional control characteristics associated with error monitoring and cognitive regulatory tasks involving working memory and inhibitory control in infancy and early childhood (Bell, 2001; Bell & Adams, 1999; Davis, Bruce, & Gunnar, 2002; Wolfe & Bell, 2004). Thus, from early development, components of attentional control and working memory appear to be coupled.

EMOTION CONTROL PROCESSES: EMOTION REGULATION

The developments in emotion regulation during infancy and early childhood are as remarkable as those in attentional control and working memory. Developmental changes in emotion regulation are demonstrated in the progression from total dependence on caregivers for regulation of emotion state to independent self-regulation of emotions (Calkins, 2004). According to Kopp (1989), early emotion regulation is influenced mainly by innate physiological mechanisms. Around 3 months of age, some voluntary control of arousal becomes evident, with more purposeful control evident by 12 months. This is when developing motor skills and communication behaviors allow for intentional interactions with caregivers. During the 2nd year, infants begin to use language skills and better impulse control and a transition from passive to active methods of emotion regulation (Calkins, 2004). Kopp (1989) considers this emotion self-control to fully emerge between ages 3 and 4.

Emotion regulation can occur prior, during, or after the elicitation of emotion (Eisenberg & Spinrad, 2004). Like working memory, emotion regulation appears to also be strongly associated with attentional control. Regulatory aspects of temperament are driven by individual differences in arousal and reactivity. The construct of effortful control, noted earlier, represents a behavioral system that emerges in the 2nd year and allocates resources for the voluntary control of arousal and emotion. Rothbart suggested that the development of executive attention might underlie the effortful control of emotion, evidenced in the finding that children who show more effortful control also tend to show less anger, fear, and discomfort (Rothbart et al., 2007).

ASSOCIATIONS BETWEEN COGNITIVE CONTROL AND EMOTION CONTROL

The impact of attentional control can be manifest in many different ways with respect to developing cognition–emotion relations. We consider two of those models here that are found in the developmental literature and propose a third model at the end of the chapter. We also provide some data to illustrate the initial model.

In the first model, attention control influences on the regulation of emotion may have an impact on cognitive control and, thus, on cognitive outcome. Working under this model, researchers may manipulate emotion in the experimental situation and inspect the effect on cognitive performance (Gray, 2001; Richards & Gross, 2000). With infants or very young children, researchers may examine normal variations in emotion reactivity and emotion regulation (i.e., temperament) among research participants to study impact of emotion on cognitive outcomes. Our initial longitudinal study used this model, and we report on some of those data below.

In the second model, attentional control influences on cognition may affect the regulation of emotion and, thus, socioemotional outcome (Lewis & Stieben, 2004). Researchers using this model may examine the effect of prefrontal cognitive inhibitory responses on emotion regulation. This is a model that we have not employed in our work, but it is one that has major implications for self-regulation associated with school functioning and performance.

Next we turn to findings from our longitudinal study focused on cognitive outcomes. In this initial work exploring cognition–emotion integration, we used temperament as a measure for both attentional control and emotion control. Children participated in our study during infancy, preschool, and early childhood.

Individual Differences in Cognitive Control at 8 Months

Diamond (2002) noted the dramatic improvements in cognitive control abilities across infancy and has speculated about the development of certain brain systems associated with frontal lobe functioning. Yet, all infants and young children do not improve in their cognitive control abilities at the same rate (Bell & Fox, 1992; Diamond et al., 1997). Our research program with infants included an investigation of three measures that have been theoretically and empirically linked with cognitive control (i.e., working memory and inhibitory control): the EEG, HR, and temperament.

Our infant cognitive control measure was a looking version of the classic A-not-B task. We have explained elsewhere that this task involves the cognitive skills of working memory and inhibitory control (Bell & Adams, 1999). The infant must constantly update memory as to the location of a hidden toy (working memory), while refraining from searching in a previously rewarded hiding location (inhibitory control). We focused on changes in EEG values from the pretask baseline recording to the task-related recording, because they would indicate cortical involvement in the task. When we divided infants into high and low performing groups (based on our working memory, inhibitory control task), only infants with high performance exhibited changes in EEG coherence from baseline to task; the low performers showed no change in EEG from baseline to task (Bell, 2009). These task-related changes were evident at frontal and posterior scalp locations (Bell, 2009). These data confirmed our previous cognitive neuroscience work associating frontal and posterior functioning with cognitive performance levels during infancy (Bell, 2001, 2002).

In this sample, the high performance group exhibited an increase in HR from baseline to task indicative of attentional processes. The low performance group did not show this effect. Thus, both brain imaging and cardiac measures of cognitive control distinguished between the high and low performance groups.

Our temperament findings were not as expected. We used Rothbart's maternal-report temperament measure (Infant Behavior Questionnaire, or IBQ) and predicted that the duration of orienting scale would correlate with cognitive control performance, but it did not. Instead, we found that infants rated by their parents as high on activity level or high on distress to limitations had better performance on the task. This counterintuitive finding, since replicated with a second longitudinal study currently in progress in our lab, has been difficult to comprehend. It may mean that these highly active or easily distressed infants require more parental support—a result that may lead to the enhanced development of their attention skills and cognitive control as they get older, if that support from the parent is appropriate and sensitive (Colombo & Saxon, 2002).

Individual Differences in Cognitive Control at 4 Years

We continued our investigation of individual differences when these same children were 4 years old with an age-appropriate working memory and inhibitory control task. Our preschool cognitive control measures were the day–night and the yes–no, similar to the Stroop test. For the day–night task

(Diamond et al, 1997), the child is shown a white card with a sun and instructed to say "night"; then she is shown a black card with a moon and instructed to say "day." Similarly, for the yes–no task, the child is instructed to say "no" when the experimenter nods her head yes, and to say "yes" when the experimenter shakes her head no (Wolfe & Bell, 2004). We averaged the scores on these two cognitive control tasks.

Again, we divided the children into high and low performance groups based on their day–night and yes–no task performance. Children in the high cognitive control performance group had higher EEG power values at both baseline and during the cognitive task than those children in the low cognitive control performance group for the frontal and temporal scalp locations. All children exhibited increases in HR from baseline to task, indicative of the cognitive stress associated with performing the task.

With respect to maternal report of temperament using Rothbart's Child Behavior Questionnaire (CBQ), we noted positive associations between performance on the cognitive control tasks and the two scales of the effortful control factor: attention focusing and inhibitory control scales. We also noted a negative relation between cognitive control performance and the anger/frustration scale, suggesting that children who perform better on the cognitive control tasks also have a greater ability to regulate their emotions of anger and frustration. We also found an unexpected, but rather robust, negative relation between cognitive control performance and parental ratings of approach/anticipation—a scale that is included in the surgency factor of the CBQ. A consideration of the CBQ items included in the approach/anticipation scale provides some insight into this negative association (e.g., gets very enthusiastic about the things he or she does, shows great excitement about opening a present, gets so excited about things he or she has trouble sitting still). Although these findings are contrary to some work comparing temperament and cognition that reports outgoing, sociable, and active children score higher on mental tasks, they are consistent with the findings of Davis et al. (2002), who reported a strong, but also unexpected, negative correlation between the Surgency factor of the CBQ and performance on inhibitory control tasks.

Individual Differences in Cognitive Control at 8 Years

Cognitive control may be especially critical to investigations of cognition–emotion relations during middle childhood because working memory and inhibitory control may be interdependent, relative to other executive function tasks (Luna, Garver, Urban, Lazar, & Sweeney, 2004; Roberts & Pennington, 1996). During the children's visits to the research lab at age 8, the cognitive control tasks were the classic Wisconsin Card Sorting Task (WCST). The children also performed the Attention Networks Task (ANT) designed to examine Posner's attentional constructs of alerting, orienting, and conflict. It is the conflict aspect of attention that is associated with the executive attention network.

We are still analyzing the data from the children's visits at age 8, but we can provide some preliminary findings. Successful performance on the WCST, as indexed by either number of categories completed or total correct, was associated with EEG power values at frontal scalp locations but not at posterior scalp locations (Bell, Wolfe, & Adkins, 2007). We have not yet prepared the cardiac data for HR analysis.

During the age-8 visit, we were able to assess child report of temperament using the child version of Rothbart's Early Adolescent Temperament Questionnaire. The children's self-report of activation control (i.e., capacity to perform an action when there is a strong tendency to avoid it) was positively correlated with cognitive control (WCST performance). Child-reported high-intensity pleasure (i.e., pleasure derived from activities involving high intensity or novelty) emerged from the surgent dimension of temperament as negative correlate of cognitive control functioning. The child report finding complements the data for 4-year-olds from this sample, in which the surgent dimension of temperament was negatively related to cognitive control performance (Wolfe & Bell, 2004). In addition, the surgent dimension of temperament has been negatively related to academic performance in school-age children, such that low levels of fear and shyness paired with high levels of intensity pleasure are indicative of lower grades and social problems (Rothbart & Jones, 1999). Perhaps the child misses relevant information because he or she is easily excited, distracted, and often impulsive.

Cognition–Emotion Integration From 8 Months to 4 Years

With our specific interests in cognitive control, we hypothesized that the attentional and regulatory aspects of infant temperament would predict working memory performance during early childhood. These data have been reported elsewhere (Wolfe & Bell, 2007). To summarize the findings at 8 months and at 4 years of age: Infant and child EEG, as well as infant and child temperament, were correlated, as expected. Infant and child cognitive control (i.e., working memory) performance measures were not correlated, however. It is important that infant temperament was a predictor of child cognitive control. Specifically, approach/anticipation at age 4 mediated the relation between 8-month soothability and 4-year cognitive control, with a positive correlation between soothability and approach/anticipation. In essence, an infant who is difficult to sooth at 8 months may be low on approach/anticipation behaviors at 4 years and thus more likely to perform well on cognitive control tasks involving controlled, inhibitory processing. As we hypothesized with the correlation between distress and cognitive control at 8 months, many parents in supporting infants during distress or fussiness attempt to soothe infants by distracting them with visual and other stimuli. This may aid in the development of attentional skills that later are key in relieving distress (Ruff & Rothbart, 1996). These attentional skills may also contribute to the attentional and regulatory abilities, such as self-control during approach/anticipation, associated with the executive attention system and later complex cognition, such as that required by cognitive control tasks in preschool years.

Cognition–Emotion Integration From 4 Years to 8 Years

Unlike the infant and preschool cognitive control tasks, working memory performance at 4 and 8 years was correlated. As with the infant and preschool data, it was important that 4-year-olds' temperament was a predictor of 8-year-olds' attentional control. Specifically, effortful control tasks in the research lab at age 4 (items from Kochanska's battery; Kochanska et al., 2000) were related to the conflict and alerting scores on the ANT. Thus, these regulatory skills associated with effortful control at preschool appear to contribute to the attentional control abilities during middle childhood.

CONCLUSION

In this chapter we have focused on cognition–emotion integration in early development by emphasizing brain mechanisms of the executive attention system associated with attentional control. We outlined our psychobiological framework, which highlighted the potential impact of attentional control on the development of working memory and emotion regulation beginning in infancy and continuing throughout early childhood. We argued that these cognitive control and emotion control processes become integrated with development. We presented some longitudinal data that illustrate our initial attempts at tracking individual differences in cognitive control by examining attentional and emotion-related influences on the development of working memory.

Our overall discussion of attentional control and the executive attention system, however, lends itself to a more encompassing model of cognition–emotion integration that does not assign primacy to either cognitive or emotion processes. Thus, the third model that we present is the focus of our current longitudinal work, and it assigns both cognition and emotion as outcomes. In this model, attentional control processes exert influence on both cognition and emotion so that they may become increasingly reciprocal over time, with interlocking developmental trajectories demonstrating the significance of both cognition and emotion as outcome measures. Informed by data from our initial longitudinal model and by research linking attentional control to both cognitive and emotion processes via the executive attention system, we are examining the development of attentional control, working memory, and emotion regulation across infancy and early childhood using both behavioral and electrophysiological measures.

Examination of the beginnings of cognition–emotion integration during infancy and early childhood is valuable for understanding the foundations of individual differences in self-regulation. In school-age children, this integration between cognitive control and emotion regulation may be essential for school achievement and for appropriate and adaptive social behavior. Thus, there is a need to investigate the development of cognitive and emotion processes and their integration across early development.

REFERENCES

Bar-Haim, Y., Fox, N. A., van Meenen, K. M., & Marshall, P. J. (2004). Children's narratives and patterns of cardiac reactivity. *Developmental Psychobiology, 44,* 238–249.

Bell, M. A. (1998). The ontogeny of the EEG during infancy and childhood: Implications for cognitive development. In B. Garreau (Ed.), *Neuroimaging in child neuropsychiatric disorders* (pp. 97–111). Berlin: Springer-Verlag.

Bell, M. A. (2001). Brain electrical activity associated with cognitive processing during a looking version of the A-not-B object permanence task. *Infancy, 2,* 311–330.

Bell, M. A. (2002). Infant 6–9 Hz synchronization during a working memory task. *Psychophysiology, 39,* 450–458.

Bell, M. A. (2009). *A neuroscience perspective on individual differences in working memory at 8 months.* Manuscript under review.

Bell, M. A., & Adams, S. E. (1999). Equivalent performance on looking and reaching versions of the A-not-B task at 8 months of age. *Infant Behavior & Development, 22,* 221–235.

Bell, M. A., & Deater-Deckard, K. (2007). Biological systems and the development of self-regulation: Integrating behavior, genetics, and psychophysiology. *Journal of Developmental & Behavioral Pediatrics, 28,* 409–420.

Bell, M. A. & Fox, N. A. (1992). The relations between frontal brain electrical activity and cognitive development during infancy. *Child Development, 63,* 1142–1163.

Bell, M. A., & Wolfe, C. D. (2004). Emotion and cognition: An intricately bound developmental process. *Child Development, 75,* 366–370.

Bell, M. A., & Wolfe, C. D., (2007). The use of the electroencephalogram in research on cognitive development. In L. A. Schmidt & S. J. Segalowitz (Eds.), *Developmental psychophysiology.* New York: Cambridge University Press.

Bell, M. A., Wolfe, C. D., & Adkins, D. R. (2007). Frontal lobe development during infancy and childhood: Contributions of brain electrical activity, temperament, and language to individual differences in working memory and inhibitory control. In D. Coch, G. Dawson, & K. W. Fischer (Eds.), *Human behavior, learning, and the developing brain: Typical development* (pp. 247–276). New York: Guilford Press.

Blair, C. (2002). School readiness: Integrating cognition and emotion in a neurobiological conceptualization of children's functioning at school entry. *American Psychologist, 57,* 111–127.

Blair, C., & Razza R. P. (2007). Relating effortful control, executive function, and false belief understanding to emerging math and literacy ability in kindergarten. *Child Development, 78,* 647–663.

Bornstein, M.H., & Suess, P. E. (2000). Physiological self-regulation and information processing in infancy: Cardiac vagal tone and habituation. *Child Development, 71,* 273–287.

Bush, G., Luu, P., & Posner, M.I. (2000). Cognitive and emotional influences in anterior cingulated cortex. *Trends in Cognitive Sciences, 4,* 215–222.

Calkins, S. D., (1997). Cardiac vagal tone indices of temperamental reactivity and behavioral regulation in young children. *Developmental Psychobiology, 31,* 125–135.

Calkins, S. D. (2004). Early attachment processes and the development of emotional self-regulation. In R. F. Baumeister & K. D. Vohs (Eds.), *Handbook of self-regulation: Research, theory, and applications* (pp. 324–339). New York: Guilford Press.

Calkins, S. D., & Fox, N. A. (2002). Self-regulatory processes in early personality development: A multilevel approach to the study of childhood social withdrawal and aggression. *Development and Psychopatholology, 14,* 477–498.

Colombo, J., & Saxon, T. F. (2002). Infant attention and the development of cognition: Does the environment moderate continuity? In H. E. Fitzgerald, K. H. Karraker, & T. Luster (Eds.), *Infant development: Ecological perspectives* (pp. 35–60). Washington, DC: Garland Press.

Davidson, M. C., Amso, D., Anderson, L. C., & Diamond, A. (2006). Development of cognitive control and executive functions from 4 to 13 years: Evidence from manipulations of memory, inhibition, and task switching. *Neuropsychologia, 44,* 2037–2078.

Davis, E. P., Bruce, J., & Gunnar, M. R. (2002). The anterior attention network: Associations with temperament and neuroendocrine activity in 6-year-old children. *Developmental Psychobiology, 40,* 43–56.

Diamond, A. (1985). Development of the ability to use recall to guide action, as indicated by infants' performance on AB. *Child Development, 56,* 868–883.

Diamond, A. (2002). Normal development of prefrontal cortex from birth to young adulthood: Cognitive functions, anatomy, and biochemistry. In D. T. Stuss & R. T. Knight (Eds.), *Principles of frontal lobe function* (pp. 466–503). Oxford, England: Oxford University Press.

Diamond, A., Prevor, M. B., Callender, G., & Druin, D. P. (1997). Prefrontal cortex cognitive deficits in children treated early and continuously for PKU. *Monographs of the Society for Research in Child Development, 62*(4, Serial No. 252).

Eisenberg, N., & Spinrad, T. L. (2004). Emotion-related regulation: Sharpening the definition. *Child Development. 75*, 334–339.

Engle, R. W. (2002). Working memory capacity as executive attention. *Current Directions in Psychological Science, 11*, 19–23.

Engle, R. W., Kane, M.J., & Tuholski, S. W. (1999). Individual differences in working memory capacity and what they tell us about controlled attention, general fluid intelligence, and functions of the prefrontal cortex. In A. Miyake & P. Shah (Eds.), *Models of working memory: Mechanisms of active maintenance and executive control* (pp. 102–134). New York: Cambridge University Press.

Fichtenholtz, H. M., Dean, H. L., Dillon, D. G., Yamasaki, H., McCarthy, G., & LaBar, K. S. (2004). Emotion–attention network interactions during visual-oddball task. *Cognitive Brain Research, 20*, 67–80.

Fox, N. A., Henderson, H. A., Marshall, P. J., Nichols, K. E., & Ghera, M. M. (2005). Behavioral inhibition: Linking biology and behavior within a developmental framework. *Annual Review of Psychology, 56*, 235–262.

Gray, J.R. (2001). Emotion modulation of cognitive control: Approach–withdrawal states double-dissociate spatial from verbal two-back task performance. *Journal of Experimental Psychology: General, 130*, 436–452.

Hajcak, G., McDonald, N., & Simons, R. F. (2003). To err is autonomic: Error-related brain potentials, ANS activity and post-error compensatory behavior. *Psychophysiology, 40*, 895–903.

Hansen, A. L., Johnsen, B. H., & Thayer, J. F. (2003). Vagal influence on working memory and attention. *International Journal of Psychophysiology, 48*, 263–274.

Henderson, H. A., & Wachs, T. D. (2007). Temperament theory and the study of cognition-emotion interactions across development. *Developmental Review, 27*, 396–427.

Kochanska, G., & Knaack, A. (2003). Effortful control as a personality characteristic of young children: Antecedents, correlates, and consequences. *Journal of Personality, 71*, 1087–1112.

Kochanska, G., Murray, K. T., & Harlan, E. (2000). Effortful control in early childhood; Continuity and change, antecedents, and implications for social development. *Developmental Psychology, 36*, 220–232.

Kopp, C. B. (1989). Regulation of distress and negative emotions: A developmental view. *Developmental Psychology, 25*, 343–354.

Kopp, C. B. (2002). The co-development of attention and emotion regulation. *Infancy, 3*, 199–208.

Levy, R., & Goldman-Rakic, P. S. (2000). Segregation of working memory functions within the dorsolateral prefrontal cortex. *Experimental Brain Research, 133*, 23–32.

Lewis, M. D., & Stieben, J. (2004). Emotion regulation in the brain: Conceptual issues and directions for developmental research. *Child Development, 75*, 371–376.

Lewis, M. D., & Todd, R. M. (2007). The self-regulating brain: Cortical–subcortical feedback and the development of intelligent action. *Cognitive Development, 22*, 406–430.

Luna, B., Carver, K. E., Urban, T. A., Lazar, N. A., & Sweeney, J. A. (2004). Maturation of cognitive processes from late childhood to adulthood. *Child Development, 75,* 1357–1372.

Marshall, P. J., Bar-Haim, Y., & Fox, N. A. (2002). Development of the EEG from 5 months to 4 years of age. *Clinical Neurophysiology, 113,* 1199–1208.

Pivik, R. T., Broughton, R. J., Coppola, R., Davidson, R. J., Fox, N. A., & Nuwer, M. R. (1993). Guidelines for the recording and quantitative analysis of electroencephalographic activity in research contexts. *Psychophysiology, 30,* 547–558.

Porges, S. W. (1991). Vagal tone: an autonomic mediator of affect. In J. Barber, & K. A. Dodge (Eds.), *The development of emotion regulation and dysregulation* (pp. 111–128). Cambridge, England: Cambridge University Press.

Porges, S. W. (1995). Orienting in a defensive world: Mammalian modifications to our evolutionary heritage: A polyvagal theory. *Psychophysiology, 32,* 301–318.

Porges, S. W., Doussard-Roosevelt, J. A., & Maiti, A. K. (1994). Vagal tone and the physiological regulation of emotion. *Monographs of the Society for Research in Child Development, 59*(2–3), 167–186.

Posner, M. I., & Rothbart, M. K. (2000). Developing mechanisms of self-regulation. *Development and Psychopathology, 12,* 427–441.

Reynolds, G. D., Richards, J. E. (2005). Familiarization, attention, and recognition memory in infancy: An event-related potential and cortical source localization study. *Developmental Psychology, 41,* 598–615.

Richards, J. M., & Gross, J. J. (2000). Emotion regulation and memory: The cognitive costs of keeping one's cool. *Journal of Personality and Social Psychology, 79,* 410–424.

Roberts, R. J., & Pennington, B. F. (1996). An interactive framework for examining prefrontal cognitive processes. *Developmental Neuropsychology, 12,* 105–126.

Rothbart, M.K. (2004). Temperament and the pursuit of an integrated developmental psychology. *Merrill-Palmer Quarterly, 50,* 492–505.

Rothbart, M. K., Derryberry, D., & Posner, M. I. (1994). A psychobiological approach to the development of temperament. In J. E. Bates & T. D. Wachs (Eds.), *Temperament: Individual differences at the interface of biology and behavior* (pp. 83–116). Washington, DC: American Psychological Association.

Rothbart, M. K. & Jones, L. B. (1999). Temperament, self-regulation and education. *School Psychology Review, 27,* 479–491.

Rothbart, M. K., Sheese, B. E., & Posner, M. I. (2007). Executive attention and effortful control: Linking temperament, brain networks, and genes. *Child Development Perspectives, 1,* 2–7.

Rueda, M. R., Posner, M. I., & Rothbart, M. K. (2004). Attentional control and self-regulation . In R. F. Baumeister & K. D. Vohs (Eds.), *Handbook of self-regulation: Research, theory, and applications* (pp. 283–300). New York: Guilford Press.

Rueda, M. R., Posner, M. I., & Rothbart, M. K. (2005). The development of executive attention: Contributions to the emergence of self-regulation. *Developmental Neuropsychology, 28,* 573–594.

Ruff, H. A., & Rothbart, M. K. (1996). *Attention in early development: Themes and variations*. New York: Oxford University Press.

Sokol, B. W., & Muller, U. (2007). The development of self-regulation: Toward the integration of cognition and emotion. *Cognitive Development, 22*, 401–405.

Stifter, C. A., & Corey J. M. (2001). Vagal regulation and observed social behavior in infancy. *Social Development, 10*, 189–201.

Suess, P. E., Porges, S. W., & Plude, D. J. (1994). Cardiac vagal tone and sustained attention in school-age children. *Psychophysiology, 31*, 17–22.

Taylor, M. J., & Baldeweg, T. (2002). Application of EEG, ERP and intracranial recordings to the investigation of cognitive functions in children. *Developmental Science, 5*, 318–334.

Thatcher, R. W. (1994). Cyclic cortical reorganization: Origins of human cognitive development. In G. Dawson & K. W. Fischer (Eds.), *Human behavior and the developing brain* (pp. 232–266). New York: Guilford Press.

Thayer, J. F., & Lane, R. D. (2000). A model of neurovisceral integration in emotion regulation and dysregulation. *Journal of Affective Disorders, 61*, 201–216.

Wolfe, C. D., & Bell, M. A. (2004). Working memory and inhibitory control in early childhood: Contributions from electrophysiology, temperament, and language. *Developmental Psychobiology, 44*, 68–83.

Wolfe, C. D., & Bell, M. A. (2007). The integration of cognition and emotion during infancy and early childhood: Regulatory processes associated with the development of working memory. *Brain and Cognition, 65*, 3–13.

8

COGNITION AND EMOTION: A BEHAVIORAL GENETIC PERSPECTIVE

KIRBY DEATER-DECKARD AND PAULA Y. MULLINEAUX

Infants typically arrive in the world ready for cognitive and affective action. Over time and with adequate socialization, most will develop into full-fledged cognitive–affective modulators, capable of showing and understanding a broad range of complex behaviors, cognitive events, and emotions. Guiding each child through this journey is a set of experiences, operating within the context of a foundation of biological mechanisms. As individuals, children differ from each other in the genotypes that they are born with and in what they experience. These distinct but sometimes correlated genetic and nongenetic sources of influence work together—hopefully to produce a well-regulated thinking and feeling person.

The concept of *self-regulation* can be a useful way to conceptualize the gene–environment mechanisms that create connections between cognition

We thank our colleagues on the Western Reserve Reading Project (WRRP), including Stephen A. Petrill, Lee A. Thompson, Laura S. DeThorne, Chris Schatschneider, and David Vandenbergh. We are grateful for support from National Institutes of Health Grants NICHD (HD38075) and NICHD/OSERS (HD46167) for WRRP. During the writing of this chapter, Kirby Deater-Deckard also received support from NICHD (HD 54481) and from the Jessie Ball duPont Fund. Portions of this chapter were presented at the annual meeting of the Association for Psychological Science in Washington, DC (May 2007).

and emotion. The capacity for self-regulation develops rapidly over infancy and early childhood, and individual differences in this capacity arise from complex transactions between biological and environmental causal factors. This variation between children can be studied at different levels of analysis and as different components of the whole integrated system of cognitive, emotional, and behavioral regulation (Baumeister & Vohs, 2004; Bell & Deater-Deckard, 2007).

Our view is that quantitative models of genetic and nongenetic influence on development can be used to elucidate certain aspects of the architecture of the cognition–emotion connection that helps define each child's self-regulatory capacity. Thus, the focus of the current chapter is on the quantitative behavioral genetic level of analysis of the development of cognitive control of emotion, using twin and adoption designs. As we hope to demonstrate, focusing on biosocial processes that link cognition and emotion can help identify the overlapping and distinctive architecture of cognition and emotion, as well as help explain how cognitive and emotional events interact and influence each other in the brain. From a behavioral genetic perspective, the question is whether there are overlapping or independent genetic and environmental influences on the cognitive and affective psychological constructs that are involved in the regulation of emotion. In other words, are the genes and environmental factors that cause variation between people in cognitive processing of information the same as, or different from, the genetic and environmental influences on emotion processes?

As a concrete illustration of this perspective, we emphasize a particular emotion regulation mechanism: attentional control of dispositional anger/frustration. Decades of human and animal neuroscience have shown distinct neural mechanisms involved in the focusing and control of attention (e.g., prefrontal cortex) and the elicitation and expression of anger (e.g., amygdala). Although these systems can be localized and clearly are anatomically separate from each other, they are connected (in terms of neural and genetic pathways) in ways that allow for the integration of activity in primitive limbic regions involved in emotion with activity in cortical regions that regulate attention and other cognitive factors (Davidson, Jackson, & Kalin, 2000; Gray, 2004; Heilman, 1997; Posner & Rothbart, 2007).

Healthy socioemotional and cognitive development requires acquisition of a set of cognitive skills that serve to regulate arousal and the affects that accompany it, including frustration and anger (Zhou et al., 2007). As children move from early childhood into the elementary school years, they typically demonstrate remarkable improvement in their capacity to exercise self-control of their frustration and anger as well as other negative emotions. Recent theory and empirical research has emphasized developmental improvement in attention and memory processes (Posner & Rothbart, 2007), as well as adoption of behavioral skills for managing frustration (Underwood, Hurley, Johanson, & Mosley, 1999). By the time children are 9 or 10 years old, most have the capacity for cognitively controlling frustration and anger when they occur, although—this age-typical developmental milestone aside—there remains wide variation among children in the effectiveness of this cognitive emotion regulation mechanism into adolescence and beyond (Bell & Deater-Deckard, 2007). The broad goal of the behavioral genetic approach and perspective is to further our understanding of the etiology of this variation. If the integration of cognitive and affective systems operates at the genetic level, we should see evidence of moderate to substantial genetic overlap between attention span/persistence and anger/frustration, as this would reflect an underlying interconnectivity between biological influences (including but not limited to genes) on each construct. At the same time, given the neurobiological evidence, there also should be independent genetic variance in attention span/persistence beyond anger/frustration.

BEHAVIORAL GENETICS

Human behavioral genetic research uses naturally occurring populations to investigate genetic similarity among individuals. Examination of specific genes (based on genotyping of DNA) is important, as well, but beyond the scope of the current chapter. The three basic behavioral genetic designs are family, adoption, and twin studies (for a detailed treatment of this subject, see Plomin, DeFries, McClearn, and McGuffin, 2001). As a first step, family studies can be used to make comparisons of parents and their children, as well as siblings within each generation of the family. Parents share 50% of their genes (i.e., particular versions of genes—*alleles*—that are identical by descent), on average, with their biological children, as do full biological siblings, and they live together in what most refer to as a *family environment* during early development years. Family studies are a first step—if family member resemblance on the cognitive or affective measure of interest is negligible, it suggests that the genetic and environmental influences on that attribute do not segregate within families. However, in most cases, family member resemblance is found.

When parent–child or sibling resemblance is found, more specified designs are required to address whether and how genetic and nongenetic influences may be operating to explain this "familiality" for the attribute being studied. The *adoption design* is one such approach, in which variance can be attributed to genetic and nongenetic influences differentially. The adoption study is based on comparisons between an adopted child and the biological parents who do not share any postnatal experiences with the child, as well as comparisons between the adopted child and adoptive parents who are genetically independent of that child. If the adopted child resembles the biological parents, then genetic influences are implicated. Similarities between the adopted child and the adoptive parents are a result of postnatal environmental influences. The adoption design also allows comparisons between genetically related and unrelated adoptive siblings for deriving estimates.

The *twin design* is the other major approach that can be used to attribute variance components to genetic and nongenetic sources. Identical or monozygotic (MZ) twins share all of their genes, whereas fraternal or dizygotic (DZ) twins (just like full siblings) on average share 50% of alleles identical by descent. MZ and DZ twins can be compared on an attribute of interest to see whether there is evidence of differential sibling resemblance based on genetic similarity. If MZ twins are more similar than DZ twins, then genetic influences are implicated. Other sibling designs are sometimes used, including comparisons of step- and half-siblings.

Comparing differences in the phenotypic correlations between groups that differ in the known degree of genetic relatedness is the foundation for the estimation of genetic and nongenetic effects. The univariate quantitative genetic model allows for the estimation of independent additive genetic effects (A), shared environment effects (C), and nonshared environment effects including error (E). Additive genetic effects are individual differences that are a result of the aggregation of alleles or loci. Shared environment effects are those environmental factors that are responsible for family member similarity. In contrast, nonshared environment effects are environmental factors that contribute to dissimilarity among family members (although this estimate also includes measurement error variance). Also represented in the univariate model are pathways between the latent variables representing the additive genetic variance or covariance, which is set at different levels that represent the degree of genetic relatedness for each group (i.e., MZ = 1.0 and DZ = .50). The shared environment pathways are set at 1.0 for all groups, whereas the nonshared environment pathways are set at 0 for all groups. In the following sections we provide an example of a multivariate extension of this model (Neale & Cardon, 1992) that allows for the estimation of independent genetic and nongenetic influences as well as an estimation of overlapping additive genetic, shared environment, and nonshared environmental sources of covariance/correlation that account for the observed phenotypic correlation between two behaviors.

COGNITION OR EMOTION

Turning now to the content of behavioral genetic studies, we must begin with a caveat. There has been little behavioral genetic work on the intersection of emotion and cognition. This may be because most prior genetic research has focused on discrete dimensions of individual variation by emphasizing measurement of personality, affect, and cognitive performance. Although there is evidence of consistent connections between certain aspects of emotion and cognition from this literature (e.g., IQ and the Big Five personality traits of Openness/Intellect and Conscientiousness), the effect sizes are small and, as a result, there has not been much behavioral genetic research on this interface (Chamorro-Premuzic & Furnham, 2005). To illustrate, we examined unpublished data from three behavioral genetic studies. In the TRACKS study of British preschool-age twins (Deater-Deckard et al., 2001), correlations between children's Stanford-Binet composite scores (Verbal, Memory, Quantitative, and Abstract/Visual Reasoning) and their negative affect and emotionality scores (based on parents' and observers' ratings) were ± .03 to .11 (n = 188–233). The same range of modest correlations is found in data from 3- to 16-year-olds (n = 292–361) in the Northeast–Northwest Collaborative Adoption Project, and on 4- to 8-year-olds (n = 393–515) in the Western Reserve Reading Project (Petrill, Deater-Deckard, Thompson, DeThorne, & Schatschneider, 2006).

This caveat aside, the extant behavioral genetic research on individual differences in emotions and cognitive performance is illuminating. With respect to emotion, much of the genetically informative research has focused on negative affects—broadly as in negative emotionality or neuroticism, and narrowly as in dispositional anger, fear, or sadness. These studies have converged to indicate that general negative affectivity as well as anger/frustration and fear/anxiety are moderately to substantially heritable by early childhood (Davidson, Putnam, & Larson, 2000; Emde, Robinson, Corley, Nikkari, & Zahn-Waxler, 2001; Goldsmith, Buss, & Lemery, 1997; Oniszczenko et al., 2003).

With respect to traditional behavioral genetic research on cognition, nearly all of the work has focused on general and specific cognitive abilities among adolescents and adults. For general cognitive ability (g), the variance attributable to additive genetic effects is around 50%, with nongenetic influences accounting for the other 50% (Bouchard & McGue, 1981). Shared environmental variance in g accounts for 20% to 40% of the variance, depending on the study design (Chipuer, Rovine, & Plomin, 1990). Developmentally, heritability increases from under 20% in infancy, to 40% to 60% from childhood through early adulthood, and up to 80% among older adults (McCartney, Harris, & Bernieri, 1990; Plomin, Fulker, Corley, & DeFries, 1997).

Throughout development, nonshared environmental variance accounts for about one third of the variance in g, although it is important to note that the nonshared environment estimate includes variance due to measurement error. In contrast, shared environmental variance decreases with development, becoming negligible by adolescence (McGue, Bouchard, Iacono, & Lykken, 1993). In early childhood, some of the shared environmental variance in cognitive performance may be attributable to aspects of the rearing environment, including maternal warmth and socioeconomic status (Petrill & Deater-Deckard, 2004), but even in infancy there is moderate genetic variance in measures of the home environment, suggesting that genetic influences pervade even measures intended to assess environmental mechanisms (Coon, Fulker, DeFries, & Plomin, 1990).

Do the changes in heritable variance from infancy through adolescence reflect continuous or discontinuous shifts in the etiology of general cognitive ability? The answer may be "both." In early childhood, stable shared environmental influences appear to account for some of the longitudinal stability of g, but this stability is accounted for by stable genetic influences as children progress through early childhood, middle childhood, and adolescence. At the same time, there is some evidence suggesting that new genetic influences may arise and contribute to change in cognitive performance during the 2nd- and 7th-year transitions (Cardon, Fulker, DeFries, & Plomin, 1992; Cherny, et al., 2001; Fulker, Cherny, & Cardon, 1993).

By middle childhood and beyond, moderate to substantial heritability estimates are also found for individual differences in performance on measures of specific cognitive abilities (e.g., spatial, verbal, memory) as well as cognitive tasks that measure such factors as processing speed, inspection, and choice reaction times (Alarcón, Plomin, Fulker, Corley, & DeFries, 1998; Cardon & Fulker, 1993; Boomsma & Somsen, 1991; McGue & Bouchard, 1989; Petrill, Thompson, & Detterman, 1995). There may be a positive association between degree of task complexity and magnitude of heritability for these specific-ability cognitive tasks (Neubauer, Spinath, Riemann, Angleitner & Borkenau, 2000; Vernon, 1989), and, like general intelligence, the heritability of specific cognitive abilities increases with age (Plomin et al., 1997).

Neural Activation

Although quantitative genetic studies of cognition and emotion have focused heavily on behavioral performance measures in the past, more recent research has taken advantage of the developing technologies for examining neural activation. One such domain of work is found in studies of brain electrophysiology. A common electrophysiological measure used in studying brain activity is the electroencephalogram (EEG), which allows researchers to measure changes in electrical impulses over the surface of the brain. EEGs can be used to indicate how long it takes the brain to process various stimuli (Kolb & Whishaw, 2003). As found for performance-based measures of g, the heritabilities of delta, theta, and alpha bands derived from EEG appear to increase from early childhood through adolescence (McGuire, Katsanis, Iacono, & McGue, 1998; Orekhova, Stroganova, Posikera, & Malykh, 2003). There also is evidence of moderate to substantial heritable variance in P3 latency and slow wave measures from event-related potential (ERP) methods (Hansell et al., 2001; van Baal, de Geus, & Boomsma, 1998). A more recent meta-analysis reported heritabilities of 81% for alpha frequency, 60%

for P300 amplitude, and 51% for P300 latency (van Beijsterveldt & van Baal, 2002).

Although electrophysiological methods such as EEG and ERP offer precise data in regard to temporal patterns of activation, their spatial resolution is poor. Other techniques such as functional magnetic resonance imaging (fMRI) are required for localizing the specific regions of activation, though fMRI is not used often with children. MRI studies have revealed moderate to substantial heritabilities for measures of white and gray matter volume and other structural aspects of brain function (Pennington et al., 2000; Thompson et al., 2001), and this heritable variance in brain volume measures accounts for a substantial portion of the genetic variance in behavioral measures of cognitive performance (Posthuma, deGeus, & Baaré, 2002). Consistent with the behavioral evidence, heritability of white matter volume probably increases over childhood and adolescence (Wallace et al., 2006).

Genes

A number of studies have focused on variations in genes known to be associated with a particular neurotransmitter operating within certain networks within the brain. These studies have focused on how different versions or alleles have different associations with measures of cognitive function and how different gene "doses" may influence behavior. The research has emphasized visual attention, working memory, and executive function, and scientists have found associations with structural variations in genes involved in the dopamine neurotransmitter system and other systems, including DBH, DRD4, DAT1, COMT, and MAOA genes (Diamond, Briand, Fossella, & Gehlbach, 2004; Egan et al., 2001; Fan, Fossella, Sommer, Wu, & Posner, 2003; Fossella et al., 2002; Reuter et al., 2005). In addition, although it has emerged from studies of dementia in older adults, the APOE gene has been found to be associated with typical variation in adult working memory performance (Greenwood & Parasuraman, 2003; Reynolds, Prince, & Feuk, 2006) and could be implicated in working memory in childhood as well.

There is some evidence of the influence of dopamine genes on negative affect (anger and fear in particular), with the DRD4 gene implicated in several studies of infants' negative emotion (Auerbach, Faroy, & Ebstein, 2001; Ebstein et al., 1998). However, most of the evidence points to serotonin neurotransmitter system genes—in particular, a serotonin transporter gene (5-HTTLPR) and the TPH gene that is involved in dampening the production of serotonin. Structural variations in these genes have been associated with trait neuroticism, anger, fear, and anxiety (Ebstein, 2006; Levinson, 2006; Manuck et al., 1999; Rujescu et al., 2002). More important to the current chapter, serotonin transporter gene variations have been associated with individual differences in neural activation in the circuitry that bridges cortical and limbic brain regions involved in the cognitive control of affective states (Pezawas et al., 2005).

It is important to bear in mind that the effect sizes in the molecular genetic studies tend to be small and multiple replications remain elusive; moreover, little of the research involves children, let alone tests of development and change. This situation is due at least in part to the fact that this research is trying to capture (in fairly simple measurement strategies) highly complex arrays of genetic and nongenetic effects. Nevertheless, the current molecular genetic literature strongly suggests that the current techniques of examining structural variations in candidate genes and individual differences in behavioral measures of cognitive functions are proving useful.

COGNITION *AND* EMOTION: GENES AND SELF-REGULATION

Comparatively little genetically informative research has examined the development of connections between cognition and emotion. As we stated at the beginning of the chapter, we believe that research on the development of self-regulation may provide a useful framework for furthering understanding of gene–environment processes that create connections between emotion and cognition. We can illustrate this perspective by describing research on gene–environment processes in the link between control of attention and anger/frustration.

Over early childhood, children develop capacities for self-regulation of their internal states and behaviors at the same time that stable individual differences in temperament are emerging. Executive control of attention and its connection with negative affectivity plays a prominent role in developing self-regulation. A number of studies of temperament and self-regulated emotion have focused on various aspects of attention and negative affect (Posner & Rothbart, 2007, pp. 19–22). However, most of this research has relied on one or two methods of assessment (usually administered in isolation and typically based on parents' reports or performance-based measures in the lab), and more research on biosocial influences on self-regulation is needed. In an effort to address these gaps, we have been striving to apply multi-informant, multi-assessment composite scores to represent interrelated aspects of attention span/persistence (a key indicator of effortful control of attention; Anderson, 2002) and anger/frustration (a key indicator of negative affectivity; Putnam & Rothbart, 2006).

One of the developmental tasks of early and middle childhood is to gain self-control over arousal and the negative emotions that can accompany it. In particular, the regulation of anger/frustration is critical to healthy socioemotional development. Children who are easily frustrated and have difficulty controlling their anger are more likely to have difficult relationships with their caregivers, teachers, and peers (Keane & Calkins, 2004;

Wilson, Gardner, Burton, & Leung, 2006). The executive attention system that develops rapidly over infancy and early childhood facilitates the cognitive control of negative affective responses (e.g., fear, anger) to the environment. Over time, the neural circuitry and affective-behavioral patterns that are associated with this attentional control become fairly stable across situations, emerging as individual differences in *effortful control* (i.e., attention control, low-intensity pleasure, and perceptual sensitivity), one of the core dimensions of temperament that emerge early in development (Kopp, 2002; Rothbart, Ellis, Rueda, & Posner, 2003).

In the developmental and clinical literatures, the regulation of attention is strongly implicated in the modulation of negative emotions and especially trait anger (Calkins & Fox, 2002; Eisenberg et al., 2005; Kochanska & Knaack, 2003). The common interpretation of the association between attention span and negative affectivity is that those with better attentional control are using attention in ways that serve to reduce the experience and expression of powerful emotional states such as anger, although it is plausible that reactive negative affect serves to modulate attention span (i.e., bidirectionality). Generally, the studies in this literature use one or sometimes two informants and methods, and typically on one occasion. We have sought to extend this literature by developing stronger composites with optimal reliability and validity by incorporating testers', observers', teachers', and parents' reports over time.

For effortful control and attention span/persistence, similar patterns of moderate to substantial genetic variance and modest to moderate nonshared environmental variance are found (Goldsmith et al., 1997; Oniszczenko et al., 2003; Emde et al., 2001; Yamagata et al., 2005), with genes in the dopamine system (Maher, Marazita, Ferrell, & Vanyukov, 2002; Schmidt, Fox, Perez-Edgar, Hu, & Hamer, 2001) and differential maternal warm scaffolding behavior (Deater-Deckard, Petrill, Thompson, & DeThorne, 2005) identified as candidate genetic and nonshared environmental factors, respectively. In addition, recent research on a dopamine receptor gene (DRD4) suggests that it interacts with maternal warm responsive behavior in its effects on attention, as well as other aspects of temperament (Bakermans-Kranenburg & van IJzendoorn, 2006; Sheese, Voelker, Rothbart, & Posner, 2007). In contrast, shared environmental influences have been found to be negligible.

By comparison, little is known about genetic and nongenetic influences on the link between attention and anger that may be indicative of a self-regulatory mechanism. To gain more understanding of these influences, we examined gene–environment processes in the connection between attention and anger (Deater-Deckard, Mullineaux, Petrill, & Thompson, 2007), using data from the Western Reserve Reading Project, an ongoing longitudinal twin study spanning middle childhood and the transition to early adolescence (Petrill et al., 2006). The sample included 111 monozygotic (MZ; 57% female) twin pairs and 154 dizygotic (DZ; 57% female) same-sex twin pairs, for all of whom there were complete data on the attention and anger/frustration measures. In this ongoing study, the children are assessed annually; they were 6 years old on average at the first assessment (ranging from 4 to 8 years of age). Parental educational attainment in the sample was widely distributed, with just over half of the sample having college degrees. The majority of the twins were Caucasian (92%), and 94% lived in two-parent households.

To examine attention and anger/frustration, we aggregated items from ratings by teachers, observers, testers, and parents across two annual assessments. Testers' and observers' ratings were based on their observations of child and parent behavior during the home visits, and mother–child interactions were videotaped while the dyad completed challenging cooperation tasks. Potential rater effects on estimates of twin similarity were minimized by having each twin rated by a different tester and observer. Teachers and parents completed questionnaires, and items or scales relevant to anger/frustration and attention span/persistence were selected from the Teacher Report Form (TRF; Achenbach, 1991) and the parent-rated Child Behavior Questionnaire—Short Form (CBQ-SF; Putnam & Rothbart, 2006). Mother and father reports were moderately to substantially correlated (range of .4–.6) and were averaged for those children with data from both parents. We aggregated composite scores that were internally consistent, based on evidence from principal components analyses (the single component accounted for at least 45% of the variance in the indicators, with loadings > .4). Indicators were standardized, averaged, and standardized again to yield an attention composite and an anger/frustration composite. Any child with at least one valid informant score was included.

There was a moderate significant association between higher attention span and less anger/frustration ($r = -.52$); this association replicated across *twin 1* (firstborn) and *twin 2* subsamples. As for twin similarity (estimated as intraclass correlations), the twins were moderately and significantly alike for both attention span/persistence ($r = .42$) and anger/frustration ($r = .48$). Furthermore, it was apparent that genetic variance was present for both constructs. The MZ twin intraclass correlations for anger/frustration (.61) and attention span/persistence (.68) were significantly greater than those for DZ twin anger (.40) and attention span (.22), based on Fisher r-to-z tests.

Next we estimated a bivariate Cholesky model to estimate variance and covariance for attention span/persistence and anger/frustration (Neale & Cardon, 1992). We examined three models—one in which all of the paths were estimated (ACE), a second in which the additive genetic and nonshared environment paths were estimated and the shared environment paths were fixed at zero (AE), and a third in which the additive shared and nonshared environment paths were estimated and the genetic paths were fixed at zero (CE).

For the full ACE model, all three paths for A (additive genetic influences) and all three paths for E (nonshared environment influences and er-

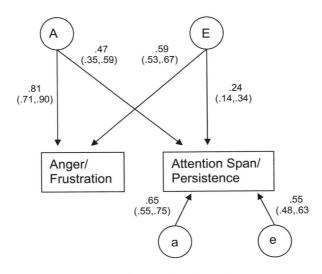

Figure 8.1. Best-fitting bivariate Cholesky decomposition with estimated path coefficients and their 95% confidence intervals. Latent variables represent additive genetic effects (A) and nonshared environment effects including error (E), as well as residual genetic (a) and nonshared environmental variance (e). The pathways between latent variables representing genetic variance and covariance across twins are set at 1 for monozygotic (MZ) twins and .5 for dizygotic (DZ) twins, and the paths for nonshared environmental variance and covariance across twins are set at 0 for MZ and DZ twins. For simplicity, only one half of the model for one twin is shown; it is duplicated for the second twin in the complete model.

ror) were significantly greater than zero. In contrast, none of the three paths for C (shared environment influences) was significant. For anger/frustration, 47% of the variance was heritable, 16% was attributable to shared environmental influences, and 37% was due to nonshared environmental influences. For attention span/persistence, these variance estimates were 62% for genetic influences, 3% for shared environmental influences, and 35% for nonshared environmental influences. Comparative model fitting showed that the model fit improved by "dropping" the C path; the AE model was the best fitting and most parsimonious model, x^2 (14) = 26.26, p = .024, AIC = –1.74, root mean square error of approximation (RMSEA) = .054. These results are shown in Figure 8.1. On the basis of this final best-fitting model, genetic influences accounted for 65% and 64% of the variance, and nonshared environment 35% and 36%, for anger/frustration and attention/persistence, respectively.

We also used the paths in the AE model to estimate genetic parameters that correspond to overlapping genetic and nongenetic variance (i.e., genetic correlation and nonshared environmental correlation). These paths accounted for the phenotypic correlation between anger/frustration and attention span/persistence and were statistically significant. The estimated genetic correlation was .58 (accounting for 73% of the phenotypic correlation between attention and anger), and the nonshared environment correlation was .40 (accounting for 27% of the phenotypic correlation). In addition, there were significant residual/independent genetic and nonshared environmental variance estimates for attention span/persistence after genetic and nonshared environmental covariance with anger/frustration was controlled, as indicated by the significant independent paths from "a" and "e" to attention span/persistence in Figure 8.1.

The finding of a moderate negative association between our measure of effortful control of attention and negative affectivity is consistent with prior studies pointing to an effect size in the –.2 to –.4 range (Kochanska & Knaack, 2003; Olson, Sameroff, Kerr, Lopez, & Wellman, 2005; Rothbart et al., 2003; Rydell, Berlin, & Bohlin, 2003). We think it unlikely that the correlation of –.52 in the current set of analyses reflects inflation due to method variance, given that we aggregated across four informants' perspectives that were based on the children's behaviors in multiple contexts (i.e., both home and school) and across several time points.

The behavioral genetic analyses replicated and extended the literature on attention span/persistence and anger/frustration. Consistent with previous studies, the univariate heritability and nonshared environmental variance estimates for both phenotypes were moderate in magnitude and significant (Goldsmith et al., 1997; Emde et al., 2001; Oniszczenko et al., 2003). More important, the novel finding from the current study was that the correlation between attention span/persistence and anger/frustration included a moderate genetic correlation of .58—an effect that accounted for nearly three quarters of the observed association between our behavioral measures of attention and anger. This suggests that there are common sets of genetic influences that partly explain the link between better attentional control and lower levels of anger/frustration. In light of the molecular genetic literature (Maher et al., 2002; Manuck et al., 1999; Rujescu et al., 2002; Schmidt et al., 2001), sets of candidate genes in the serotonin and dopamine neurotransmitter systems are logical places to look for the source of these overlapping genetic effects. However, it also is clear from the bivariate genetic model results that not all of the genetic variance in attention span/persistence and anger overlaps. There remained significant residual genetic variance even after the genetic correlation was estimated, indicating the presence of independent genetic influences on attention span/persistence compared with anger/frustration. This is not surprising given that it is unlikely that all of the genetic variance in attention span/persistence and anger/frustration would be overlapping.

ENVIRONMENT

Genetic factors figure prominently in accounting for the etiology of the bridge between cognitive control and emotion regulation. These genetic influences are evident as moderate to large heritability estimates and genetic correlations, as dopamine and serotonin neurotransmitter system genes involved in cognitive and emotion "actions," and as neural activation in cortical and limbic regions that appear to be primarily responsible for the effortful regulation of thoughts, emotions, and other internal states. We have focused on behavioral genetic approaches to the study of the connections between cognition and emotion, with particular emphasis on the genetic underpinnings of these connections and their development. However, behavioral genetic studies are just as useful for highlighting the importance of nongenetic influences; the critical importance of contextual factors on the development of well-regulated cognitions and emotions cannot be overlooked. We know from decades of research that the child's caregiving environment is important to the development of self-regulation (Calkins & Hill, 2007; Kochanska, Coy, & Murray, 2001). Most recently, experimental work by Posner and Rothbart (2007) suggests that effortful visual attention skills and their associated neural systems can be improved through intervention in early childhood.

However, these nongenetic sources of influence on the links between cognition and emotion are not likely to operate to produce family-member resemblance (through shared environmental mechanisms) but rather are most likely to produce within-family differences. With few exceptions, nearly all of the nongenetic variance in all of the cognitive and affective attributes that are studied is nonshared. In the behavioral genetic analysis of the correlation between attention span/persistence and anger/frustration described earlier, we found a significant nonshared environment correlation of .40. This suggests the presence of nongenetic influences that operate systematically to produce sibling differences in covarying attention and anger. To our knowledge, there are no studies that have identified specific environmental factors that might account for this nonshared environment correlation, nor are there any studies on the nonshared environmental variance in the separate cognitive or affective attributes.

Yet there are hints in the literature about some nonshared environment factors in the home environment that are potential candidates for study. For instance, parents of infants and toddlers sometimes manipulate their children's attention in an effort to reduce distress. A common strategy for reducing distress in a young child is to distract her and focus her attention on an engaging and more pleasurable attractor such as the parent's face or an interesting object or a favorite toy (Posner & Rothbart, 2007, p. 58). These and other parent–child interaction factors could operate as powerful socialization experiences that work differentially within families to produce different outcomes for siblings. Even if the actual environmental factors that explain the nonshared environment correlation between attention and anger eventually are identified, *why* those factors serve to differentiate siblings remains a critically important question to be answered. Also, caution is warranted because some of the nonshared environment correlation could represent error variance that is correlated across the two constructs.

CONCLUSIONS AND IMPLICATIONS

Most children are provided with many opportunities to learn to use their cognitive capacities (and attention and working memory skills, in particular) to control their negative emotions. As they develop, children can rely less on objects and caregivers to regulate their arousal for them. As a result, by middle childhood most children have strategies of self-regulation in place, including the application of regulated attention and memory mechanisms to control anger and other negative emotions. However, there are wide-ranging individual differences in control of attention and expression of affect that remain throughout the life span. These individual differences arise from complex transactions between genetic and environmental influences. On the biological side, these include dopamine and serotonin neurotransmitter system genes and central nervous system activation and connectivity involving prefrontal cortical and limbic brain regions. Some of these influences overlap and some are independent in their effects on these and other components of regulated cognitive and affective control. Behavioral genetic research informs us about the ways in which experiences—some of which arise from active and evocative person–environment processes (e.g., selection of peers, eliciting accepting or rejecting behaviors from others)—further reinforce or dampen the effects of genetic and nonshared environmental influences on covarying cognitive and emotional mechanisms.

We wish to emphasize two implications in regard to basic and applied genetically informative research on the integration of cognition and emotion. First, individual differences in cognitive control of emotion are malleable. The cognitive–affective–behavioral processes connecting cognition and emotion can be modified as a result of changes in environments, although the nature and specificity of these mechanisms of change remain to be identified. Experimental evidence is emerging to support this view. There is excitement among developmental scientists about promising results showing that children's attentional control and self-regulation can be modified (Diamond, Barnett, Thomas, & Munro, 2007; Posner & Rothbart, 2007). Also, psychological and behavioral interventions with children who are highly anxious and fearful of people and school (fairly common childhood phobias) are proving to be successful, with rapidly graduated exposure proving highly effective in reducing children's fearfulness and arousal (Ollendick & March, 2004).

Second, the integration of cognitive and affective processes likely stems in part from multiple pleiotropic genes, whereby each relevant gene has multiple influences on multiple phenotypes (rather than only one type of effect on one specific phenotype). Thus, the genes that are involved in the cognitive control of emotion may be involved in cognitive control of information processing generally—whether or not the information that is being processed is affective (for a discussion of "generalist genes," see Kovas & Plomin, 2006). Similarly, the genes involved in the expression and regulation of specific positive and negative emotions—anger/frustration to boredom to pleasure—probably overlap; specific genes for specific affects almost certainly will not be found. The exciting challenge that lies ahead for developmental science is to understand precisely how a set of "phenotype general" gene–environment processes can result in specific cognitive regulation mechanisms of distinct emotions.

REFERENCES

Achenbach, T. M. (1991). *Manual for the Teacher's Report Form and 1991 Profile.* Burlington: University of Vermont, Department of Psychiatry.

Alarcón, M., Plomin, R., Fulker, D. W., Corley, R., & DeFries, J. C. (1998). Multivariate path analysis of specific cognitive abilities data at 12 years of age in the Colorado Adoption Project. *Behavior Genetics, 28,* 255–264.

Anderson, P. (2002). Assessment and development of executive function (EF) during childhood. *Child Neuropsychology, 8,* 71–82.

Auerbach, J. G., Faroy, M., & Ebstein, R. (2001). The association of the dopamine D4 receptor gene (DRD4) and the serotonin transporter promoter gene (5-HTTLPR) with temperament in 12-month-old infants. *Journal of Child Psychology and Psychiatry, 42,* 777–783.

Bakermans-Kranenburg, M. J., & van IJzendoorn, M. H. (2006). Gene-environment interaction of the dopamine D4 receptor (DRD4) and observed maternal insensitivity predicting externalizing behavior in preschoolers. *Developmental Psychobiology, 48,* 406–409.

Baumeister, R. F., & Vohs, K. D. (2004). *Handbook of self-regulation: Research, theory, and applications.* New York: Guilford Press.

Bell, M. A., & Deater-Deckard, D. (2007). Biological systems and the development of self-regulation: Integrating behavior, genetics, and psychophysiology. *Journal of Developmental and Behavioral Pediatrics, 28,* 409–420.

Boomsma, D. I., & Somsen, R. J. M. (1991). Reaction times measured in a choice reaction time and a double task condition: A small twin study. *Personality and Individual Differences, 12,* 519–522.

Bouchard, T. J., Jr., & McGue, M. (1981, May 29). Familial studies of intelligence: A review. *Science, 212,* 1055–1059.

Calkins, S. D., & Fox, N. A. (2002). Self-regulatory processes in early personality development: A multilevel approach to the study of childhood social withdrawal and aggression. *Development & Psychopathology, 14,* 477–498.

Calkins, S. D., & Hill, A. (2007). Caregiver influences on emerging emotion regulation: Biological and environmental transactions in early development. In J. J. Gross (Ed.), *Handbook of emotion regulation* (pp. 229–248). New York: Guilford Press.

Cardon, L. R., & Fulker, D. W. (1993). Genetics of specific cognitive abilities: Nature, nurture, and psychology. In R. Plomin & G. E. McClearn (Eds.), *Nature, nurture, and psychology* (pp. 99–120). Washington, DC: American Psychological Association.

Cardon, L. R., Fulker, D. W., DeFries, J. C., & Plomin, R. (1992). Continuity and change in general cognitive ability from 1 to 7 years of age. *Developmental Psychology, 28,* 64–73.

Chamorro-Premuzic, T., & Furnham, A. (2005). *Personality and intellectual competence.* Mahwah, NJ: Erlbaum.

Cherny, S. S., Fulker, D. W., Emde, R. N., Plomin, R., Corley, R. P., & DeFries, J. C. (2001). Continuity and change in general cognitive ability from 14 to 36 months. In R. N. Emde & J. K. Hewitt (Eds.), *Infancy to early childhood: Genetic and environmental influences on developmental change* (pp. 206–220). New York: Oxford University Press.

Chipuer, H. M., Rovine, M. J., & Plomin, R. (1990). LISREL modeling: Genetic and environmental influences on IQ revisited. *Intelligence, 14,* 11–29.

Coon, H., Fulker, D. W., DeFries, J. W., & Plomin, R. (1990). Home environment and cognitive ability of 7-year-old children in the Colorado Adoption Project: Genetic and environmental etiologies. *Developmental Psychology, 26,* 459–468.

Davidson, R. J., Jackson, D. C., & Kalin, N. H. (2000). Emotion, plasticity, context, and regulation: Perspectives from affective neuroscience. *Psychological Bulletin, 126,* 890–909.

Davidson, R. J., Putnam, K. M., & Larson, C. L. (2000, July 28). Dysfunction in the neural circuitry of emotion regulation: A possible prelude to violence. *Science, 289,* 591–594.

Deater-Deckard, K., Mullineaux, P. Y., Petrill, S. A., & Thompson, L. A. (2007, May). *Attention span and anger/frustration in childhood: A behavioral genetic analysis.* Poster presented at the Association for Psychological Science, Washington, DC.

Deater-Deckard, K., Petrill, S. A., Thompson, L., & DeThorne, L. (2005). A cross-sectional behavioral genetic analysis of task persistence in the transition to middle childhood. *Developmental Science, 8,* F21–F26.

Deater-Deckard, K., Pike, A., Petrill, S. A., Cutting, A., Hughes, C., & O'Connor, T. G. (2001). Nonshared environmental processes in social-emotional development. *Developmental Science, 4,* F1–F6.

Diamond, A., Barnett, W. S., Thomas, J., & Munro, S. (2007, November 1). Preschool program improves cognitive control. *Science, 318,* 138–1388.

Diamond, A., Briand, L., Fossella, J., & Gehlbach, L. (2004). Genetic and neurochemical modulation of prefrontal cognitive functions in children. *American Journal of Psychiatry, 161,* 125–132.

Ebstein, R. P. (2006). The molecular genetic architecture of human personality: Beyond self-report questionnaires. *Molecular Psychiatry, 11*, 427–445.

Ebstein, R., Levine, J., Geller, V., Auerbach, J., Gritsenko, I., & Belmaker, R. H. (1998). Dopamine D4 receptor and serotonin transporter promoter in the determination of neonatal temperament. *Molecular Psychiatry, 3*, 238–246.

Egan, M. F., Goldberg, T. E., Kolachana, B. S., Callicott, J. H., Mazzanti, C. M., Straub, R. E., et al. (2001). Effect of COMT Val[108/158]Met genotype on frontal lobe function and risk for schizophrenia. *Proceedings of the National Academy of Sciences, USA, 98*, 6917–6922.

Eisenberg, N., Sadovsky, A., Spinrad, T. L., Fabes, R. A., Losoya, S. H., Valiente, C., et al. (2005). The relations of problem behavior status to children's negative emotionality, effortful control, and impulsivity: Concurrent relations and prediction of change. *Developmental Psychology, 41*, 193–211.

Emde, R. N., Robinson, J. L., Corley, R. P., Nikkari, D., & Zahn-Waxler, C. (2001). Reactions to restraint and anger-related expressions during the second year. In R. N. Emde & J. K. Hewitt (Eds.), *Infancy to early childhood: Genetic and environmental influences on developmental change* (pp. 127–140). New York: Oxford University Press.

Fan, J., Fossella, J., Sommer, T., Wu, Y., & Posner, M. I. (2003). Mapping the genetic variation of executive attention onto brain activity. *Proceedings of the National Academy of Sciences, USA, 100*, 7406–7411.

Fossella, J., Sommer, T., Fan, J., Wu, Y., Swanson, J. M., Pfaff, D. W., & Posner, M. I. (2002). Assessing the molecular genetics of attention networks. *BMC Neuroscience, 3*, 14.

Fulker, D. W., Cherny, S. S., & Cardon, L. R. (1993). Continuity and change in cognitive development. In R. Plomin and G. E. McClearn (Eds.), *Nature, nurture, and psychology* (pp.77–97). Washington, DC: American Psychological Association.

Goldsmith, H. H., Buss, K. A., & Lemery, K. S. (1997). Toddler and childhood temperament: Expanded content, stronger genetic evidence, new evidence for the importance of environment. *Developmental Psychology, 33*, 891–905.

Gray, J. R. (2004). Integration of emotion and cognitive control. *Current Directions in Psychological Science, 13*, 46–48.

Greenwood, P. M., & Parasuraman, R. (2003). Normal genetic variation, cognition, and aging. *Behavioral and Cognitive Neuroscience Reviews, 2*, 278–306.

Hansell, N. K., Wright, M. J., Geffen, G. M., Geffen, L. B., Smith, G. A., & Martin, N. G. (2001). Genetic influence on ERP slow wave measures of working memory. *Behavior Genetics, 31*, 603–614.

Heilman, K. M. (1997). The neurobiology of emotional experience. *Journal of Neuropsychiatry & Clinical Neuroscience, 9*, 439–448.

Keane, S. P., & Calkins, S. D. (2004). Predicting kindergarten peer social status from toddler and preschool problem behaviors. *Journal of Abnormal Child Psychology, 32*, 409–423.

Kochanska, G., Coy, K. C., & Murray, K. T. (2001). The development of self-regulation in the first four years of life. *Child Development, 72,* 1091–1111.

Kochanska, G., & Knaack, A. (2003). Effortful control as a personality characteristic of young children. *Journal of Personality, 71,* 1087–1112.

Kolb, B., & Whishaw, I. Q. (2003). *Fundamentals of human neuropsychology* (5th ed.). New York: Worth.

Kopp, C. B. (2002). Commentary: The codevelopments of attention and emotion regulation. *Infancy, 3,* 199–208.

Kovas, Y., & Plomin, R. (2006). Generalist genes: Implications for the cognitive sciences. *Trends in Cognitive Sciences, 10,* 198–203.

Levinson, D. F. (2006). The genetics of depression: A review. *Biological Psychiatry, 60,* 84–92.

Maher, B. S., Marazita, M. L., Ferrell, R. E., & Vanyukov, M. M. (2002). Dopamine system genes and attention deficit hyperactivity disorder: A meta-analysis. *Psychiatric Genetics, 12,* 207–215.

Manuck, S. B., Flory, J. D., Ferrell, R. E., Dent, K. M., Mann, J. J., & Muldoon, M. F. (1999). Aggression and anger-related traits associated with a polymorphism of the tryptophan hydroxylase gene. *Biological Psychiatry, 45,* 603–614.

McCartney, K., Harris, M. J., & Bernieri, F. (1990). Growing up and growing apart: A developmental meta-analysis of twin studies. *Psychological Bulletin, 107,* 226–237.

McGue, M. & Bouchard, T. J., Jr. (1989). Genetic and environmental determinants of information processing and special mental abilities: A twin analysis. In R. J. Sternberg (Ed.), *Advances in the psychology of human intelligence* (Vol. 5, pp. 7–45). Hillsdale, NJ: Erlbaum.

McGue, M., Bouchard, T. J., Jr., Iacono, W. G., & Lykken, D. T. (1993). Behavioral genetics of cognitive ability: A life-span perspective. In R. Plomin & G. E. McClearn (Eds.), *Nature, nurture, and psychology* (pp. 59–76). Washington, DC: American Psychological Association.

McGuire, K. A., Katsanis, J., Iacono, W. G., & McGue, M. (1998). Genetic influences on the spontaneous EEG: An examination of 15-year-old and 17-year-old twins. *Developmental Neuropsychology, 14,* 7–18.

Neale, M. C., & Cardon, L. R. (1992). *Methodology for genetic studies of twins and families.* Dordrecht, Netherlands: Kluwer Academic.

Neubauer, A. C., Spinath, F. M., Riemann, R., Angleitner, A., & Borkenau, P. (2000). Genetic and environmental influences on two measures of speed of information processing and their relation to psychometric intelligence: Evidence from the German Observational Study of Adult Twins. *Intelligence, 28,* 267–289.

Ollendick, T., & March, J. (2004). *Phobic and anxiety disorders in children and adolescents.* Oxford, England: Oxford University Press.

Olson, S. L., Sameroff, A. J., Kerr, D. C. R., Lopez, N. L., & Wellman, H. M. (2005). Developmental foundations of conduct problems in young children: The role of effortful control. *Development & Psychopathology, 17,* 25–45.

Oniszczenko, W., Zawadzki, B., Strelau, J., Riemann, R., Angleitner, A., & Spinath, F. M. (2003). Genetic and environmental determinants of temperament: A comparative study based on Polish and German samples. *European Journal of Personality, 17,* 207–220.

Orekhova, E. V., Stroganova, T. A., Posikera, I. N., & Malykh, S. B. (2003). Heritability and "environmentability" of electroencephalogram in infants: The twin study. *Psychophysiology, 40,* 727–741.

Pennington, B. F., Filipek, P. A., Lefly, D., Chhabildas, N., Kennedy, N., Simon, J. H., et al. (2000). A twin MRI study of size variation in the human brain. *Journal of Cognitive Neuroscience, 12,* 223–232.

Petrill, S. A., & Deater-Deckard, K. (2004). Task orientation, parental warmth, and SES account for significant proportion of the shared environmental variance in general cognitive ability in early childhood. *Developmental Science, 7,* 25–32.

Petrill, S. A., Deater-Deckard, K., Thompson, L., DeThorne, L., & Schatschneider, C. (2006). Reading skills in early readers: Genetic and shared environmental influences. *Journal of Learning Disabilities, 39,* 48–55.

Petrill, S. A., Thompson, L. A., & Detterman, D. K. (1995). The genetic and environmental variance underlying elementary cognitive tasks. *Behavior Genetics, 25,* 199–209.

Pezawas, L., Meyer-Lindenberg, A., Drabant, E. M., Verchinski, B. A., Munoz, K. E., Kolachana, B. S., et al. (2005). 5-HTTLPR polymorphism impacts human cingulate–amygdala interactions: A genetic susceptibility mechanism for depression. *Nature Neuroscience, 8,* 828–834.

Plomin, R., DeFries, J. C., McClearn, G. E., & McGuffin, P. (2001). *Behavioral genetics* (4th ed.). New York: Worth.

Plomin, R., Fulker, D. W., Corley, R., & DeFries, J. C. (1997). Nature, nurture, and cognitive development from 1 to 16 years: A parent–offspring adoption study. *Psychological Science, 8,* 442.

Posner, M. I., & Rothbart, M. K. (2007). *Educating the human brain.* Washington, DC: American Psychological Association.

Posthuma, D., de Geus, E. J. C., & Baaré, W. F. C. (2002). The association between brain volume and intelligence is of genetic origin. *Nature Neuroscience, 5,* 83–84.

Putnam, S., & Rothbart, M. K. (2006). Development of short and very short forms of the Children's Behavior Questionnaire. *Journal of Personality Assessment, 87,* 103–113.

Reuter, M., Peters, K., Schroeter, K., Koebke, W., Lenardon, D., Bloch, B., & Hennig, J. (2005). The influence of the dopaminergic system on cognitive functioning: A molecular genetic approach. *Behavioral Brain Research, 164,* 93–99.

Reynolds, C. A., Prince, J. A., & Feuk, L. (2006). Longitudinal memory performance during normal aging: Twin association models of APOE and other Alzheimer candidate genes. *Behavior Genetics, 36,* 185–194.

Rothbart, M. K., Ellis, L. K., Rueda, M. R., & Posner, M. I. (2003). Developing mechanisms of temperamental effortful control. *Journal of Personality, 71,* 1113–1143.

Rujescu, D., Giegling, I., Bondy, B., Gietl, A., Zill, P., & Moller, H. J. (2002). Association of anger-related traits with SNPs in the TPH gene. *Molecular Psychiatry, 7*, 1023–1029.

Rydell, A., Berlin, L., & Bohlin, G. (2003). Emotionality, emotion regulation, and adaptation among 5- to 8-year-old children. *Emotion, 3*, 30–47.

Schmidt, L. A., Fox, N. A., Perez-Edgar, K., Hu, S., & Hamer, D. (2001). Association of DRD4 with attention problems in normal childhood development. *Psychiatric Genetics, 11*, 25–29.

Sheese, B. E., Voelker, P. M., Rothbart, M. K., & Posner, M. I. (2007). Parenting quality interacts with genetic variation in dopamine receptor DRD4 to influence temperament in early childhood. *Development and Psychopathology, 19*, 1039–1046.

Thompson, L. A. (1993). Genetic contributions to intellectual development in infancy and childhood. In P. A. Vernon (Ed.), *Biological approaches to the study of human intelligence* (pp. 95–138). Norwood, NJ: Ablex.

Thompson, P. M., Cannon, T. D., Narr, K. L., van Erp, T., Poutanen, V. P. Huttunen, M., et al. (2001). Genetic influences on brain structure. *Nature Neuroscience, 4*, 1253–1258.

Underwood, M. K., Hurley, J. C., Johanson, C. A., & Mosley, J. E. (1999). An experimental, observational investigation of children's responses to peer provocation: Developmental and gender differences in middle childhood. *Child Development, 70*, 1428–1446.

van Baal, G. C. M., de Geus, E. J. C., & Boomsma, D. I., (1998). Longitudinal study of genetic influences on ERP-P3 during childhood. *Developmental Neuropsychology, 14*, 19–45.

van Beijsterveldt, C. E. M., & van Baal, G. C. M. (2002). Twin and family studies of the human electroencephalogram: A review and meta-analysis. *Biological Psychology, 61*, 111–138.

Vernon, P. A. (1989). The heritability of measures of speed of information-processing. *Personality and Individual Differences, 10*, 573–576.

Wallace, G. L., Schmitt, J. E., Lenroot, R., Viding, E., Ordaz, S., Rosenthal, M. A., et al. (2006). A pediatric twin study of brain morphometry. *Journal of Child Psychology and Psychiatry, 47*, 987–993.

Wilson, C., Gardner, F., Burton, J., & Leung, S. (2006). Maternal attributions and young children's conduct problems. *Infant and Child Development, 15*, 109–121.

Yamagata, S., Takahashi, Y., Kijima, N., Maekawa, H., Ono, Y., & Ando, J. (2005). Genetic and environmental etiology of effortful control. *Twin Research and Human Genetics, 8*, 300–306.

Zhou, Q., Hofer, C., Eisenberg, N., Reiser, M., Spinrad, T. L., & Fabes, R. A. (2007). The developmental trajectories of attention focusing, attentional and behavioral persistence, and externalizing problems during school-age years. *Developmental Psychology, 43*, 369–385.

9

UNDERSTANDING THE SOCIAL WORLD: A DEVELOPMENTAL NEUROSCIENCE APPROACH

MARK H. JOHNSON

One of the main features of the human brain is its specialized processing of social stimuli. Adults have regions of the brain specialized for processing and integrating information about the appearance, behavior, and intentions of other humans, a network often referred to as the *social brain*. The activity of this network may be regulated by emotional states. Although the social brain has been the subject of much study in adults, exactly how these neural and cognitive specializations emerge during development is still poorly understood. Indeed, one of the major debates in human cognitive neuroscience concerns the phylogenetic and ontogenetic origins of the social brain network. In this chapter, I show that the role of ontogeny in the emerging specificity of the social brain has been relatively neglected, with evidence suggesting that each developing child's brain adapts afresh to capture the regularities inherent in the social world.

I acknowledge financial support from Medical Research Council (UK) Grant G0701484 and Birkbeck College, London, England. This chapter is a revised and updated version of Johnson (2005b) and incorporates material from Grossman and Johnson (2007). I also thank my collaborators for their specific and general contributions to the work and ideas presented.

A widely held assumption about the emerging social brain is that specific genes are expressed in particular parts of cortex and consequently "code for" specific patterns of neural wiring intrinsic to a region and therefore particular to certain computational functions. Although this type of explanation appears to be valid for specialized computations within subcortical structures, a variety of genetic, neurobiological, and cognitive neuroscience evidence indicates that it is, at best, only part of the story for many human cognitive functions dependent on cerebral cortex (for a review, see Johnson, 2005a). This requires a shift of explanatory power from phylogeny toward ontogeny (Johnson, 2005a). Just one example of this is that, in human adults, experience in particular domains changes the extent of cortical tissue activated during performance of a task. In this chapter, I consider the development of the social brain network from three different perspectives before going on to review empirical evidence from several domains of social perception and cognition.

THREE PERSPECTIVES ON THE FUNCTIONAL DEVELOPMENT OF THE HUMAN BRAIN

Relating changes in the neuroanatomy of the brain during development to the remarkable transitions in motor, perceptual, and cognitive abilities during the first years of life presents a considerable challenge. In previous work I have outlined three approaches to this issue (Johnson 2001, 2005a): (a) a maturational perspective, (b) a skill-learning viewpoint, and (c) interactive specialization (IS).

The maturational perspective has motivated much research in developmental cognitive neuroscience in which the goal is to relate the underlying maturation of particular regions of the brain, usually regions of cerebral cortex, to the emergence of novel sensory, motor, and cognitive functions. Commonly, evidence concerning the neuroanatomical development of different brain regions is used to determine an age when a particular region comes "online," or is otherwise functional. Success in a new behavioral task at this age is then attributed to the underlying brain maturation. From this perspective, postnatal functional brain development is essentially the reverse of adult neuropsychology, with the only difference being that specific brain regions (and their corresponding computational modules) are added instead of being knocked out. In the social brain network, different regions or modules could come online at different postnatal ages to enable more sophisticated functions to be computed.

Although the maturational approach is intuitively appealing, it fails to explain some important aspects of human functional brain development. For example, some of the cortical regions that are slowest to develop in their neuroanatomical connections also can be activated from shortly after birth (for review, see Johnson 2005a). Furthermore, where brain function during a behavioral transition has been assessed by functional magnetic resonance imaging (fMRI), multiple cortical and subcortical areas appear to change their response pattern (e.g., Luna et al., 2001), as opposed to one or two previously inactive regions becoming active. Finally, associations between neural and cognitive changes based on their having a similar age of onset are unconstrained because of the great variety of different neuroanatomical and neurochemical measures that change at different times in different regions of the brain.

The second perspective on human functional brain development, skill learning, involves the assumption that the changes in neural activity seen during functional brain development in infants and children as they acquire new perceptual or motor abilities correspond with, or are similar to, those involved in the more complex perceptual and motor skill tasks we undertake as adults. For example, Gauthier has shown that extensive training of adults with *greebles* (i.e., artificially created objects that do not exist in the natural world) eventually results in activation of a cortical region previously associated with face processing, the so-called fusiform face area (Gauthier, Tarr, Anderson, Skudlarski, & Gore, 1999). This example of neural changes resulting from acquired perceptual expertise raises the possibility that the region is normally activated by faces in adults, not because it is prewired to process faces but rather because we have extensive perceptual expertise with this type of stimulus (see Gauthier & Nelson, 2001). Although the degree to which parallels can be drawn between adult expertise and infant development still remains unclear, to the extent that the skill learning hypothesis is correct, it presents a view of continuity of mechanisms of plasticity and learning throughout the life span.

The third perspective, IS, assumes that postnatal functional brain development, at least within cerebral cortex, involves a process of organizing patterns of interregional interactions (Johnson 2001, 2005a). According to this view, the response properties of a specific region are partly determined by its patterns of connectivity to other regions and by these regions' patterns of activity. During postnatal development, changes in the response properties of cortical regions occur as they interact and compete with each other to acquire their role in new computational abilities. According to IS, at least some cortical regions begin with very broadly defined functions and are consequently partially activated in a wide range of different contexts and tasks. During development, activity-dependent interactions between regions sharpens the functions of regions such that activation becomes restricted to a narrower set of circumstances (e.g., a region originally activated by a wide variety of visual objects may come to confine its response to upright human faces). The onset of new behavioral competencies during infancy will therefore be associated with changes in activity over several regions and not just with the onset of activity in one or more additional region(s).

Different key assumptions underlie the three approaches just outlined. The first of these concerns Gottlieb's (1992) two approaches to the study of development, *deterministic epigenesis,* in which it is assumed that there is a unidirectional causal path from genes to structural brain changes to psychological function, and *probabilistic epigenesis,* in which interactions between genes, structural brain changes, and psychological function are viewed as bidirectional, dynamic, and emergent. The maturational approach assumes deterministic epigenesis; region-specific gene expression is assumed to effect changes in intraregional connectivity that, in turn, allow new functions to emerge. A related assumption of the maturational approach is that there is a one-to-one mapping between brain and cortical regions and particular cognitive functions, such that specific computational modules come online following that maturation of circuitry intrinsic to the corresponding cortical region. In some ways, this view parallels so-called mosaic development at the cellular level, in which simple organisms (such as *C. elegans*) are constructed through cell lineages that are largely independent of each other (Elman et al., 1996). Similarly, different cortical regions are assumed to have different and independent maturational timetables, thus enabling new cognitive functions to emerge at different ages in relative isolation (Mareschal et al., 2007).

An assumption underlying the skill learning approach is that there is a continuity of the circuitry underlying skill acquisition from birth through to adulthood. This skill acquisition circuit is likely to involve a network of structures that retains the same basic function across developmental time (involving a static brain-cognition mapping). However, other brain regions may respond to training with dynamic changes in functionality similar or identical to those hypothesized within the IS framework.

Several underlying assumptions of IS (Johnson 2001, 2005a) differ from the other views. With regard to Gottlieb's (1992) distinction, an assumption of probabilistic epigenesis is coupled with the view that cognitive functions are the emergent product of interactions between different brain regions and also between the whole brain and its external environment. It is assumed that different brain regions do not develop independently but that their development is heavily constrained by interactions with their neighboring regions. This latter assumption follows recent trends in adult functional neuroimaging. For example, Friston and Price (2001) pointed out that the response properties of a region are determined by its patterns of connectivity to other regions, and it may be an error to assume that particular functions can be localized within a certain cortical region. Similar views have been expressed by Carpenter et al. (2001), who stated,

> In contrast to a localist assumption of a one-to-one mapping between cortical regions and cognitive operations, an alternative view is that cognitive task performance is subserved by large-scale cortical networks that consist of spatially separate computational components, each with its

own set of relative specializations, that collaborate extensively to accomplish cognitive functions. (p. 360).

Applying these ideas to development, the IS approach emphasizes dynamic changes in interregional connectivity, as opposed to the maturation of intraregional connectivity (Fair et al., 2007). Where the maturational approach may be analogous to mosaic cellular development, the IS view corresponds to the regulatory development seen in higher organisms in which cell–cell interactions are critical in determining developmental fate. In the same way as the brain is shaped by developing within a body (*embodiment*), the development of each brain region is constrained by its development within the whole brain (i.e., *embrainment*; Johnson, 2005a; Mareschal et al., 2007).

Another assumption of the IS view is that the mapping between structure and function can change during development. This is in contrast to much previous work in the field that has assumed that the relation between brain structure and cognitive function is static during development. For example, taking a maturational view, researchers assume that when new structures come online, the existing (already mature) regions continue to support the same functions that they did at earlier developmental stages. This is partly why it is acceptable to study developmental disorders in adulthood and then extrapolate back in time to early development. Contrary to this view, the IS approach suggests that when a new computation or skill is acquired, there is a reorganization of interactions between brain different structures and regions. This reorganization process could even change how previously acquired cognitive functions are represented in the brain. Thus, the same behavior could potentially be supported by different neural substrates at different ages during development.

Assuming that structure–function relations can change with development raises the important further questions of how and why this occurs. Fortunately, the view that there is competitive specialization of regions during development gives rise to more specific predictions about the types of changes in structure–function relations that should be observed. Specifically, as regions become increasingly selective in their response properties during infancy, the overall extent of cortical activation during a given task may therefore decrease. This is because regions that previously responded to a range of different stimuli (e.g., complex animate and inanimate objects) come to confine their activity to a particular class of objects (e.g., upright human faces) and therefore no longer respond to stimuli or tasks contexts in the same way as before. Evidence in support of these predictions will be discussed later. It is important to emphasize that, according to the IS view, given a typical social environment and initial biases in regional functionality and connectivity, most individuals will follow the same developmental trajectory, resulting in similar patterns of cortical specialization by adulthood. In other words, what is inherited is not a rigid maturational plan for functional brain development but a developmental pathway or trajectory with a predictable outcome in most cases (Carroll, 2005).

Having reviewed the three basic perspectives on human functional brain development, I return to the topic of the ontogeny of the social brain network and examine which of the perspectives I have outlined best accounts for the existing evidence. I begin with one of the most basic visual functions of the social brain: the detection and perception of faces.

FACE PERCEPTION

Several regions within the cortical social brain network, including regions of the fusiform gyrus, lateral occipital area, and superior temporal sulcus have all been implicated in neuroimaging studies as being face-sensitive regions involved in aspects of encoding/detecting facial information (Adolphs, 2003; Kanwisher, McDermott, & Chun, 1997). The adult stimulus specificity of response has been most extensively studied for the *fusiform face area* (FFA), a region that is more activated by faces than by many other comparison stimuli, including houses, textures, and hands (Kanwisher et al., 1997). Although the greater activation of the FFA to faces than to other objects has led some to propose it is a face module (Kanwisher et al., 1997), others call this view into question (Haxby et al., 2001). However, the observation remains that faces activate the FFA more than any other visual object and that the distribution of activity over the ventral cortex for faces differs from that for other types of objects in that it is more focal and less influenced by attention (Haxby et al., 2001). Given this example of adult cortical specialization, we can inquire into how this specialization arises and ask why face-sensitive regions tend to be located in particular regions of cortex. The three perspectives outlined earlier provide different answers to this question.

According to the maturational view, specific genes are expressed within particular cortical regions (such as the FFA) and prewire the circuitry within those areas for face processing. One of several problems with this argument is that differential gene expression within the mammalian cerebral cortex tends to be on a much larger scale than the functional regions identified in imaging studies (for a review, see Johnson, 2005a). According to the skill learning view, much of the adult social brain network is better characterized as a perceptual skill network, and this coincides with social processing because most human adults are experts with this type of stimulus. Finally, according to the IS view, the social brain emerges from other (nonsocial) brain networks as a result of interactions among different brain regions and between the whole brain and the typical child's external world.

Face Perception in Newborns

A number of studies have shown that newborn infants (in some studies within the 1st hour of life) preferentially look toward facelike patterns (e.g.,

Johnson, Dziurawiec, Ellis, & Morton, 1991; Valenza, Simion, Cassia, & Umiltà, 1996; for a review, see Johnson, 2005c). There has been considerable debate over the specificity of the mechanisms (or representations) that underlie this primitive behavior. At one extreme is the view that such preferences are simply due to the fact that faces contain the optimal psychophysical properties as visual stimuli for the newborn visual system (a view consistent with a skill-learning perspective). At the other extreme is the view that newborns' processing of faces is substantially similar to that observed in adults and can include well-specified representations of individual faces (consistent with one version of the maturational perspective). An intermediate between these extremes was advanced by Johnson and Morton (1991), who proposed that newborns' brains possess the minimum necessary information to elicit adaptive behavior toward faces. Specifically, they argued for a mechanism they termed CONSPEC that might contain a representation as simple as three high-contrast blobs in the locations of the eyes and mouth. They suggested that this skeletal representation may be sufficient to "bootstrap" other developing systems by providing them with the appropriate input. In this respect the two-process theory advanced by Johnson and Morton (1991) is generally consistent with the IS approach.

Since these theories were proposed, several laboratories have focused on determining the representation that underlies the tendency of newborns to orient to faces, through empirical investigation and neural network modeling. With regard to the latter, results from neural network simulations suggest that a representation for CONSPEC as simple as three high-contrast blobs can account for the majority of the newborn behavioral data collected to date, involving a variety of different schematic and naturalistic face stimuli (see Bednar & Miikkulainen, 2003). Current debate centers on whether the minimal representation supporting CONSPEC involves the three high-contrast blobs, as originally proposed by Johnson and Morton (1991), or whether the representation supports a preference for arrays with a greater number of elements in the upper half of a stimulus (Turati, Simion, Milani, & Umiltà, 2002). However, recent evidence from adult cognitive neuroscience encourages the former view (discussed later). In both cases the neural representation is probably close to the minimum sufficient to elicit orienting to faces within the natural environment of the newborn, given the constraints of the newborn visual system.

Several lines of evidence suggest that this newborn preference is not mediated by the same cortical structures as are involved in face processing in adults and that it may be due to subcortical structures such as the amygdala, superior colliculus, and pulvinar (Johnson, 2005c). Recent cognitive neuroscience studies suggest that the same pathway may exist as a "quick and dirty" route for face processing in adults (Johnson, 2005c). One purpose of the newborn bias to fixate on faces may be to elicit bonding from adult caregivers. However, I suggest that an equally important purpose is to bias the visual input to cortical circuits that show developmental plasticity. This biased sampling of the visual environment over the first days and weeks of life may ensure the appropriate specialization of later-developing cortical circuitry (Morton & Johnson, 1991; Johnson, 2005c). In addition, the subcortical route may project to particular cortical regions that become recruited into the social brain network.

The Neurodevelopment of Face Processing

Although the current evidence on newborn face preferences is difficult to reconcile with a strictly skill-learning view of functional brain development, it is not entirely inconsistent with either the maturational or IS approach. According to at least some versions of the maturational approach, primitive abilities in the newborn would be augmented by more sophisticated modules maturing at later ages. According to the IS approach, a primitive brain system like CONSPEC bootstraps later developing experience-dependent systems by providing the appropriate input for them. Given that newborn behavior alone cannot discriminate between at least two of the perspectives on functional brain development, I now consider developmental changes over the first few months of life. Specifically, I address the question of whether subsequent developmental changes in brain functions look more like the addition of new components or the gradual specialization of circuitry for processing of social stimuli.

Following the logic of studying the development of a specific neural response in adults, several labs have examined changes in event-related potentials (ERPs) in face processing. In particular, attention has focused on the N170, an ERP component that has been strongly associated with face processing in a number of studies on adults (for a review, see de Haan, Johnson, & Halit, 2003). More specifically, the amplitude and latency of this ERP component varies according to whether faces are present in the visual field of the adult volunteer under study. As mentioned by de Haan et al. (2003), an important aspect of the N170 in adults is that it has a highly selective response. For example, the N170 shows a different response to human upright faces than to perceptually very similar stimuli such as inverted human faces and upright monkey faces (de Haan, Pascalis, & Johnson, 2002). Although the exact underlying brain generators of the N170 are currently still debated, the specificity of response of the adult N170 can be taken as an index of the degree of specialization of cortical processing for human upright faces. For this reason, we and others have studied the development of the N170 over the first weeks and months of postnatal life.

The first issue we addressed in our developmental studies was the age at which the face-sensitive N170 emerged. In a series of experiments, we have identified a component in the infant ERP that has many of the properties associated with the adult N170 but is of a slightly longer latency (240–290 ms; de Haan et al., 2002; Halit, de Haan & Johnson, 2003). It is not unusual for prominent ERP components in infants to have longer latencies than those in adults. In studying the response properties of this ERP component at 3, 6, and 12 months of age, we discovered that (a) the component is present from at least 3 months of age (although its development continues into middle childhood), (b) the component becomes more finely tuned to human upright faces with increasing age, and (c) there is clearer evidence for adult-like lateralization of the component at older ages. Thus, study of the component is consistent with the predictions of the IS view of increased specialization and localization resulting from development.

More direct evidence for increased specialization and localization comes from several recent fMRI studies of the neural basis of face processing in children as compared with adults (for a review, see Cohen-Kadosh & Johnson, 2007). For example, in at least one study, children activated a larger extent of cortex around face-sensitive areas than did adults during a face-matching task (Passarotti et al., 2003), and other studies have found evidence for increasing specialization of face-sensitive cortical tissue (Cohen-Kadosh & Johnson, 2007). Similar conclusions were drawn from a PET study conducted on 2-month-old infants, in which a large network of cortical areas were activated when infants viewed faces compared with a moving dot array (Tzourio-Mazoyer, et al., 2002).

With regard to face perception, the evidence from newborns allows us to rule out the skill-learning hypothesis, and the evidence on neurodevelopment over the first months and years is consistent with the types of dynamic changes in processing predicted from the IS approach. Thus, the emerging picture from this initial example of face processing is consistent with the view that a variety of constraints operate on a process of emerging specialization, such that cortical regions specialized for face processing, such as the FFA, are the inevitable result of the typical developmental trajectory. In other words, given a typical starting point of regional brain biases and connectivity, taken together with a typical early social environment, the specialization of FFA for faces is ensured.

THE EYES AND BEYOND

Obviously the adult social brain network processes much else besides the basic perceptual analysis of faces. Although most of these computations remain to be investigated from a neuroscience approach, one facet of the social world for which there are data concerns processing information about the eyes of other humans. Two important aspects of processing information about the eyes are (a) detecting the direction of another's gaze in order to direct your own attention to the same object or spatial location (*gaze following* or *gaze cueing*) and (b) detecting eyes that are looking directly at you (*eye contact*). In adults, perception of averted gaze can elicit an automatic shift of attention in the same direction (Driver et al., 1999), allowing the establishment of *joint attention* (Butterworth and Jarrett, 1991). Caregivers' and infants' joint attention to objects is thought to be crucial for a number of aspects of cognitive and social development, including word learning. The detection of direct gaze enables eye contact to take place between the viewer and the perceived face. Eye contact is the main mode of establishing a communicative context between humans and is believed to be important for normal social development (e.g., Kleinke, 1986; Symons, Hains, & Muir, 1998). It is commonly agreed that eye gaze perception is important for mother–infant interaction and that it provides a vital foundation for subsequent social development (e.g., Jaffe, Stern, & Peery , 1973; Stern, 1974).

Which regions of the social brain network are important for these computations? The superior temporal sulcus (STS) has been identified in several imaging studies of eye gaze perception and processing in adults (for a review, see Adolphs, 2003). As with the cortical streams of face processing described previously, in adults the response properties of this region are highly specialized (tuned) in that the region does not respond to superficially similar nonbiological motion (e.g., Puce, Allison, Bentin, Gore, & McCarthy, 1998). Thus, the narrow response tuning of the region in adults potentially provides another example of specialization within the cortical social brain network and may result from IS processes similar to those that shaped the emergence of FFA.

Investigating eye gaze processing from the IS perspective led us to hypothesize that eye gaze processing and other aspects of face processing will share more common processing early in development when relevant cortical circuits are less specialized. Specifically, with increasing specialization of functions and pathways within the social brain network, eye gaze processing will become increasingly differentiated from other aspects of face processing during postnatal development. This may become evident as differential patterns of activation within the social brain when information about the eyes is being processed, compared with other face-relevant tasks. We have begun to examine this hypothesis in several lines of investigation.

In the first line of work, we studied the importance of a period of eye contact with a face for two important developmental functions in infants: the cueing of attention by gaze direction and the recognition of individual faces. As mentioned earlier, gaze cues are able to trigger an automatic and rapid shifting of the focus of the adult viewer's visual attention (Driver et al., 1999; Friesen & Kingstone, 1998; Langton & Bruce, 1999). However, it remains unknown when the ability to use eye gaze direction as an attention cue first emerges. Previous work with human infants has indicated that they start to discriminate and follow adults' direction of attention at the age of 3 or 4 months (Hood, Willen, & Driver, 1998; Vecera & Johnson, 1995). In our studies we examined further the visual properties of the eyes that enable infants to follow the direction of the gaze. We tested 4-month-olds using a cueing paradigm adapted from Hood et al. (1998). Each trial began with the eyes in the stimulus face blinking (to attract attention), before the pupils shifted to either the right or the left for a period of 1,500 ms. A target stimulus was then presented either in the same position where the stimulus face eyes were looking (congruent position) or in a location incongruent with the direction of gaze. By measuring the saccadic reaction time of infants to orient to the target, we demonstrated that the infants were faster to look at the location congruent with the direction of gaze of the face.

In a subsequent series of experiments, my colleagues and I (Farroni, Johnson, Brockbank, & Simion, 2000) found that a variety of types of lateral motion induced cueing effects in infants but only when preceded by a short period of direct gaze. Taken together with other findings, these results suggest that it is only following a period of eye contact with an upright face that cueing effects are observed in infants. In other words, eye contact with an upright face may engage mechanisms of attention such that the viewer is more likely to be cued by subsequent motion. Further, the finding that infants are as effectively cued by lateral motion of features other than the eyes provides general support to the hypothesis, predicted by the IS view, that their STS may be less specialized in its response properties than it is in adults.

Recent behavioral studies in adults have demonstrated that direct gaze can modulate other aspects of face processing, and this has recently been termed the *eye contact effect* (Senju & Johnson, 2009). For example, eye contact with a viewed face can affect both the speed of online gender judgments and the accuracy of incidental recognition memory of faces (Vuilleumier, Gorge, Lister, Armoni, & Driver, 2005), and performance in face memory tasks can be influenced by gaze direction both at the encoding and at the retrieval levels (Hood, Macrae, Cole-Davies, & Dias, 2003). In the latter case, Hood and colleagues tested children and adults on a forced-choice face recognition task in which the direction of eye gaze was manipulated over the course of the initial presentation and subsequent test phase of the experiment. To establish whether there are any effects of direct gaze on the encoding or retrieval of individual faces, participants were presented with faces displaying either direct or averted gaze and with their eyes closed during the test phase (i.e., encoding manipulation) or with faces presented initially with eyes closed and tested with either direct or averted gaze (i.e., retrieval manipulation). The results demonstrated that direct gaze facilitated the encoding process in both children and adults. Faces with direct gaze also enhanced the retrieval process, although this effect was stronger for adults.

In a follow-up to this work, my colleagues and I (Farroni, Massaccesi, Menon, & Johnson, 2007) investigated whether direction of gaze has any effect on face recognition in 4-month-old infants. The infants were shown faces with both direct and averted gaze and subsequently given a preference test involving the same face and a novel one. A novelty preference during test was found only after initial exposure to a face with direct gaze. Further, individual face recognition was also generally enhanced for faces both with direct and averted gaze when the infants started the task with the direct gaze condition. Taken together, these results indicate that eye contact modulates face processing even in early infancy.

In a further series of experiments, we attempted to gain converging evidence for the differential processing of direct gaze in infants, by recording ERPs from the scalp as infants viewed faces. We studied 4-month-old babies with similar stimuli as those described above and found a difference between the two gaze directions at the time and scalp location of the previously identified face-sensitive component of the infant ERP (N240/N290; de Haan et al., 2002). As mentioned earlier, this component of the infant ERP is thought to be the equivalent of the well-studied adult face-sensitive N170 component. In infants the component is sensitive to changes in the orientation and species of a face by at least 12 months of age (Halit et al., 2003). Thus, eye contact enhances the neural processing of faces in 4-month-old infants. Further experiments demonstrated that this modulating effect of gaze direction is found only when gaze occurs within the context of an upright face.

Although modulation of face-sensitive components of the ERP is seen in infants as described above, when we used the same paradigm with adult participants we did not find any modulation of the ERP by gaze direction (Grice et al., 2005). This negative result was confirmed when we tested a group of young children 2 to 5 years old. Why did we find an effect in infants that then disappeared at older ages? One possibility, predicted by the IS view, is that although processes related to face processing are relatively unspecialized early in life, eye gaze processing and other aspects of face processing share common mechanisms and are heavily intertwined. According to the IS view, as a result of development (and increased specialization), eye gaze processing becomes partially distinct and thus ceases to modulate more general aspects of face processing. If this is the case, it is possible that certain disorders of development that involve social cognition will entail a delay or aberrant specialization process. That is, the normal factors that constrain the emergence of components of the social brain network are disturbed in some way. In this case, we may observe gaze direction modulation of the ERP at ages at which this does not occur in typically developing children. Grice et al. (2005) tested this prediction of the IS view in a group of young children with autism (2 to 5 years old). These children showed modulation of the N170 in response to direct gaze in a way very similar to that previously observed in typically developing 4-month-old infants. This modulatory effect was not seen in age-matched controls.

Recent experiments with 4-month-old infants have advanced the study of the neural basis of eye gaze perception in infants by analyzing high-frequency EEG bursting in the gamma (40 Hz) range (Grossman et al., 2007). Gamma oscillations are of interest partly because they correlate with the blood oxygen level dependent (BOLD) response used in fMRI (Niessing et al., 2005; Foucher, Otzenberger, & Gounot, 2003; Fiebach, Gruber, & Supp, 2005). Grossmann, Johnson, Farroni, and Csibra (2007) predicted a burst of gamma oscillation over prefrontal sites in response to direct gaze if gamma oscillations are indeed related to detecting eye contact/communicative intent. as suggested by adult fMRI work (Kampe, Frith, & Frith,2003; Schilbach et al., 2006). Because the right intraparietal sulcus (IPS) and right STS are sensitive to averted gaze in the adult brain (Hoffman & Haxby, 2000), we further hypothesized that some activity over right temporo-parietal regions would be associated with the perception of averted gaze. In addition, another group of 4-month-old infants was presented with the same face stimuli upside down, which is thought to disrupt configural face processing (Rodriguez et al., 1999; Turati, Sangrioli, Ruel, & de Schonen, 2004) and infants' preference for eye contact (Farroni, Menon, & Johnson, 2006). Thus, we predicted that inverted faces would not induce activity in the gamma band that differs as a function of eye gaze.

The data revealed that gamma oscillations varied as a function of gaze direction only in the context of an upright face, which extends the previous ERP results (Farroni, Csibra, Simion, & Johnson, 2002; Farroni, Johnson, & Csibra, 2004; Johnson et al., 2005). In support of our hypotheses, specific effects with distinct spatial and temporal characteristics were observed depending on whether gaze within an upright face was directed at or away from the infant. Direct gaze compared with averted gaze evoked early (100 ms) increased gamma activity (20–40 Hz) at occipital channels. Short-latency phase-locked oscillatory evoked gamma responses have been described in the visual modality in response to brief static stimuli in infant and adult EEG (Csibra, Davis, Spratling, & Johnson, 2000; Tallon-Baudry & Bertrand, 1999). In adults, evoked gamma activity is significantly larger for items that match memory representations (Herrmann, Lenz, Junge, Busch, & Maess, 2003; Herrmann, Munk, & Engel, 2004). For infants, a face with direct gaze may represent a more familiar and prototypical face (Farroni et al., 2007), which is closer to what is represented in memory than a face with averted gaze, and therefore elicits an enhanced evoked oscillatory response. This interpretation is supported by the findings described earlier showing enhanced neural processing (Farroni et al., 2002) and better recognition of upright faces with direct gaze in infants (Farroni et al., 2007). The modulation of the evoked gamma response in this study was observed much earlier (100 ms) than the effect in the previous ERP study (290 ms; Farroni et al., 2002, 2004). This indicates that gamma activity may be a more sensitive measure of some aspects of very early brain processes related to the discrimination of gaze direction.

As predicted, direct gaze within an upright face also elicited a late (300 ms) induced gamma burst over right prefrontal channels. As mentioned earlier, eye contact serves as an important ostensive signal in face-to-face interactions that helps to establish a communicative link between two people. Successful communication between two people may well depend crucially on the ability to detect the intention to communicate conveyed by signals directed at the self such as making eye contact (Kampe et al., 2003). On a neural level, the medial prefrontal cortex (MPFC) is consistently activated when gaze is directed at, but not when gaze is averted from, the self (Kampe et al., 2003; Schilbach et al., 2006). Since gamma oscillations measured with EEG are correlated with the BOLD response used in fMRI (Fiebach et al., 2005; Foucher et al., 2003), eye contact detection in 4-month-old infants may well recruit some of the same brain regions as in adults. However, the gamma burst distributed over right frontal cortex in infants might reflect less localized functional activity than in adults, suggesting a more diffuse to a more focal pattern of cortical activity with age.

According to the IS view, a network as a whole becomes specialized for a particular function. Therefore, we suggest that the "eye region" of the STS does not develop in isolation, or in a modular fashion, but that its functionality emerges within the context of interacting regions involved in either general face processing or in motion detection recently termed *embrainment* (Mareschal et al., 2007). Viewed from this perspective, STS may be a region that integrates motion information with the processing of faces (and other body parts). Although STS may be active in infants, we propose that it is not yet efficiently integrating motion and face information. In other words, although the 4-month-old has good face processing and general motion perception, he or she has not yet integrated these two aspects of perception together into adult-style eye gaze perception. By this account, making eye contact with an upright face fully engages face processing, which then facilitates the orienting of attention by lateral motion. At older ages, eye gaze perception becomes a fully integrated function in which even static presentations of averted eyes are sufficient to facilitate gaze.

THE PERCEPTION OF HUMAN ACTION

Although the face and eyes are important for interpersonal communication, another function of the social brain network is to perceive and predict the behavior of other humans on the basis of their actions. Although this area has been intensively studied with behavioral methods, a developmental neuroscience approach has begun to be taken to two aspects of the perception of action: biologically possible versus impossible actions, and goal-directed versus incomplete actions.

The issue of whether young infants can detect biologically impossible human action promises to inform us about the extent to which learning processes are involved in the perception of human action. Behavioral studies of infant perception of biomechanical motion have been conducted for more than a decade. Initial studies such as that by Bertenthal, Proffitt, and Cutting (1984) used point-light-displays (PLDs), first used by Johansson (1973). Using such stimuli, researchers have shown infants as young as 3 months to be sensitive to configural information related to movement (Bertenthal et al., 1984). Research with PLDs demonstrates that there is considerable change in infant perception of point light motion throughout the 1st year. Even though such stimuli may be useful in investigating the perception of movement, PLDs are unnatural and intrinsically novel stimuli for infants. Developments in video technology allow for manipulation of still frames from video, thus allowing for the creation of realistic human movements that are, nonetheless, biologically impossible.

Reid, Belsky, and Johnson (2005) investigated infant perception of possible and impossible movements of the human body and attempted to relate this to the perceptual experience and motor abilities of the individual infant. To assess potential differences in individual experience, they measured the extent of "motionese" displayed by the mother during play interaction with the infant. Research suggests that parents present objects to infants in a manner different from the way in which they present objects to other adults. This activity is characterized by a deliberate enhancing of structure in object manipulation in order to allow infants greater understanding of the action involved in the object manipulation; hence the term *motionese* (Brand, Baldwin, & Ashburn, 2002). Such results suggest that the amount of exaggerated object manipulation, or motionese, that is displayed to infants is variable between infants, although this does not provide information about what aspect of visual experience is critical for the perception of biomechanical movement.

Reid et al. (2005) used both behavioral (visual preference) and electrophysiological measures to examine (a) the environment provided by mothers (as indexed by degree of maternal motionese), (b) infant motor abilities. (c) assessment of infant mental and motor abilities per standardized measures of development, and (d) infants' processing of biological movement (as indexed by looking times and gamma-band time-frequency analysis of EEG). In their first experiment it was found that, as a group, 8-month-old infants looked longer at video clips of impossible body movements than at clips of possible movements. However, this effect turned out to be mainly due to the subset of infants with relatively high fine motor skills. In a second experiment we assessed the contribution of general developmental maturation by repeating the first experiment with the addition of the Bayley Scales of Infant Development (Bayley, 1993). The overall looking time effect was replicated from the first experiment, but this effect did not correlate with Bayley mental or motor scores, allowing us to exclude general maturational factors. In our third and final experiment in this series, gamma frequency analysis of EEG resulting from passive viewing of possible and impossible action indicated that it was only those infants with relatively high fine motor skills that processed these stimuli differently. When taken together, these studies suggest a relation between the infant's own ability to perform fine motor action and the perception of biologically possible human movement.

Beyond the detection of biological possibility (or otherwise) of a single action, there is the need to segment sequences of actions into appropriate chunks and to use this information to predict the intentions of others. Research on adults has established that parsing of action sequences is partly based on understanding the intentions of the actor and the goals of the action. The issue of what cues infants use to parse action has generated debate, with behavioral results indicating that markers of intentionality may be critical. Certainly by 14 months infants are capable of discerning intentional from accidental action (Carpenter, Akhtar, & Tomasello, 1998). Other behavioral studies suggest that infants of 9 months can detect intentions in actions and that infants take an intentional stance toward an agent (Gergely, Nadasdy, Csibra, & Bíró, 1995), with this skill possibly not evident at 6 months (Csibra, Bíró, Koós, & Gergely, 2003).

Reid, Csibra, Belsky, and Johnson (2007) initially conducted a behavioral study in which they established that 8-month-old infants looked longer at an incomplete action involving a pouring event than they did at the complete action. In the latter action, the goal of the actor involved was clear, whereas in the former action sequence it was not. A subsequent gamma-range EEG analysis revealed a significant difference between conditions over left frontal regions shortly after the complete and incomplete action sequences diverged. The direction of the difference indicated that the incomplete condition yields greater power in the same frequency range than does the complete condition.

One explanation for the results of the EEG experiment is that the increased gamma over left frontal channels reflects a more specific basis for the perception of an action sequence by infants. For example, increased gamma may reflect the resetting of infant brain processes to prepare for new information once action resumes. Another potential explanation along this line is that the infant brain attempts to continue the action despite visual cues suggesting that the action is not taking place ("forward mapping"). This latter explanation may be consistent with research into object permanence indicating that gamma power in infants increases when an object unexpectedly disappears (Kaufman, Csibra, & Johnson, 2003).

A final study pitted the importance of possible biological motion against the infants' ability to parse action sequences into sensible, goal-directed chunks of action events (Southgate, Csibra, & Johnson, 2008). In this study, having been habituated to an event in which a human arm behaves efficiently to obtain a small ball, 6-month-old infants then saw two test events in which a box now obstructed a direct reach for the ball. In the first test event, infants watched the arm move the box out of the way and then reach for the ball. In the second test event, the human arm was seen snaking around the box in a biologically impossible manner. However, if it were possible, the second event would be a more efficient route to the goal, as it would not require the effort of moving the box out of the way first. Six-month-olds looked significantly longer at the possible (but less efficient) than the impossible (but more efficient) test event. This is a striking finding because it suggests that familiarity is not a prerequisite for goal attribution (infants could not be familiar with an action that is biologically impossible) and that goal attribution in this case is driven by the recognition of an efficient action relative to the goal state.

CONCLUSIONS AND FUTURE PROSPECTS

In this chapter, I have considered evidence on the development of the social brain network in relation to three perspectives on human functional brain development. For the relatively well-studied case of face perception, when evidence from several developmental ages is taken into account, I argued that the IS view of functional brain development can best account for the available data. In the less well-studied case of eye gaze processing, the evidence obtained so far is also consistent with the IS approach (but without clearly ruling out alternatives). In the third section of the chapter, I reviewed some initial studies on the perception and parsing of sequences of human action. Future work will determine whether the development of this and other complex aspects of social brain function can also be accounted for within the IS framework, but the evidence for the effects of individual experience on the perception of human action in infants is certainly consistent with this view.

Although this chapter has traced the patterns of emerging specialization in the social brain, it is likely that the neural, perceptual, and cognitive transitions observed occur more rapidly for the social brain network than for other domain-relevant systems in the brain. One reason for this is the critical importance to the infants' brain development of learning through and from their caregivers and other conspecifics (Grossmann & Johnson, 2007). It is likely that intergenerational transmission of information plays an important role in the specialization of other neural systems that support cognition in nonsocial domains and, thus, that specialization of the social brain is prioritized in early postnatal life.

REFERENCES

Adolphs, R. (2003). Cognitive neuroscience of human social behaviour. *Nature Reviews Neuroscience, 4*, 165–178.

Bayley, N. (1993). *Bayley Scales of Infant and Toddler Development* (2nd ed.). San Antonio, TX: Harcourt Assessment.

Bertenthal, B., Proffitt, D., & Cutting, J. (1984). Infants' sensitivity to figural coherence in biochemical motions. *Journal of Experimental Child Psychology, 37*, 213–230.

Bednar, J. A., & Miikkulainen, R. (2003). Learning innate face preferences. *Neural Computation, 15*, 1525–1557.

Brand, R. J., Baldwin, D. A. & Ashburn, L. A. (2002). Evidence for "motionese": Modifications in mothers' infant-directed action. *Developmental Science, 5*, 72–83.

Butterworth, G., & Jarrett, N. (1991). What minds have in common is space: Spatial mechanisms serving joint visual attention in infancy. *British Journal of Developmental Psychology, 9*, 55–72.

Carroll, S. (2005). *Endless forms most beautiful: The new science of Evo Devo.* New York: Norton.

Carpenter, M., Akhtar, N., & Tomasello, M (1998). Fourteen-through 18-month-old infants differentially imitate intentional and accidental actions. *Infant Behavior and Development, 21*, 315–330.

Carpenter, P. A., Just, M. A., Keller, T., Cherkassky, V., Roth, J. K., & Minshew, N. (2001). Dynamic cortical systems subserving cognition: fMRI studies with typical and atypical individuals. In J. L. McClelland & R. S. Siegler (Eds.), *Mechanisms of cognitive development: Behavioral and neural perspectives. Carnegie Mellon Symposia on Cognition* (pp. 353–383). Mahwah, NJ: Erlbaum.

Cohen-Kadosh, K., & Johnson, M. H. (2007). Developing a cortex specialized for face perception. *Trends in Cognitive Neuroscience, 11*, 367–369.

Csibra, G., Bíró, S., Koós, S., & Gergely, G. (2003). One-year-old infants use teleological representations of actions productively. *Cognitive Science, 27*, 111–133.

Csibra, G., Davis, G., Spratling, M.W., & Johnson, M.H. (2000, November 24). Gamma oscillations and object processing in the infant brain. *Science, 290*, 1582–1585.

de Haan, M., Johnson, M. H., & Halit, H. (2003). Development of face-sensitive event-related potentials during infancy: A review. *International Journal of Psychophysiology, 51*, 45–58.

de Haan, M., Pascalis, O. & Johnson, M. H. (2002). Specialization of neural mechanisms underlying face recognition in human infants. *Journal of Cognitive Neuroscience, 14*, 199–209.

Driver, J., Davis, G., Ricciardelli, P., Kidd, P., Maxwell, E., & Baron-Cohen, S. (1999). Gaze perception triggers reflexive visuospatial orienting. *Visual Cognition, 6*, 509–540.

Elman, J., Bates, E. A., Johnson, M. H., Karmiloff-Smith, A., Parisi, D. & Plunkett, K. E. (1996). *Rethinking innateness: A connectionist perspective on development.* Cambridge, MA: MIT Press.

Fair, D. A., Dosenbach, N. U. F., Church, J. A., Cohen, A. L., Brahmbhatt, S., Miezin, F. M., et al., (2007). Development of distinct control networks through segregation and integration. *Proceedings of the National Academy of Sciences, USA, 104*, 13507–13512.

Farroni, T., Johnson, M. H., Brockbank, M. & Simion, F. (2000). Infant's use of gaze direction to cue attention: The importance of perceived motion. *Visual Cognition, 7*, 705–718.

Farroni, T., Csibra, G., Simion, F., & Johnson, M. H. (2002). Eye contact detection in humans from birth. *Proceedings of the National Academy of Sciences, USA, 198*, 9602–9605.

Farroni, T., Johnson, M. H., & Csibra, G. (2004). Mechanisms of eye gaze perception during infancy. *Journal of Cognitive Neuroscience, 16*, 1320–1326.

Farroni, T., Menon, E., & Johnson, M. H. (2006). Factors influencing newborns' face preferences for faces with eye contact. *Journal of Experimental Child Psychology, 95*, 298–308.

Farroni, T., Massaccesi, S., Menon, E., and Johnson, M. H. (2007). Direct gaze modulates face recognition in young infants. *Cognition, 102*, 396–404.

Fiebach, C. J., Gruber, T., & Supp, G. G. (2005). Neuronal mechanisms of repetition priming in occipitotemporal cortex: Spatiotemporal evidence from functional magnetic imaging and electronencephalography. *Journal of Neuroscience, 25*, 3414–3422.

Foucher, J. R., Otzenberger, H., & Gounot, D. (2003). The BOLD response and gamma oscillations respond differently than evoked potentials: An interleaved EEG-fMRI study. *BMC Neuroscience, 4*, 22.

Friesen, C. K., & Kingstone, A. (1998). The eyes have it! Reflexive orienting is triggered by nonpredictive gaze. *Psychonomic Bulletin & Review, 5*, 490–495.

Friston, K. J., & Price, C. J. (2001). Dynamic representations and generative models of brain function. *Brain Research Bulletin, 54*, 275–285.

Gauthier, I., Tarr, M. J., Anderson, A. W., Skudlarski, P., & Gore, J. C. (1999). Activation of the middle fusiform 'face area' increases with expertise in recognizing novel objects. *Nature Neuroscience, 2*, 568–573.

Gauthier, I., & Nelson, C. A. (2001). The development of face expertise. *Current Opinion in Neurobiology, 11*, 219–224.

Gergely, G., Nadasdy, Z., Csibra, G., & Bíró, S. (1995). Taking the intentional stance at 12 months of age. *Cognition, 56*, 165–193.

Gottlieb, G. (1992). *Individual development and evolution: The genesis of novel behavior*. London: Oxford University Press.

Grice, S. J., Halit, H., Farroni, T., Baron-Cohen, S., Bolton, P., & Johnson, M. H. (2005). Neural correlates of eye-gaze detection in young children with autism. *Cortex, 41*, 342–353.

Grossmann, T., & Johnson, M. H. (2007). The development of the social brain in human infancy. *European Journal of Neuroscience, 25*, 909–919.

Grossmann, T., Johnson, M. H., Farroni, T., & Csibra, G. (2007). Social perception in the infant brain: Gamma oscillatory activity in response to eye gaze. *Social Cognitive & Affective Neuroscience, 2*, 284–291.

Halit, H., de Haan, M., & Johnson, M. H. (2003). Cortical specialisation for face processing: face-sensitive event-related potential components in 3- and 12-month-old infants. *NeuroImage, 19*, 1180–1193.

Haxby, J. V., Gobbini, M. I., Furey, M. L., Ishai, A., Schouten, J. L., & Pietrini, P. (2001, September 28). Distributed and overlapping representations of faces and objects in ventral temporal cortex. *Science, 293*, 2425–2430.

Hermann, C. S., Lenz, D., Junge, S., Busch, N. A., & Maess, B. (2003). Memory-matches evoke human gamma responses. *BMC Neuroscience, 5*, 13.

Hermann, C. S., Munk, M. H. J., & Engel, A. K. (2004). Cognitive functions of gamma band activity: Memory match and utilization. *Trends in Cognitive Science, 8*, 347–355.

Hoffman, E. A., & Haxby, J. V. (2000). Distinct representations of eye gaze and identity in the distributed human neural system for face perception. *Nature Neuroscience, 3*, 80–84.

Hood, B. M., Macrae, C. N., Cole-Davies, V., & Dias, M. (2003). Eye remember you: The effects of gaze direction on face recognition in children and adults. *Developmental Science, 6*, 67–71.

Hood, B. M., Willen, J. D., & Driver, J. (1998). Adult's eyes trigger shifts of visual attention in human infants. *Psychological Science, 9*, 131–134.

Ishai, A., Ungerleider, L. G., Martin, A., Schouten, J. L., & Haxby, J. V. (1999). Distributed representation of objects in the human ventral visual pathway. *Proceedings of the National Academy of Sciences, USA, 96*, 9379–9384.

Jaffe, J., Stern, D. N., & Peery, J. C. (1973). "Conversational" coupling of gaze behavior in prelinguistic human development. *Journal of Psycholinguistic Research, 2*, 321–329.

Johansson, G. (1973). Visual perception of biological motion and a model of its analysis. *Perception and Psychophysics, 14*, 201–211.

Johnson, M. H. (2001). Functional brain development in humans. *Nature Reviews Neuroscience, 2*, 475–483.

Johnson, M. H. (2005a). *Developmental cognitive neuroscience: An introduction.* Oxford, England: Blackwell.

Johnson, M. H. (2005b). The ontogeny of the social brain. In U. Mayr, E. Awh, & S. W. Keele (Eds.), *Developing individuality in the human brain: A tribute to Michael Posner* (pp. 125–140). Washington, DC: American Psychological Association..

Johnson, M. H. (2005c). Subcortical face processing. *Nature Reviews Neuroscience. 6*, 766–774.

Johnson, M. H., Dziurawiec, S., Ellis, H. & Morton, J. (1991). Newborns' preferential tracking of face-like stimuli and its subsequent decline. *Cognition, 40*, 1–19.

Johnson, M. H., Griffin, R., Csibra, G., Halit, H., Farroni, T., de Haan, M., et al. (2005) The emergence of the social brain network: Evidence from typical and atypical development. *Developmental Psychopathology, 17*, 599–619.

Johnson, M. H., & Morton, J. (1991). *Biology and cognitive development: The case of face recognition.* Oxford, England: Blackwell.

Kampe, K., Frith, C. D., & Frith, U. (2003). "Hey John": Signals conveying communicative intention toward self activate brain regions associated with "mentalizing," regardless of modality. *Journal of Neuroscience, 12*, 5258–5263.

Kanwisher, N., McDermott, J., & Chun, M. M. (1997). The fusiform face area: A module in human extrastriate cortex specialized for face perception. *Journal of Neuroscience, 17,* 4302–4311.

Kaufman, J., Csibra, G., & Johnson, M. H. (2003). Representing occluded objects in the human infant brain. *Proceedings of the Royal Society B: Biology Letters, 270/ S2,* 140–143.

Kleinke, C. L. (1986). Gaze and eye contact: A research review. *Psychological Bulletin, 100,* 78–100.

Langton, S. R. H., & Bruce, V. (1999). Reflexive visual orienting in response to the social attention of others. *Visual Cognition, 6,* 541–567.

Luna, B., Thulborn, K. R., Munoz, D. P., Merriam, E. P., Garver, K. E., Minshew, N. J. et al., (2001). Maturation of widely distributed brain function subserves cognitive development. *NeuroImage, 13,* 786–793.

Mareschal, D., Johnson, M. H., Sirois, S., Spratling, M., Thomas, M., & Westermann, G. (2007). *Neuroconstructivism: Vol. 1. How the brain constructs cognition.* Oxford, England: Oxford University Press.

Morton, J., & Johnson, M. H. (1991). CONSPEC and CONLERN: A two-process theory of infant face recognition. *Psychological Review, 98,* 164–181.

Niessing, J., Ebisch, B., Schmidt, K. E., Niessing, M., Singer, W., & Galuske, R. A. W. (2005, August 5). Hemodynamic signals correlate tightly with synchronized gamma oscillations. *Science, 309,* 948–951.

Passarotti, A. M., Paul, B. M., Bussiere, J. R., Buxton, R. B., Wong, E. C., & Stiles, J. (2003). The development of face and location processing: An fMRI study. *Developmental Science, 6,* 100–117.

Puce, A., Allison, T., Bentin, S., Gore, J. C., & McCarthy, G. (1998). Temporal cortex activation in humans viewing eye and mouth movements. *Journal of Neuroscience, 18,* 2188–2199.

Reid, V .M., Belsky, J., & Johnson, M. H. (2005). Infant perception of human action: Toward a developmental cognitive neuroscience of individual differences. *Cognition, Brain, Behavior* 9(2), 35–52.

Reid, V. M., Csibra, G., Belsky, J., & Johnson, M. H. (2007). Neural correlates of the perception of goal-directed action in infants. *Acta Psychologica 124,* 129–138.

Rodriguez, E., George, N., Lachaux, J. P, Martinere, J., Renault, B., & Varela, F. (1999, February 4). Perception's shadow: Long distance synchronization of human brain activity. *Nature, 397,* 430–433.

Schilbach, L., Wohlschlager, A. M., Newen, A., Shah, N. J., Fink, G. R., & Vogeley, K. (2006). Being with virtual others: Neural correlates of social interaction. *Neuropsychologica, 44,* 718–730.

Senju, A., & Johnson, M. H. (2009). The eye contact effect: Mechanisms and development. *Trends in Cognitive Sciences, 13,* 127–134.

Southgate, V., Johnson, M.H., & Csibra, G. (2008). Infants attribute goals even to biomechanically impossible actions. *Cognition, 107,* 1059–1069.

Stern, D.N. (1974). Mother and infant at play: The dyadic interaction involving facial, vocal, and gaze behaviors. In Ñ. M. Lewis & L. Rosenblum (Eds.), *The effect of the infant on its caretaker* (pp. 187–213). New York: Wiley.

Symons, L. A., Hains, S. M. J., & Muir, D. W. (1998). Look at me: Five-month-old infants' sensitivity to very small deviations in eye-gaze during social interactions. *Infant Behavior and Development, 21,* 531–536.

Tallon-Baudry, C., & Bertrand, O. (1999). Oscillatory gamma activity in humans and its role in object representation. *Trends in Cognitive Science, 3,* 151–162.

Turati, C., Sangrioli, S., Ruel, J., & de Schonen, S. (2004). Evidence of the face inversion effect in 4-month-old infants. *Infancy, 6,* 275–297.

Turati, C., Simion, F., Milani, I., & Umiltà, C. (2002). Newborns' preference for faces: What is crucial? *Developmental Psychology, 38,* 875–882.

Tzourio-Mazoyer, N., De Schonen, S., Crivello, F., Reutter, B., Aujard, Y., & Mazoyer, B. (2002). Neural correlates of woman face processing by 2-month-old infants. *NeuroImage, 15,* 454–461.

Valenza, E., Simion, F., Cassia, V. M., & Umiltà, C. (1996). Face preference at birth. *Journal of Experimental Psychology: Human Perception and Performance, 22,* 892–903.

Vecera, S. P., & Johnson, M. H. (1995). Eye gaze detection and the cortical processing of faces: Evidence from infants and adults. *Visual Cognition, 2,* 101–129.

Vuilleumier, P., Gorge, N., Lister, V., Armoni, J., & Driver, J. (2005). Effects of perceived mutual gaze and gender on face processing and recognition memory. *Visual Cognition, 12,* 85–101.

10

DESIRE, DOPAMINE, AND CONCEPTUAL DEVELOPMENT

MARC D. LEWIS

Developmentalists generally recognize that emotions influence learning. Developmentalists who study emotions examine their influence on personality development (e.g., Izard & Malatesta, 1987; Malatesta & Wilson, 1988), and neo-Piagetians have tried to grapple with the interplay between emotions and normative cognitive acquisitions (e.g., Case, Hayward, Lewis, & Hurst, 1988; Fischer, Shaver, & Carnochan, 1990; Pascual-Leone, 1987). Both of these domains of development—personality development and normative cognitive development—are built up through the acquisition of new concepts. Thus, emotion can be seen as influencing the learning of concepts, that is, conceptual development. The impact of emotion on conceptual development is particularly interesting from an individual difference perspective. Children's conceptual repertoires are not all the same, and sometimes differences in the concepts they bring to important life events have enormous consequences for their behavior, their competence, and their success in social and educational situations. However, even normative conceptual development may depend on particular emotional processes, such that emotional anomalies may have drastic effects on the normal trajectory of cognitive development. Yet we don't know enough about *how* emotion affects concept formation to understand its influence on development. At least since Herbert Simon's (1967) seminal article on the subject, psychologists have recognized that emotion influences the scope, style, and contents of cognition. And research by emotion theorists (e.g., Isen, 1985; Mathews, 1990; Wood, Mathews, & Dalgleish, 2001) has demonstrated systematic effects of emotion on the breadth and focus of attention and on the encoding and retrieval of information in memory, often under the rubric of motivated attention (e.g., Derryberry & Tucker, 1994; Niedenthal, Setterlund, & Jones, 1994). If emotion affects the style and contents of attention in real time, then this influence must accumulate across occasions, and this simple logic should help us understand the impact of emotion on conceptual development.

However, as usual, the devil is in the details. What is the precise mechanism by which emotion shapes cognitive activity in general and attention in particular? What emotional processes support encoding and long-term change—necessary components of learning? And what kinds of emotions fashion what kinds of conceptual assemblies? Are positive emotions necessary for learning, do negative emotions suffice, or is a particular kind of emotion or motive needed for long-term consolidation? Recently, Izard (2007) proposed that the emotion of interest has a preeminent role in shaping developmental outcomes. For him, interest is the default positive emotion that appears when other emotional responses don't override or replace it. And it has a particular affinity for cognitive processes and thus for learning. This proposal is highly congenial with the theme of this chapter. Yet it is more or less untested. The problem for developmental psychologists is that emotion-cognition interaction is so subtle, so rapid, and so inaccessible to conscious awareness that neither observation nor self-report is an adequate empirical method for plumbing its mysteries. As with many other phenomena of interest to psychologists, a neural level of analysis seems to be the next logical step. Thus, the premise of this chapter is that the new field of developmental neuroscience is poised to bring specificity to models of cognition–emotion relations, dispel myths, and promote new insights into how emotion actually shapes conceptual development.

The chapter has a somewhat unusual structure. Instead of presenting a theory or integrating ideas from the (almost nonexistent) literature on neural mediators of emotion in early development, my approach is to present qualitative data from the observation of my two young children, review literature on the neural substrates of approach motivation, and then derive a neuropsychological model based on the integration of these two accounts. The plan is as follows.

I first argue that interest, desire, and craving reflect different levels of intensity along a single dimension of approach emotion. I next present a qualitative observational account of approach emotions and conceptual advances displayed my two twin sons between birth and 2 years of age. I catalogue the observations that any parent might make and reflect on what they represent in terms of affects, appraisals, and goals. These observations point to recurrent associations between approach emotions and new conceptual acquisitions, and these associations are considered as a phenomenon that needs to be explained.

Next, I set out a psychological model of the relations among goal seeking, approach motivation, and concept formation that is based on principles of cognition–emotion interaction and on specific insights gleaned from a dynamic systems approach. Then, I review research on neural systems mediating approach motivation (or desire), goal pursuit, and learning. I focus especially on corticostriatal systems and the role of the neuromodulator dopamine. I then show how synaptic change in corticostriatal circuits is an outcome of goal-seeking behavior and a key mediator of learning and development. Finally, I construct a neuropsychological model that permits a parsimonious and detailed explanation of the observational data recorded.

DESIRE AND CONCEPTUAL DEVELOPMENT

The emotional quality associated with approach behavior or reward-seeking can be summed up by the term *desire*. As any poet will tell you, desire is not always fun. Nevertheless, it can initiate cognitive advances, from Romeo's oratory achievements to the pursuit of beauty, goodness, and truth. This everyday emotion, meat and potatoes to poets, remains a mystery to psychologists. How should we classify desire? Very few emotion theorists include desire as a basic emotion. Arnold (1960) and Frijda (1986) are the exceptions, and Parrot (2001) described desire as a feature of lust, nested under the basic emotion of love. Desire is generally not considered a basic emotion because it does not correspond to any facial expression and it is not short-lived, two criteria emphasized by Ekman (1984). Yet desire is nothing if not basic. First, it is subserved by a distinct neural mechanism (Berridge & Robinson, 1998; Depue & Collins, 1999; Panksepp, 1998), a critical criterion proposed by Barrett (2006) for basic emotions viewed as "natural kinds." Second, it is evident early in the life span, a criterion emphasized by Izard (1993). Third, it seems to have a specific functional impact on cognition in the moment (prolonged attention and approach) and on cognitive development (increasing skill formation and knowledge) over repeated occasions, as also emphasized by Izard (1993, 2007). Fourth, it has a distinct action tendency: that of behavioral approach. Desire may be too specific a term for the emotional accompaniments of reward seeking. It may be useful to subdivide this affective dimension into interest, at the less intense end, and craving, at the more intense end. Desire, as it is generally understood, is very close to what Izard (e.g., 2007) has called *interest*. In fact, Izard's emphasis on interest, Panksepp's (1998) portrayal of the "SEEKING" system, and my focus on desire are largely overlapping. Regardless of the terminology one uses, the feeling of "wanting" is fundamental.

There are many definitions of *concept formation*, but by this term I simply mean the acquisition of a general schema or category that refers to a subset of events or objects, such that those events or objects are viewed as similar (e.g., instantiations of a schema, members of a category, tokens of a type of thing). Conceptual development is then the accumulation of new concepts that together form an integrated and meaningful representation of the experienced world. For infants, concepts must be sensorimotor, and because infants don't have language, one can only infer their concepts by observing their behavioral orientation toward particular sets of events or objects. Moreover, sensorimotor concepts must include not only the child's actions or intended actions but also the effects they are expected to have on sensory feedback from the world (Neisser, 1976). I report on the acquisition of several key sensorimotor concepts because it was relatively easy for me to watch them develop. Then, as my boys passed from the sensorimotor stage into the stage of symbolic thought and language (at about 18–20 months), I was able to track concepts represented by words and phrases. Reporting on these concepts requires another lens, permitting greater specificity but posing additional problems and questions.

Both psychological and neuropsychological accounts of conceptual development restrict themselves to cognitive factors, ignoring emotion completely (e.g., Leslie & Thaiss, 1992; Neisser, 1987). On the contrary, I argue that the emotional states of interest or desire often lead to conceptual change, as unknown objects or classes of events become known. Sustained desire leading to conceptual change (or concept formation) may generally be facilitated by goals that remain temporarily out of reach. I propose that continual efforts to achieve these goals generate recurrent activation at synapses, modifying networks that come to represent objects, events, and situations in novel ways (cf. Lewis, 2000).

OBSERVATIONS AND REFLECTIONS ABOUT DESIRE AND CONCEPT FORMATION

In this section, I describe a sequence of conceptual acquisitions denoted by new behavior patterns or verbal labels along with my interpretations of their emotional underpinnings.

Behavioral Concepts

The Breast

Watching my sons Julian and Ruben learn to nurse at the breast has been quite an education on the relationship between desire and concept formation. At 2 months of age, the most noticeable thing about nursing was the lunging toward the nipple, accompanied by sideways shaking of the head very similar to what a terrier does, grabbing the nipple (or whatever makes contact) in the mouth, holding onto it intensely, going back to it immediately when it is lost, and sucking on it consistently, at the exclusion of any other activity or distraction: the only game in town. However, the motivation to suck at the breast does not start out this strong. Rather, it becomes more intense day by day. In the 1st few days of life, babies have to be encouraged to nurse. This somewhat counterintuitive observation may epitomize the evolution of a basic reflex through learning and recognition—in short, concept formation. Indeed, Ruben and Julian treated the breast almost lethargically for the 1st week, sucking when the nipple was placed in their mouths but just as likely to let go of it if the nipple was just a little bit off center or if it required an extra hoist to get their bodies in position for a good latch. Their passion for the breast, their intense preoccupation with it, targeting it, zeroing in on it, grabbing it, and so forth, all developed over days and weeks. Not until 1 month to 6 weeks did this interest start to plateau. Most important, it was only after several weeks that the breast, or nursing-at-the-breast, became a concept that was accessible even in the absence of the breast; that is, it became a memory, an association, triggered by other stimuli or capable of being recalled when hunger arose.

Motivation in the moment seems to come in two flavors. The first, in the presence of the object, is *while* the goal is being achieved; that is *wanting and getting*. The second is when the object is absent; that boils down to *wanting and not getting*. The first case is usually short-lived. All the emotional behaviors indicative of desire dissipate rapidly if the goal is in hand (or in mouth). But the second case may last for some time; this must be the period in which the memory of the goal supplies enough information to maintain the state of anticipation, attentional focus, motivation, and so forth required for conceptual development (Lewis, 2000). This seems like an important point for analysis. The breast may indeed be the infant's first long-term memory, as emphasized by psychoanalytically oriented developmentalists (Mahler, Pine, & Bergman, 1975; Winnicott, 1992), but from the perspective of contemporary cognitive psychology, it would qualify as a motivated memory. Tucker (e.g., 2001, 2007) has described all memory as motivated memory because of the overlapping functions of motivation and memory ascribed to limbic structures. With newborns, memory is obviously motivated. Even 10 minutes after a good feed, when he could not possibly be hungry yet, the edge of the blanket would touch Ruben's chin while he was moving or yawning, and then his mouth would start to open and close, he would make sucking motions with his lips and jaws, his brows would crease, and he would begin thrashing about. If this behavior were simply the expression of a reflex, why would it be so much more sophisticated, forceful, and directed than it was after a week? Why would it include the creasing of the brows? Some learning must have taken place by now, and so it seems to me that Ruben was remembering the breast and wanting it at the same time. This memory would have a sensory and a motor component, but also a motivational component. It is a memory of something that counts.

Graspable Objects

From 2 to 4 months, approximately, babies become more and more interested in objects that move, that stand out from their backgrounds, or that otherwise present themselves for exploration. But they have no idea which of those objects is manipulable or graspable until they develop the coordination to reach out for objects and grasp them, clutch them, and bring them toward themselves, usually for a good suck. According to Case's (1985) theory of cognitive development, this two-part coordination is not available until after the age of 4 months, and indeed it was at 4 to 5 months that Ruben and Julian began to take a special interest in graspable objects. Not only did they squirm and wriggle with excitement as they got the object in their sights—they had been doing that sporadically for months. Now they would also reach their hands out toward it with intense concentration. In one episode, Ruben lay back in his baby chair. His whole body quivered with excitement. His eyes were open wide. His hand reached out and made contact with the dangling puppet. His eyes widened still further, as if about to burst. The other hand reached forward now as well, and he grasped the object between his pincers. His eyes widened still further, and his brows arched. He got the puppet firmly in his grip, and now his mouth opened and fluttered, as if he were about to devour the puppet. He was smiling slightly as he struggled to bring the toy closer to his mouth. He was completely intent on it. His gaze did not waver from the puppet in his grasp.

These dramatic moments ushered in a period of about 2 months during which graspable objects grabbed both boys' attention like beacons in a busy harbor. These objects are scattered about the world without rhyme or reason at first, but gradually their whereabouts become predictable. They sit on table tops, in piles on the playroom floor, in the toy bins in the shelves. The boys dragged their bodies and crept within reach if they possibly could, grunting and quivering with excitement. And then, contact! Now the grasping-of-the-object, which was, after all, the goal, shifted from future to present tense. And the concept of the object could be dispensed in favor of the far more gratifying state of experiencing it directly with their hands, manipulating it with their fingers, and bringing it to their mouths for further exploration.

Crawling

The concept of crawling is so fundamental that to developmentalist Joe Campos, it is this sole physical act that initiates a major shift in cognitive development—the famous shift to object permanence, joint attention, and social referencing that occurs at about 9 months (e.g., Campos et al., 2000). Julian learned to crawl at 8½ months, Ruben at 10 months, and for both there was a common sequence. The idea dawns that some graspable object at the far side of the room can actually be acquired in moments if one can just get one's body to cooperate. And so begins a clumsy, elephantine movement of loosely coordinated hands and knees propelling the baby across the floor, interrupted by numerous spills leaving the baby flat on his face. Many things have to be coordinated: the rhythm of steps, the thrust of the hindquarters pushing forward at the right moment between steps, the duet of hands and knees having to cooperate for the first time ever. All this effortful action is carried out to the cheers of parents. (Julian's eyes were fixed on the goal: the destination. He did not look around at distractions. He gazed ahead at the stuffed penguin he was determined to reach.) Crawling is difficult, and it takes all of a baby's attention at first. This works well because the motive to move one's entire body through space, to its destination, is so attractive, so inviting, so riveting, that there is rarely anything to compete with it. It took many months before crawling was taken for granted.

By 23 months, Ruben and Julian were getting the idea that just about anything could be put into words. Of course, this in itself is an incredible concept: the idea that language is available to bridge our experience with that of others, to share whatever it is we are thinking and feeling. It is a concept that brings with it great excitement and urgency. The boys would burst into chatter from the moment they woke up, and they would thrust themselves against the bars of their crib to communicate whatever was on their minds. Following are examples of specific words and phrases that have voiced some of their more cherished concepts. I use present tense because these concepts are still emerging at this writing.

A fundamental feature of development is that concepts start off global and overextended and only through practice become whittled down to their more specific and precise meanings. It is interesting to speculate that even this feature of concept acquisition may stem from its motivational basis. We want what we want in large chunks, not specific bits. Wanting may start off global until we get close to the target, the goal, at which point proximal cues cause us to narrow it down. Perhaps that's why young children's words imply phrases and maybe even whole paragraphs! Only later do words stand for specific objects and relations that can be assembled into highly articulate representations of what we are after.

Linguistic Concepts

'Nodder One

Starting at 22 months, I give Ruben a book to read at the table, and he says, "'nodder one." So I give him another one, and says "'nodder one." Each time he says it, he looks at me, beseechingly. His vocal tone is strained, his body tense, as though he is on the verge of distress. Will I give it to him? Will I understand? More to the point, will he get it? He is waiting for his wish to be fulfilled: his wish to have a great pile of books beside him. I imagine that it is only my hesitation that thwarts his goal, amplifying the urgency of his request. The concept consolidating in his attention is apparently the image of a pile of books, a series, a sequence. And his urgency makes each book inadequate: The next one becomes the goal. By 24 months, "'nodder one" is used in a great variety of circumstances—another icicle to kick, another sock to put on, another rock to place in the toy dump truck. This evolution seems to be typical of conceptual development: Over time, concepts are differentiated outward but also abstracted and generalized. This permits more variants of the concept to be coordinated with other concepts or goals. The concepts of "more" and "next" will crystallize eventually. Also over time, urgency is reduced but not gone. Even after just a few months, "'Nodder one" has come to describe the world more as it really is than in that frenzied state of wishing it were so.

Many!

The boys began to say "Many!" at about 20 months. I am handing out Cheerios as snacks, and Julian sees that there is a whole bowl of them. I give him three or four. He looks at the bowl and says "Many!" The concept has developed in the context of wanting as many treats as he can have. "Many!" is always shouted with urgency and even desperation. If I'm divvying up pieces of chicken, Julian might look at his plate and then at Ruben's plate and shout "Many!" If Lego blocks are piled high between the two boys and I'm dividing them up, both boys might call for "many!" Within 2 months, the word was being used to refer to any quantity of objects, whether mice on the page of a book or cars in a parking lot. "Many!" went from referring to a desired goal of greedy acquisition to the first of several words used to denote quantity. But it's still "Many!" with an exuberant and eager optimism about the bounty soon to appear.

My Do It

Julian says "My do it!" often, and Ruben has begun to use the phrase as well. It means "I'll do it"—and that actually means, "Don't do it for me! Let me do it myself!" Ruben sometimes says "Buben do it!" As with so many other utterances at this age, children's meanings turn out to be more comprehensive and less differentiated than they will be in another few weeks or months. But the meaning is clear. Julian looks anxious, even desperate, and he raises his hands in front of him, fingertips up, palms facing out, to literally block me from trying to help him. He sometimes pushes me away if I get too close to him when he's trying to put on his pajama bottoms himself. We hear this utterance most when the boys are trying to put on their coats by themselves. Sometimes they just do not want help, and "My do it!" means

"I'm doing it. Leave me alone. Step back!" It is always spoken in a sharp, urgent tone, and always when one or the other parent approaches the boys in action.

Together

"Together" came into their vocabularies at about 21 months. It is a wonderful word because it captures the image of doing things as a pair (the two brothers) or as a family. Ruben will say "Together" when I'm putting on his boots to go out. He might say, "Go car. Papa go. Together." He wants to make sure that we will all be going out together and that he will not have to say good-bye. Or Julian will say it when Ruben comes to join him to stand side by side at their little toy kitchen. The tone of the utterance is one of eagerness, insistence, demand, and excitement. Doing things together is far from neutral. It is a cherished goal, and it appears to take over Ruben's thoughts and feelings when there is any chance of becoming separated. The concept has also evolved and become more refined from 21 to 24 months. At 24 months, it is spoken more matter-of-factly. "Together!" We are going to go shopping together. Of course we are. There is less urgency and more assuredness in the boys' tone now.

Common Features

With these examples in mind, I now list the common features of the behaviors and situations involved when motivated attention leads to concept formation. This list provides an important segue to the neurobiological modeling soon to come:

- a context of uncertainty before a goal has been attained, when its attainment is still unpredictable;
- sustained, narrow focus of attention;
- indication of a very specific expected outcome;
- approach behavior or maintenance of engagement until the goal is attained;
- behavior directed solely to the target of attention; resistance to distraction, until the goal is attained;
- growing emotional intensity, urgency, tension, desperation, accelerating concern, excitement, anxiety, or all of these, until the goal is attained;
- emotional intensity of the quest, amplified (within seconds) by any delay or obstacle, usually evident as growing anxiety and/or frustration;
- growth, differentiation, or generalization in the meaning of the concept, usually by extension to other variants of the original event or experience; and

- a gradual reduction in emotional intensity, once the concept has stabilized and has become a permanent fixture in the repertoire, over weeks or months.

I conclude this section by returning to the question of how to characterize approach motivation and its link with concept formation. The examples cited suggest that the breast, or graspable object, or '"nodder one" are motivationally loaded concepts. But they are concepts that apply not to the present moment but to a future moment, to what is about to occur: They are expectancies. I see the boys with their mouths open, their hands extended, their bodies arched or their brows creased. The concept seems to express, "I *will* be sucking on this breast!" or "I *will* grasp this fascinating object!" When Ruben says, "Together," as I put on his coat, he is thinking about the future, about how we will be together in the car. There is a seamless continuity that links the present moment to an image of sitting in the car together, putting on music, singing together, arriving somewhere together, being unbuckled and taken in our arms—in the future. The concept does not differentiate between a present tense and a future tense: It captures the thrusting forward of intention, as Walter Freeman (e.g., 1995) has written, so it is anchored in the present but is concerned with the future. And it is emotionally concerned with the future, the emotion very often being excitement and/or anxiety: Because the future is never certain, its emotional color ranges between hope and gut-wrenching concern.

There probably is not much conceptualizing going on *during* the event itself. One does not conceptualize graspability when grasping—one just experiences it. And if attention is not fully taken up by the experience, then it shifts to the next concept, perhaps to putting the object in the mouth. Thus, emerging concepts are bridges between a present goal and a future outcome— emotional bridges. The concept is of an expected, rewarded event that is remembered, when the breast, the object, or the car ride is still some distance off, or the object is out of reach. It is an event or object that is desired, hoped for, not only anticipated but yearned for.

On reflection, then, it seems as if motivation and concept formation are each defined in terms of the other. A concept must be motivated, at least in what I have described so far, and a motive cannot help bring forth the concept that can satisfy it. Perhaps concept acquisition becomes a drier affair by the age of 4 or 5 years. But is it ever free of motivation? Now, at 2 years, I hear Ruben's voice get thick with desire and excitement when a goal—a concept—materializes in his mind (presumably) and his speech. Julian's allotment of two pretzels brings on an emotional avalanche of unfulfilled desire and anxiety, and he shouts "Many! Many!" I say, "No, only two," and he replies with escalating desperation, "Many!!!" There is an irony here. The good things in life, the things we desire, the things that make us happy, elicit not joy but misery, at least at first. Desire is not fun! But it must surely be productive.

A PSYCHOLOGICAL MODEL

Let us consider a simple model for the relation between desire and conceptualization, between desire and thought. Dynamic systems approaches in psychology have shown that complex systems in nature, including the embodied computer of the brain, function through self-iterating processes, feedback, reciprocal causation, and the emergence of order from chaos or disorder. Esther Thelen has explained the A-not-B error as a product of feedback between perceptual highlighting and the strength of the memory trace (e.g., Thelen, Schöner, Scheier, & Smith, 2001). Linda Smith (e.g., 1995) sees all language acquisition as experience-dependent hypotheses feeding back with a shared linguistic environment. And I have written numerous articles on cognition–emotion feedback, modeling the self-organization of stable appraisals, or emotional interpretations, through coupling among the components of feeling states and cognitive associations (e.g., Lewis, 1996, 2000, 2005). If stable but elaborate mental contents arise through feedback of this sort, then the relation between desire (a motivational state) and conceptualization is not difficult to model: In real time, desire brings a thought or image to mind or sharpens or refines the thought or image that is already there (involving retrieval from long-term memory into working memory). The thought or image instantiates or concretizes an emergent goal, a goal in the process of becoming articulated. That means that a motor intention is also arising. Emotions (desire, but perhaps other emotions, such as anxiety or anger, as well) become increasingly elaborated and intensified as the goal organizes cognitive activity. In turn, this cognitive articulation enhances desire because it crystallizes the path to the goal state to which desire stretches forth (in Freeman's terms; e.g., Freeman, 1995). This constitutes a feedback cycle that simply runs itself. To be more specific, the anticipated goal generates an increasingly articulated appraisal (as emotion theorists call it) that coemerges with an action plan. The appraisal and the action plan maintain and reinforce one another, and they concurrently strengthen the state of desire from which they were generated. When the goal is attained, if it is attained, the mental image (or *protoconcept*) dissipates in favor of something else. A sketch of this cycle is presented in Figure 10.1.

The developmental picture is not complicated, either. Each time a thought or image crystallizes in working memory, it must leave a change in the psychological apparatus: an augmented memory, a stronger association, or some other indication of enhanced storage rights. I borrow the phrase *storage rights* from Tucker (2001), who used it to connote the need for emotional highlighting to select what gets remembered from among the myriad pieces of information we process. The increased strength of the memory trace, or the increasing articulation of the image or thought being remembered, increases the probability of the same thought or image becoming activated the next time around. Hence, the goal to which desire points will tend to

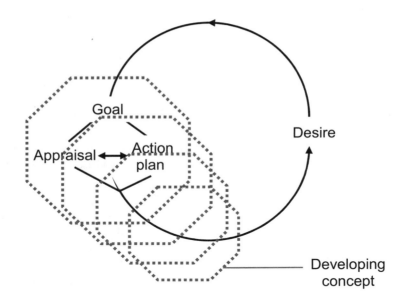

Figure 10.1. A sketch of the feedback loop that entrains desire with goals that embed cognitive events (appraisals and action plans), each augmenting the other. This feedback loop is proposed to drive conceptual development in the early years and perhaps over the life span. Smooth lines indicate real-time feedback cycle, and dotted lines indicate consolidation over development.

become all the more elaborated, articulated, and refined. It will achieve greater and greater salience on future occasions. Therefore, on each successive occasion, the real-time process of iteration (the cycle shown in Figure 10.1) can now get under way more rapidly, with more predictability. Developmentalists with a dynamic systems orientation refer to this as the deepening of an attractor on the behavioral state space (Thelen & Smith, 1994). This real-time "advantage" once again contributes to the consolidation of the image in memory, fashioning a feedback loop between one occasion and the next—a developmental feedback relation.

Yet this psychological modeling leaves one unsatisfied. The terms *memory, emotion, goal, image, appraisal,* and *plan* are too vague. The mechanisms proposed to connect them—highlighting, articulation, elaboration, strengthening, consolidation—are too abstract. They lack concreteness. Psychologists can propose any number of boxes, connected by any number of arrows, without ever approaching the real, fleshy, biological reality of human computation. Curved arrows in sketched feedback loops are a step toward greater realism, but only a small step. That is why psychologists are turning to neuroscience: to test their models, to concretize them, to correct them, to fill in the details, and ultimately to establish them in the material bedrock of measurable bodily processes.

THE NEUROBIOLOGY OF DESIRE

Psychologists' understanding of desire can be greatly aided by an investigation of the neural systems that mediate it. The human brain is well crafted to attend to and pursue goals—potential future states that are rewarding. A particular neural assembly at the core of the brain, the striatum (a subset of the basal ganglia), is involved in directing behavior toward acquiring rewards, by motivating the selection of actions and arranging them in a goal-directed sequence. Through its afferents from the prefrontal cortex (PFC), the striatum is attuned to reinforcement contingencies and goals. Through its efferents to the PFC, it organizes effortful control and working memory, both of which involve the sequencing of steps and both of which are crucial elements of executive attention. Moreover, synaptic alterations resulting from corticostriatal activity are fundamental to learning (Kelley, Smith-Roe, & Holahan, 1997; Kerr & Wickens, 2001; Shohamy et al., 2004). Thus, goal pursuit, learning, and the emotions that propel them are products of an integrated neural system that allows animals to maximize their successes in the moment and over the life span.

Neuroscientists who study motivation often focus on a component of the striatum called the *nucleus accumbens* (NAS). This ventral striatal system has been referred to as the *motivation-to-action interface* (Goto & O'Donnell, 2001), and it is known to be activated in states of positive affect related to the anticipation of reward (Burgdorf & Panksepp, 2006), especially immediate reward. The NAS constitutes part of a motivational loop (which includes the ventral tegmental area and ventral pallidum) providing forward thrust or surgency (Depue & Collins, 1999; see the review by Lewis, 2005). But what the NAS motivates is the selection of actions leading to an expected reward. This motivation-to-action interface is supported by cooperation between the NAS and dorsal regions of the striatum (or *neostriatum*) that are specifically involved in motor control, such as the caudate nucleus. The caudate may also be activated by static or long-term rewards (for a review, see Graybiel, 2005). Streams of activity from both regions are integrated in an ongoing cycle that includes the thalamus and several areas of cortex. The NAS receives inputs from many regions of prefrontal cortex but especially the orbitofrontal cortex (OFC), which recruits it for specific goals and rewards (Depue & Collins, 1999; Horvitz, 2002; Rolls, 1999). The OFC can be thought of as having its own fundamental appraisal system and/or working memory—by which potential rewards (or punishments) can be represented for some period of time (Depue & Collins, 1999; Rolls, 1999). The NAS also receives inputs from the amygdala, which enhances its activation based on emotional salience (Cardinal, Parkinson, Hall, & Everitt, 2002), from the hippocampus (Kelley & Domesick, 1982), which is involved in contextualizing present events within known routines or plans, and from the ventral tegmental area (VTA), a small region of midbrain that supplies the

NAS with dopamine (Haber, Kunishio, Mizobuchi, & Lynd-Balta, 1995; Oades & Halliday, 1987). Outputs from the NAS travel back to the PFC to help organize cognitive and motor activity. Some of these outputs are routed through the thalamus, from where they are integrated with cortical activities supporting motor articulation as well as attention to goals (Depue & Collins, 1999; Rolls, 1999). Outputs from the NAS also target the VTA, in a reciprocal fashion, to keep the dopamine pump going (Depue & Collins, 1999). Meanwhile, dorsal striatal structures feed specific motor information through the thalamus to the supplementary motor area where action routines are orchestrated.

Dopamine is a critical fuel for the striatum, including the NAS, and for the OFC, with which it is intimately connected. But what exactly does dopamine do? The neuromodulator dopamine, usually associated with the evaluation (appraisal) and pursuit (planning) of goals, is necessary for synaptic activation within the striatum and between the striatum and other structures, including the PFC. Dopamine projections from the VTA to the OFC and NAS correspond with degree of incentive motivation. The relation between dopamine and incentive motivation is epitomized by the self-administration of stimulating drugs (e.g., cocaine) that are thought to increase dopamine activity in corticostriatal circuits. However, dopamine activation does not necessarily feel good. First, VTA dopamine travels to the amygdala as well as the striatum, where it may enhance activation relative to anticipated threats, not just rewards. Second, high levels of incentive salience, mediated by the striatum, are probably experienced as desire and even craving rather than the euphoria produced by psychostimulant drugs. A critical distinction between wanting and liking is now accepted by many neuroscientists, based mostly on the work of Berridge (e.g., Berridge & Robinson, 1998), and these authors have convincingly demonstrated that dopamine is critical for wanting something, but liking something may depend more on opioid systems (Berridge & Robinson, 1998; Panksepp, 1981). Finally, the incentive-sensitization theory of drug addiction builds on the idea that wanting and craving fall along the same continuum of dopamine response, indexing need or desire but not pleasure or satisfaction (Robinson & Berridge, 1993).

The incentive properties of dopamine are further demonstrated by the fact that dopamine projections to the NAS are triggered by anticipated rewards, not by rewards that are already available. Dopamine is also thought to enhance associations between stimuli and responses, thus facilitating learning, in the presence of potential rewards (Depue & Collins, 1999). In the study of self-initiated brain stimulation, dopamine surges corresponded with enhanced firing rates in striatal cells whose activation precedes delivery of the reward (Cheer et al., 2007). In fact, dopamine specifically enhances learning based on feedback or reinforcement (stimulus–response links), mediated by the ventral striatum, and not learning based on associations among stimuli, mediated by the dorsal striatum (Shohamy et al., 2004). Dopamine activation is proportional to the effort animals expend to gain reinforcers (Salamone

& Correa, 2002). Again, this function is thought to be based on the capacity of dopamine to enhance the salience of an incentive, or what one may simply think of as an enhanced sense of value—not on the increased predictability of a particular positive outcome (Berridge & Robinson, 1998). In fact, as predictability increases, dopamine activation wanes. Of particular importance when considering learning as a sequence, dopamine response is activated by increasingly early predictors of reward, once proximal cues are learned (Schultz, Dayan, & Montague, 1997). In sum, dopamine can enhance incentive motivation, initiate locomotion, and facilitate the learning of strings of activities that eventually lead to reinforcement.

Dopamine activation of corticostriatal circuits was initially thought to be the basis of organized motor activity. Now, however, it is considered critical for the organization of thinking, planning, and learning as well. Wickens (e.g., Wickens, Begg, & Arbuthnott, 1996) has emphasized that the sequential activation of cell assemblies in prefrontal cortex requires the participation of dopamine-activated striatal neurons. Moreover, the learning deficits experienced by children with attention-deficit/hyperactivity disorder (ADHD) and adults with Parkinson's disease appear to result from attentional lapses caused by deficits in dopamine metabolism. Dopamine-enhanced learning results from the modification of synapses within striatal and corticostriatal circuits (see the review by Wickens, Horvitz, Costa, & Killcross, 2007). Dopamine increases the sensitivity of striatal synapses to excitatory inputs (mediated by the neurotransmitter glutamate). It may boost strong concurrent glutamate inputs while minimizing weak inputs (Horvitz, 2002). These inputs arrive primarily from the PFC (e.g., OFC) but also from the hippocampus, amygdala, midbrain, and thalamus. Over several occasions, dopamine-induced augmentation in the plasticity of striatal and corticostriatal neurons may facilitate learning through long-term potentiation (LTP), a chief candidate for synaptic change based on glutamate uptake (Kelley et al., 1997; Kerr & Wickens, 2001). Dopamine-glutamate interactions may thus be the principal means by which new skills or motor responses are acquired (see the review by Graybiel, 2005). According to one model, dopamine may also serve to decouple striatal neurons from ongoing cortical activity, making them more sensitive to novel inputs. As a result, novel inputs would take over firing activity in the striatum more easily (Wickens et al., 2007). Whatever the precise mechanism, converging evidence suggests that striatal neurons become enlisted both in the anticipation of reward and in feedback-based learning as a result of synaptic changes that are supported by dopamine activation.

One more word is in order concerning the reward-action circuits of the brain. I proposed three macroscopic systems of reciprocally connected structures in a model of neural self-organization: an object evaluation loop, a self-monitoring loop, and a motivated action loop (Lewis, 2005). It is the last of these loops that has been described in detail in the foregoing paragraphs. There is something unique about this loop, fundamental to its character:

Motivation and action fashion a *directional* stream of activity. That is, a sequence of neural events continues to cycle while action unfolds continuously. The connections linking the structures in this loop—the striatum, thalamus, motor cortex, and prefrontal cortex—form an ongoing sequence. Despite reciprocal connections between many elements in this loop, and despite the supporting roles played by the amygdala and hippocampus, inserting meaning and memory into the stream of action, the loop has a unidirectional flow that keeps motivated action moving forward in time. It cycles from (OFC-mediated) goal processing, to (striatally mediated) motivational gating and action selection, to (thalamocortically mediated) motor generation and output, and then back to goal processing, in a sequence by which action is continually generated, shaped, and refined. Animals are always in the process of acting, even when at rest, even when they are merely anticipating action, even when they are dreaming. That is because goal attainment is the point of cognitive activity. It is the criterion for connecting with the real world, the world outside our bodies. Whether we are engaged in anticipating, planning, or generating action, the striatal–thalamic–cortical loop propels us forward in a seamless integration with a world that is constantly changing—largely as a result of our actions. Like the interlacing teeth of a zipper, motivated action continuously synchronizes our mental processes with the momentum of reality. And for intelligent animals with good memories and a penchant for generalization and symbol formation, the by-product of this synchronizing momentum is concept formation—a growing repertoire of mental events that maintain a fixed correspondence with the elements of that reality.

Although I have not elaborated this issue, it should be noted that the neurobiological basis of many concepts must include activation in specific sensory regions where the physical attributes of concepts are processed (Barsalou, 2008). Much of the current emphasis in the study of concepts is on these sensory systems, and the assumption is that neural networks interconnecting these sensory sites are the actual locus of concepts in the brain. Here I am emphasizing the goal- or action-oriented aspects of concepts. Further discussion of sensory systems would make the modeling too complicated. But there is no reason to think that the orbitostriatal circuits involved in the action-oriented thrust of early concepts should not be connected to posterior sensory regions that represent the perceptual attributes of these concepts. In fact, dense fiber bundles send messages from the sensory cortices to the OFC for processing.

A NEUROPSYCHOLOGICAL MODEL OF MOTIVATED CONCEPT FORMATION

Now, with these neural parts and processes mapped out in some detail, the simple psychological model of desire, goal-pursuit, and concept formation set out earlier can be translated into precise biological terms. Let us consider the emergence of the concept *many!* when it is still a new developmental acquisition. At the core of the model is the reciprocal (two-way) amplification of a motivational state and a thought or image in the mind. This is the self-augmenting feedback loop through which desire grows rapidly along with the appraisal and plan for getting the thing being desired. When Julian shouts "Many!" there is a welling up of desire for—what?—a mound, an ocean perhaps, of little pretzels. The desire increases rapidly, soon joined by anxiety, as evidenced by his creased brows, the sudden shrillness of his voice, the way he thrusts his body forward, and his desperate reaching in the direction of the countertop. At the same time, one can infer that an image of a mound of pretzels—an appraisal of quantity—materializes in his mind, cued by the meager presence of one or two pretzels being cautiously shaken out of the bag and onto the counter by a parent whose own goals concern preserving Julian's appetite for supper. A few pretzels activate the memory of a mound of pretzels in corticohippocampal circuits. Then a variety of prefrontal regions become involved as the image of pretzels is embedded in an appraisal held in working memory. Among these regions, the reinforcing value of the *mound* of pretzels is represented in the OFC by synapses linking the image of that mound with an expectancy of good taste and perhaps the anticipated satisfaction of hoarding. In turn, OFC neurons send messages to VTA cells (in the midbrain) that release dopamine, while at the same time activating the NAS, giving rise to a motivational thrust indicated by eager, intentional reaching. Dopamine from the VTA enhances glutamate transmission in the OFC, thus increasing throughput from the OFC to the NAS and other parts of the striatum. These signals bolster awareness of the present contingency—the appraisal that it is possible to gain more pretzels—while the striatum devises a motor sequence or plan to attain the goal: shouting "Many!" to a responsive parent. And there it is: the concept of *many!*—an image, a label, and an intended action held together by desire. Meanwhile, the salience of the imagined goal—the pile of pretzels glimmering like a pot of gold—is boosted by the wash of dopamine to the NAS and related structures.

At this point, a state of desire has rapidly coemerged with a goal, the pile of pretzels, while the appraisal (of potential reinforcement, temporarily obstructed) consolidates in the OFC and the action plan (of shouting "Many!") consolidates in striatal synapses. The cell bodies fed by those synapses send axons to the thalamus, where the next layer of cells synapse on neurons in the supplementary motor area. Now the selected action is represented as an intention, and that representation is fed forward to the premotor and motor cortices for execution in the form of articulated mouth movements (with the participation of speech centers, such as Broca's area). During and after execution of the vocal response, activated thalamic neurons also target a variety of other regions, but especially the PFC. The PFC can now integrate information about the motor (speech) action being generated and the sensory awareness of a look of stubborn refusal on the face of the parent. The appraisal of the situation becomes further refined. There are still only two pretzels on the countertop! Perhaps at this point the amygdala becomes activated by the appraisal of being ignored. The situation looks dire! The parent's face shows no signs of capitulation; the parent's hands continue to restrict the flow of pretzels. Now efferent pathways from the amygdala to the NAS convey the threatening nature of the situation while pathways from the amygdala to the VTA induce the release of more dopamine (while pathways to other brainstem regions release a surge of norepinephrine, typical of intense emotional states). The surge of dopamine further supports the motivation-to-action function of the NAS, which continues to work toward realization of the anticipated reward—the replenishment of the supply of pretzels. Note that any increase in the likelihood of the reward—such as the moment when the parent begins to listen to Julian's demands—increases dopamine flow and corresponding reward salience still further. That is why, as any parent knows, one had better not even begin to register a toddler's demands unless one plans to follow through. Julian notices that the parent is noticing him, and the resultant dopamine surge makes the desire for "many!" almost unbearable; if he could articulate it, he might say, "Oh, if only I had a big pile of pretzels. I so want there to be MANY!!!" The cycle continues, with dopamine enhancing the sensitivity of striatal synapses to convergent information about the goal and any changes in its accessibility. These result, in turn, in changes in the vocal musculature, elicited by communication between the striatum, speech areas, and motor cortex, as Julian's voice becomes increasingly demanding, shrill, and insistent.

But how does the concept of *many!* actually emerge and crystallize in development? This is the question that this chapter was intended to answer. Consider the first few occasions in which Julian shouted "Many!" On each of these occasions, there was a convergence of information at the synapses of striatal circuits. The information came from the hippocampus, the OFC, other regions of PFC, the amygdala, and most important, the VTA. It is the convergence of messages from these regions that sets up a self-augmenting, self-reinforcing feedback loop. The reward-relevant signals from the OFC, the threshold changes induced by dopamine from the VTA, the excitatory inputs from the amygdala, and so forth, select and reinforce each other, creating a macro-network state that is coherent and enduring. This brain state is the biological foundation underpinning (in psychological terms) the amalgam of attention, desire, and action. Each time this state coheres in real time, corticostriatal synapses are modified, as a result of recurring glutamate activity at the synapses where dopamine and glutamate work together. Whether by LTP or some other mechanism, the synapses that are activated by the convergence of all these sources of information are strengthened, and new synapses may be formed between cells that are coactivated by the convergence. In other words, it is the convergence of information flow that creates the concept—*many!*—or, more precisely, that creates the specificity and closure of neural activity that mediates the emerging concept within occasions. And it is this very convergence that grows and strengthens the synapses that subserve conceptual development across occasions. The concept is acquired by the repeating convergence of specific corticostriatal patterns on a number of occasions, and this convergence becomes increasingly probable because the synapses that support it increase in number and strength. This depiction conveys the developmental feedback loop I described earlier, by which the use of a concept on a given occasion yields the growth of that concept across occasions, while that growth increases the probability of the concept arising on any future occasion.

Evidence in support of this model has already been presented, but here I want to summarize it succinctly. Synaptic modification is thought to underlie all learning. Thus, it follows that the learning of a new concept depends on synaptic modification. It is also widely acknowledged that synaptic plasticity, resulting from neuromodulator action, is a necessary precursor to synaptic modification (Adamec, Kent, Anisman, Shallow, & Merali, 1998; Centonze, Picconi, Gubellini, Bernardi, & Calabresi, 2001; Flood, Baker, Hernandez, & Morley, 1990; Izquierdo, 1997; Izumi & Zorumski, 1999). Thus, it makes sense that the synaptic changes underlying concept formation are supported by dopamine uptake. Recent research indicates that the learning of instrumental behaviors in animals depends on dopamine activity and the interaction of dopamine and other neurotransmitters (especially glutamate) in the striatum (e.g., the nucleus accumbens; Kelley et al., 1997; Kerr & Wickens, 2001). Thus, the learning of concepts through intentional behavior and environmental feedback may depend on similar neurochemical activities in similar regions in humans. Finally, dopamine activation in corticostriatal circuits has been found to correspond with the anticipation of rewards, not their presence, and a sudden increase in the probability of reward acquisition results in increased dopamine release (Burgdorf & Panksepp, 2006; Graybiel, 2005). Thus, concept acquisition may only be possible in states of anticipation, when a goal is being sought but not yet acquired. All of these findings support the biological model I have outlined, and the model itself is based on inference and extension from these findings, integrated with my behavioral observations of my children.

What is most interesting about this model is its implications for the psychology of conceptual development. A key psychological concomitant of accumbens dopamine is a feeling state: desire, or at least an emotion somewhere on the continuum between interest and craving, where desire marks some sort of middle ground. This mapping is further supported by the idea that striatal dopamine is the foundation of wanting, not liking, and by Berridge and Robinson's (1998) model of incentive salience as the key function of dopamine in goal-directed behavior. It also resonates with Panksepp's (1998) depiction of a SEEKING system, one of the core motivational systems in the brain and one that is fundamental for attraction, engagement, and action in all mammals. Finally, it agrees with Izard's (2007) recent emphasis on *interest* as a sort of default emotional state, which lends itself most easily to the cognitive concomitants of learning. Thus, concept acquisition may depend on a very specific emotional state, experienced in the context of goal seeking. From this perspective, there is nothing dry about conceptual development, and one can only hope to model it accurately if one considers the role of emotion as well as that of cognition.

In modeling conceptual development, the contributions of intention, desire, and striving, as well as other motivational components, including anxiety, frustration, and perhaps even hope (Tucker, 2007), suggest critical implications for the larger picture of human development and human experience. First, it is fascinating to think that conceptual development, the hallmark of our intellectual activity, is a result of the activity of motivational systems that evolved for the purpose of pursuing and acquiring simple goals. Second, an existential conundrum is implied: Concept formation and conceptual development may stem from strivings that are never entirely fulfilled or satisfied. Thus, shared meaning may be considered a by-product of fundamental strivings for what is never completely attainable. Third, personality development, viewed as individual variation in the assembly of expectancies, concepts, and interpretations, would seem to be highly sensitive to differences in emotional states (e.g., Lewis & Ferrari, 2001). Small differences in emotional experiences might have major impacts on the conceptual acquisitions that distinguish one sort of person from another. And finally, the trajectory of normative conceptual development (or "cognitive development") might be located in the common space of what interests, excites, and attracts most or all members of our species.

CONCLUSION

The chief implication of the current neuropsychological model is that concept development is embedded in emotion. The emotion at its core is one that thrusts a person forward into the world: bodily at first, in our striving for the breast and for objects to grasp and suck on, and then mentally, symbolically, in our striving to extract verbal categories from the continuous wash of familiar experiences. This striving is not a function of pleasure or pain, so the language of behaviorism is not much help in understanding it. Rather, it embodies an urge that is perhaps more basic than either pleasure or pain, namely, attraction: the fundamental gravity exerted by the world on our sense of ourselves.

In this chapter I have focused on early concept acquisition, as motivated by my own attraction to the conceptual landscape that continues to blossom, day by day, in my children's development. I have also focused on the more extreme expressions of desire so obvious in the behavior of toddlers, extremes that make us laugh and hug them as we watch them struggle with the boundaries of what they can and can't have. But there is much more to the cognitive consequences of desire than the wedge of early concept acquisition (as if that were not enough). I think that striatal dopamine embodies the leading edge of much of our intentional cognitive activity—perhaps all of it. After concepts are acquired, they are then called up and used—revised, elaborated, and differentiated into mental constellations of great complexity, power, beauty, and sometimes ugliness. The emotional pulse that propels us through these creative cognitive acts may be so subtle as to barely register in consciousness or to be entirely inaccessible to appraisal and evaluation. Rather than the conspicuous craving for "'nodder one," adult conceptual advances may be motivated by the wisp of reward—a flavor or hue that imbues objects, events, ideas, actions, and even people with a modicum of value. And perhaps without that wisp, that hue, there would simply be no point to engaging with and understanding the world and its components.

Whether the current model of concept formation has any lasting value is uncertain. It may provide an early step toward more sophisticated models that rely on more precise neural information synchronized with behavioral measurement. Models continue to be revised, eventually beyond recognition, or simply discarded, as new ideas and new data arrive on the scene. But my hope is that this modeling exercise encourages readers to think about the brain to clarify their thinking about the mind. The vague abstractions we usually use to discuss cognition–emotion relations can easily be replaced with interpretations that are more vivid, detailed, and biologically precise. It is the attraction of that goal that may call to us as scientists, compelling us to explore the brain with enthusiasm and perseverance.

REFERENCES

Adamec, R., Kent, P., Anisman, H., Shallow T., & Merali, Z. (1998). Neural plasticity, neuropeptides and anxiety in animals: Implications for understanding and treating affective disorder following traumatic stress in humans. *Neuroscience and Biobehavioral Reviews, 23*, 301–318.

Arnold, M. B. (1960). *Emotion and personality: Vol. 1. Psychological aspects.* New York: Columbia University Press.

Barrett, L. F. (2006). Are emotions natural kinds? *Perspectives on Psychological Science, 1*, 28–58.

Barsalou, L. W. (2008). Cognitive and neural contributions to understanding the conceptual system. *Current Directions in Psychological Science, 17*, 91–95.

Berridge, K. C., & Robinson, T. E. (1998). What is the role of dopamine in reward: Hedonic impact, reward learning, or incentive salience? *Brain Research Reviews, 28*, 309–369.

Burgdorf, J., & Panksepp, J. (2006). The neurobiology of positive emotions. *Neuroscience and Biobehavioral Reviews, 30*, 173–187.

Campos, J. J., Anderson, D. I., Barbu-Roth, M. A., Hubbard, E. M., Hertenstein, M. J., & Witherington, D. (2000). Travel broadens the mind. *Infancy, 1*, 149–219.

Cardinal, R. N., Parkinson, J. A., Hall, J., & Everitt, B. J. (2002). Emotion and motivation: the role of the amygdala, ventral striatum, and prefrontal cortex. *Neuroscience and Biobehavioral Reviews, 26*, 321–352.

Case, R. (1985). *Intellectual development: Birth to adulthood.* New York: Academic Press.

Case, R., Hayward, S., Lewis, M. D., & Hurst, P. (1988). Toward a neo-Piagetian theory of cognitive and emotional development. *Developmental Review, 8*, 1–51.

Centonze, D., Picconi, B., Gubellini, P., Bernardi, G., & Calabresi, P. (2001). Dopaminergic control of synaptic plasticity in the dorsal striatum. *European Journal of Neuroscience, 13*, 1071–1077.

Cheer, J. F., Aragona, B. J., Heien, M. L. A. V., Seipel, A. T., Carelli, R. M., & Wightman, R. M. (2007). Coordinated accumbal dopamine release and neural activity drive goal-directed behavior. *Neuron, 54*, 237–244.

Depue, R. A. & Collins, P. F. (1999) Neurobiology of the structure of personality: Dopamine, facilitation of incentive motivation and extraversion. *Behavioral and Brain Sciences, 22*, 491–569.

Derryberry, D., & Tucker, D. M. (1994). Motivating the focus of attention. In P. M. Niedenthal & S. Kitayama (Eds.), *The heart's eye: Emotional influences in perception and attention* (pp. 167–196). San Diego, CA: Academic Press.

Ekman, P. (1984). Expression and the nature of emotion. In K. Scherer & P. Ekman (Eds.), *Approaches to emotion* (pp. 319–344). Hillsdale, NJ: Erlbaum.

Fischer, K. W., Shaver, P. R., & Carnochan, P. (1990). How emotions develop and how they organize development. *Cognition and Emotion, 4*, 81–127.

Flood, J. F., Baker, M. L., Hernandez, E. N., & Morley, J. E. (1990). Modulation of memory retention by neuropeptide K. *Brain Research, 520*, 284–290.

Freeman, W. V. (1995). *Societies of brains: A study in the neuroscience of love and hate.* Hillsdale, NJ: Erlbaum.

Frijda, N. H. (1986). *The emotions.* Cambridge, England: Cambridge University Press.

Goto, Y., & O'Donnell, P. (2001). Network synchrony in the nucleus accumbens in vivo. *Journal of Neuroscience, 21*, 4498–4504.

Graybiel, A. M. (2005). The basal ganglia: Learning new tricks and loving it. *Current Opinion in Neurobiology, 15*, 638–644.

Haber, S. N., Kunishio, K., Mizobuchi, M., & Lynd-Balta, E. (1995). The orbital and medial prefrontal circuit through the primate basal ganglia. *Journal of Neuroscience, 15*, 4851–4867.

Horvitz, J. C. (2002). Dopamine, Parkinson's disease, and volition. *Behavioral and Brain Sciences, 25*, 586.

Isen, A. M. (1985) The asymmetry of happiness and sadness in effects on memory in normal college students. *Journal of Experimental Psychology: General, 114*, 388–391.

Izard, C. E. (1993). Four systems for emotion activation: Cognitive and noncognitive processes. *Psychological Review, 100*, 68–90.

Izard, C. E. (2007). Basic emotions, natural kinds, emotion schemas, and a new paradigm. *Perspectives on Psychological Science, 2*, 260–280.

Izard, C. E., & Malatesta, C. (1987). Perspectives on emotional development I: Differential emotions theory of early emotional development. In J. D. Osofsky (Ed.), *Handbook of infant development* (pp. 494–554). New York: Wiley.

Izquierdo, I. (1997). The biochemistry of memory formation and its regulation by hormones and neuromodulators. *Psychobiology, 25*, 1–9.

Izumi, Y., & Zorumski, C. F. (1999). Norepinephrine promotes long-term potentiation in the adult rat hippocampus in vitro. *Synapse, 31*, 196–202.

Kelley A. E., & Domesick V. B. (1982). The distribution of the projection from the hippocampal formation to the nucleus accumbens in the rat: An anterograde- and retrograde-horseradish peroxidase study. *Neuroscience, 7*, 2321–2335.

Kelley, A. E., Smith-Roe, S. L., & Holahan, M. R. (1997). Response-reinforcement learning is dependent on N-methyl-D-aspartate receptor activation in the nucleus accumbens core. *Proceedings of the National Academy of Sciences, 94*, 12174–12179.

Kerr, J. N. D., & Wickens, J. R. (2001). Dopamine D-1/D-5 receptor activation is required for long-term potentiation in the rat neostriatum in vitro. *Journal of Neurophysiology, 85*, 117–124.

Leslie, A. M., & Thaiss, L. (1992). Domain specificity in conceptual development: Neuropsychological evidence from autism. *Cognition, 43*, 225–251.

Lewis, M. D. (1996). Self-organising cognitive appraisals. *Cognition and Emotion, 10*, 1–25.

Lewis, M. D. (2000). Emotional self-organization at three time scales. In M. D. Lewis & I. Granic (Eds.), *Emotion, development, and self-organization: Dynamic systems approaches to emotional development* (pp. 37–69). New York: Cambridge University Press.

Lewis, M. D. (2005). Bridging emotion theory and neurobiology through dynamic systems modeling (target article). *Behavioral and Brain Sciences, 28*, 169–194.

Lewis, M. D., & Ferrari, M. (2001). Cognitive–emotional self-organization in personality development and personal identity. In H. A. Bosma & E. S. Kunnen (Eds.), *Identity and emotions: A self-organizational perspective* (pp. 177–198). Cambridge, England: Cambridge University Press.

Mahler, M. S., Pine, F., & Bergman, A. (1975). *The psychological birth of the human infant.* New York: Basic Books.

Malatesta, C. Z., & Wilson, A. (1988). Emotion/cognition interaction in personality development: A discrete emotions, functionalist analysis. *British Journal of Social Psychology, 27*, 91–112.

Mathews, A. (1990). Why worry? The cognitive function of anxiety. *Behaviour Research and Therapy, 28,* 455–468.

Neisser, U. (1976). *Cognition and reality : Principles and implications of cognitive psychology.* San Francisco: Freeman.

Neisser, U. (1987). From direct perception to conceptual structure. In U. Neisser (Ed.), *Concepts and conceptual development: Ecological and intellectual factors in categorization* (pp. 11–24). Cambridge, England: Cambridge University Press.

Niedenthal, P. M., Setterlund, M. B., & Jones, D. E. (1994). Emotional organization of perceptual memory. In P. M. Niedenthal & S. Kitayama (Eds.), *The heart's eye: Emotional influences in perception and attention* (pp. 87–113). San Diego, CA: Academic Press.

Oades, R. D., & Halliday, G. M. (1987). Ventral tegmental (A10) system: Neurobiology. 1. Anatomy and connectivity. *Brain Research, 434,* 117–165.

Panksepp, J. (1981). The ontogeny of play in rats. *Developmental Psychobiology, 14,* 327–332.

Panksepp, J. (1998). *Affective neuroscience: The foundations of human and animal emotions.* New York: Oxford University Press.

Parrott, W. (2001). *Emotions in social psychology.* Philadelphia: Psychology Press.

Pascual-Leone, J. (1987). Organismic processes for neo-Piagetian theories: A dialectical causal account of cognitive development. *International Journal of Psychology, 22,* 531–570.

Robinson, T. E., & Berridge, K. C. (1993). The neural basis of drug craving: An incentive-sensitization theory of addiction. *Brain Research Reviews, 18,* 247–291.

Rolls, E. T. (1999). *The brain and emotion.* Oxford, England: Oxford University Press.

Salamone, J. D., & Correa, M. (2002). Motivational views of reinforcement: Implications for understanding the behavioral functions of nucleus accumbens dopamine. *Behavioural Brain Research, 137,* 3–25.

Schultz, W., Dayan, P., & Montague, P. R. (1997). A neural substrate of prediction and reward. *Science, 275,* 1593–1599.

Shohamy, D., Myers, C. E., Grossman, S., Sage, J., Gluck, M. A., & Poldrack, R. A. (2004). Cortico-striatal contributions to feedback-based learning: Converging data from neuroimaging and neuropsychology. *Brain, 127,* 851–859.

Simon, H. A. (1967). Motivational and emotional controls of cognition. *Psychological Review, 74,* 29–39.

Smith, L. B. (1995). Self-organizing processes in learning to learn words: Development is not induction. In C. A. Nelson (Ed.), *Minnesota Symposia on Child Psychology: Vol. 28. New perspectives on learning and development* (pp. 1–32). New York: Academic Press.

Thelen, E., Schöner, G., Scheier, C., & Smith, L. B. (2001). The dynamics of embodiment: A field theory of infant perseverative reaching. *Behavioral and Brain Sciences, 24,* 1–86.

Thelen, E., & Smith, L. B. (1994). *A dynamic systems approach to the development of cognition and action*. Cambridge, MA: MIT Press/Bradford.

Tucker, D. M. (2001). Motivated anatomy: A core-and-shell model of corticolimbic architecture. In G. Gainotti (Ed.), *Handbook of neuropsychology: Vol. 5. Emotional behavior and its disorders* (2nd ed., pp. 125–160). Amsterdam: Elsevier.

Tucker, D. M. (2007). *Mind from body: Experience from neural structure*. New York: Oxford University Press.

Wickens, J. R., Begg, A. J., & Arbuthnott, G. W. (1996). Dopamine reverses the depression of rat corticostriatal synapses which normally follows high-frequency stimulation of cortex in vitro. *Neuroscience, 70*, 1–5.

Wickens, J. R., Horvitz, J. C., Costa, R. M., & Killcross, S. (2007). Dopaminergic mechanisms in actions and habits. *Journal of Neuroscience, 27*, 8181–8183.

Winnicott, D. W. (1992). *Through paediatrics to psycho-analysis: Collected papers*. Philadelphia: Brunner/Mazel.

Wood, J., Mathews, A. & Dalgleish, T. (2001) Anxiety and cognitive inhibition. *Emotion, 1*, 166–181.

III

IMPLICATIONS FOR CLINICAL AND EDUCATIONAL RESEARCH

11

SELF-REGULATION AND ACADEMIC ACHIEVEMENT IN THE TRANSITION TO SCHOOL

FREDERICK J. MORRISON, CLAIRE CAMERON PONITZ, AND MEGAN M. McCLELLAND

Understanding of children's cognitive and social development has advanced significantly over the past 3 decades. Particularly with regard to those skills critical for academic success, research has revealed that multiple interacting factors in the child, home, school, and larger sociocultural context all contribute to children's literacy, numeracy, language, and social skills, starting early in life and continuing throughout the school years (Morrison, Bachman, & Connor, 2005). One factor, self-regulation, has surfaced recently as a crucial skill that uniquely predicts children's early school success. Poor self-regulation has been linked to high rates of expulsion, most dramatically in preschool classrooms (Gilliam & Shahar, 2006).

Self-regulation refers to a complex of acquired, intentional skills involved in controlling, directing, and planning one's cognitions, emotions, and behavior (Schunk & Zimmerman, 1997). In investigations beyond the class-

Funding for this chapter was supported by National Institute of Child and Human Development Grant R01 HD27176 and National Science Foundation Grant 0111754. Additional funding was provided by U.S. Department of Education, Institute for Education Sciences Grant R305B060009.

room, scientists from a broad range of perspectives have reached consensus on the centrality of successful self-regulation as a marker of adaptive development. Findings have demonstrated, at an emerging level of specificity, how biological and neurological processes interact with psychological and experiential factors to determine how children regulate themselves in a given setting. Biological factors such as *temperament*, that is, an individual's predisposed reactivity and regulation of reactions to stimuli, underpin these additive and interactive processes. Self-regulation also develops through early experiences and social interactions, in which caregivers and other significant individuals structure and shape children's trajectories (Grolnick & Farkas, 2002; Kopp, 1982).

In this chapter, we examine self-regulation and its role in academic development, focusing on the transition to formal schooling. We posit that adaptive development in the school context depends on children's ability to manage their reactions and specifically their task-related behaviors. Moreover, successfully self-regulating depends on environmental influences and interactions with others as well as child factors and predispositions. We focus on the construct of *behavioral self-regulation*, which is closely aligned with executive function and which we define as the execution and manifestation of cognitive processes in overt behavior. Remembering and using information, attending to and understanding what others are saying, directing motor actions, and persisting toward goals are all indicators of adaptive behavioral regulation (McClelland, Cameron, Wanless, & Murray, 2007).

Our goals in the chapter are to examine behavioral regulation in the context of early childhood and the transition to school, elucidating how children's skills contribute to achievement. First, we demonstrate links between behavioral regulation and academic achievement prior to formal schooling and throughout elementary school; second, we summarize evidence on the relations between behavioral regulation and emotion regulation; third, we discuss individual differences and proximal influences on regulatory skill growth; fourth, we explore risk factors in the school setting important for the development of behavioral regulation. We end the chapter with a discussion of practical implications and suggestions for future research.

BEHAVIORAL REGULATION AND ACADEMIC ACHIEVEMENT

Multiple underlying cognitive skills are involved in overt behavioral regulation. This complex of cognitive processes involves processing and manipulating stimuli (working memory); inhibiting automatic reactions to stimuli while initiating unnatural yet adaptive reactions (inhibitory control); and managing one's attention to appropriate stimuli, including resisting distraction and shifting tasks when necessary (attentional or cognitive flexibility).

Evidence has linked these individual cognitive components to achievement prior to formal schooling (Blair, 2002; Blair & Razza, 2007; McClelland, Cameron, Connor, et al., 2007) and throughout elementary school (Alexander, Entwisle, & Dauber, 1993; McClelland, Morrison, & Holmes, 2000; McClelland, Acock, & Morrison, 2006). For example, the National Institute for Child Health and Human Development Early Child Care Research Network (2003) found that better attention on a tedious computer task predicted better reading and math achievement in 54-month-old children. In another study, kindergarteners with better attention scored significantly higher than those with poorer attention skills on achievement tests (Howse, Lange, Farran, & Boyles, 2003). A third study of working memory showed that children who could keep better track of the number of dots on multiple cards had higher mathematics achievement. Finally, Blair and Razza (2007) found that preschool levels of inhibitory control predicted kindergarten reading and mathematics achievement.

Such studies have demonstrated that performing well on tasks that require focused, vigilant attention, remembering multiple pieces of information, and inhibiting automatic actions to activate nonautomatic responses predicts correspondingly higher levels of early achievement. These individual cognitive components together form a critical aspect of school readiness. The construct of *executive function* (EF), widely used in the neuropsychological and cognitive literatures, refers to these multiple components operating together (Miyake, Friedman, Emerson, Witzki, & Howerter, 2000; Zelazo, Müller, Frye, & Marcovitch, 2003). The quintessential measure of EF is the Dimensional Change Card Sort (DCCS) task, in which children must first sort cards with pictures of red and blue trucks and boats by color and then switch and sort by shape (Müller, Dick, Gela, Overton, & Zelazo, 2006). Another popular EF measure is the Tower of London or Tower of Hanoi, in which children are presented with rings of varying size on a three-pegged board; they must move the rings from one peg to another and match a particular ring sequence using as few moves as possible (Bull, Espy, & Senn, 2004). These tasks require remembering rules or holding ring/peg locations in mind, inhibiting the tendency to use the old rule or move a peg incorrectly, and attending to the current rule or ring sequence.

Kindergarten teachers agree that similar skills—such as following directions, paying attention, and working independently—although critical for school success, are deficient in many children. The studies by McClelland et al. (2000) and Rimm-Kaufman et al. (2000) have supported such observations and have highlighted a practical need to bridge the gap between findings from the laboratory and from the classroom to understand how behavioral regulation develops over the school transition. More recently, researchers have been developing structured observational measures that can be used in school settings over the transition years but do not require use of computers or specialized equipment (Griffin, 2008). The Head-to-Toes Task (HTT) is one such measure, which activates multiple cognitive skills (Ponitz et al., 2008). The task requires children to remember and respond to two conflicting spoken commands with gross motor actions (i.e., children are instructed to touch their toes when the examiner tells them to touch their head, and vice versa). Results indicate that higher prekindergarten behavioral regulation scores in the fall significantly predict stronger achievement levels in the spring. More strikingly, greater behavioral regulation gains over the prekindergarten year predict greater gains in early mathematics, literacy, and vocabulary skills after controlling for fall achievement levels (McClelland, Cameron, Connor, et al., 2007).

A follow-up study in kindergarten used a more complex version of the HTT, called Head-Toes-Knees-Shoulders (HTKS). This version builds on the HTT by requiring children to remember and respond to four (vs. two) different behavioral commands in conflict with the correct response (Ponitz, McClelland, Matthews, & Morrison, 2009). Findings revealed that stronger levels of behavioral regulation in the fall predict higher fall and spring levels of mathematics, literacy, and vocabulary skills, as well as teacher-rated classroom behavioral regulation. Behavioral regulation gains also predicted mathematics gains (controlling for fall mathematics levels).

Multiple explanations may be offered for the consistent association between behavioral regulation tasks and academic success. First, they require EF, which is a strong predictor of cognitive ability and academic performance (Mazzocco & Kover, 2007; Miyake et al., 2000). Second, they require responses similar to behaviors required in classrooms: For example, the inhibition required in HTT generically taps processes similar to remembering to raise one's hand before speaking in class. Third, instructions and commands are delivered in the school setting, by an adult in authority. The first explanation has been well established in the literature, whereas the second and third have received less attention. Studies that examine differences in trial delivery (e.g., an examiner taps a pencil, states a command, or provides a laptop or other object to deliver the trial stimulus) and task response modality (e.g., fine motor, gross motor, oral responses) would further illuminate the measures that most closely map onto school-related outcomes (Diamond, 2000).

Undoubtedly, EF and behavioral regulation overlap—indeed, it is fair to ask whether both terms are necessary. To indicate the manifestation of multiple cognitive processes in overt behavior, we use the higher order term *behavioral regulation* instead of *executive function* (McClelland, Cameron, Wanless, & Murray, 2007). In the literature, behavioral regulation has been typically situated within naturalistic, nonlaboratory contexts such as the classroom, which may present unique regulatory challenges (Calkins, 2007; Howse, Calkins, Anastopoulos, Keane, & Shelton, 2003). For example, in the classroom, children need to maintain attention on one project and remember to clean up before moving to free choice activity. A child might score well on the DCCS when it is administered in an individualized setting, but the same child may have difficulty completing the classroom project and cleaning up. In the rare studies using traditional EF measures along with behavioral regulation assessments, correlations among EF measures and behavioral outcomes that have been documented are modest (Blair, 2003; Lan & Morrison, 2008). For example, Blair (2003) found that teacher ratings of preschoolers' on-task behavior correlated $r = .24$ (ns) with EF performance on the peg-tapping and day/night tasks.

Providing further impetus to understand the development and effective measurement of behavioral regulation, or "executive function in context," is mounting evidence establishing that behavioral regulation contributes significant, unique variance to children's academic achievement and growth trajectories across preschool years, elementary school, middle school, and even high school. In one study that followed children to middle school, kindergarten behavioral regulation (as part of a broader learning-related skills construct measured by teacher report) predicted reading and math achievement between kindergarten and sixth grade and growth in literacy and math from kindergarten to second grade (McClelland et al., 2006). Another inquiry spanning early childhood to young adulthood showed that kindergarteners with poor behavioral regulation (teacher-rated attention problems and hyperactivity) were less likely to graduate from high school than their well-regulated peers (Vitaro, Brendgen, Larose, & Trembaly, 2005).

THE INTERSECTION OF EMOTION AND BEHAVIORAL REGULATION

Children's self-regulation extends to managing their emotions as well as their actions (Calkins, 2007; Eisenberg & Spinrad, 2004). We adopt Eisenberg and Spinrad's definition of *emotion regulation* as the deliberate modification and modulation of emotional reactions. Considerable evidence links children's effective management of their emotions to positive behavioral and academic outcomes (Eisenberg, Smith, Sadovsky, & Spinrad, 2004; Graziano, Reavis, Keane, & Calkins, 2006; Howse, Lange, et al., 2003). In contrast, children who cannot control their emotions are more likely to act out, behave aggressively, and oppose the perspectives and requests of others (Graziano et al., 2006; Raver, 2004).

Theoretical efforts (e.g., Blair, 2002) have sought to identify conceptual and empirical relations between emotional and behavioral regulation (and its underlying executive processes). For example, Blair has noted that stronger negative emotional reactions (e.g., anger, anxiety) may impede children's ability to regulate their behavior in school settings, where they need to deploy attention and persist in their work. Calkins (2007) concurred that variability in emotion regulation is related to, and may challenge or enhance, children's ability to manage their task-related behavior. For example, children who are easily angered will have more difficulty concentrating on schoolwork than those who can effectively modulate their emotional reactions. An emerging theme from this and other work is that strong behavioral regulation, particularly attentional flexibility, may ameliorate the otherwise negative effects of poor emotion regulation. Thus, the link between emotion regulation and other developmental outcomes depends on children's choices about where to direct their attention and overt behavior (Henderson & Fox, 1998; Rothbart, Posner, & Kieras, 2006).

For example, one study of toddlers found that those with strong negative emotionality actually achieved greater readiness for school (measured by knowledge related to colors, letters, counting, shapes, and conceptual comparisons) but only when the children had strong attention skills (Belsky, Friedman, & Hsieh, 2001). Another recent study revealed that teacher ratings of children's emotional regulation in kindergarten positively predicted first-grade teachers' ratings of attention, which then predicted first-grade achievement (Trentacosta & Izard, 2007). These findings indicate that extreme emotional lability—although previously considered a risk factor—need not be detrimental if children handle their extreme reactions in an adaptive way, such as directing their attention to something else. Thus, compared with emotional regulation, behavioral regulation may be the operable determinant of adjustment and academic success. Howse, Calkins, et al. (2003) found that preschool behavioral regulation mediated the contribution of emotion regulation on kindergarten mathematics and literacy achievement. Together, these findings provide empirical support for a hierarchical conceptualization of self-regulation, whereby children who react strongly emotionally, but who can successfully control their attention and behavior, fare better than children with little capacity to regulate their behavior.

SOURCES OF INFLUENCE

In this section, we distinguish among child factors (i.e., those originating and measured within the child) and external factors (i.e., those originating and measured in the child's environment). Throughout, we note how individual factors interrelate with environmental influences in their associations with self-regulation. We consider biological findings first, then parenting, and then move to a discussion of the emerging evidence on the role of schooling in the development of self-regulation.

Child and Family Factors

Neurological and biological influences, includng temperament, have been implicated as child-related influences, and parent–child attachment and parenting styles have emerged as family sources of growth on self-regulation.

Brain and Biological Development

Early work seemed to suggest that higher order skills underlying executive function did not really emerge until at least preadolescence (Golden, 1984). At present, it is clear that executive skills emerge early in life and grow steadily through at least early adolescence, with this position corroborated by evidence from neurological research (Diamond, 2000). Three major cycles paralleling data on cortical development have been identified: 18 months to 5 years, 5 to 10 years, and 10 to 14 years, with the cycle from late preschool through elementary school being perhaps the most dynamic. During early childhood, the parts of the brain that help children control, direct, and plan their actions undergo significant maturation, including myelination and pruning. In addition, research on brain–behavior relations has revealed that site-specific cortex activation co-occurs with particular behavioral responses (Blair, 2002; Shonkoff & Phillips, 2000). For example, deliberate cognitive processing operates through dorsolateral prefrontal pathways, whereas spontaneous responses to emotionally relevant stimuli operate through ventromedial pathways (Zelazo, Müller, & Goswami, 2002). These processes together contribute to a child's regulatory functioning (Rothbart et al., 2006).

In a recent review of findings from brain research, Lewis and Todd (2007) suggested that optimal regulation means the coordination of activation in different areas of the brain. Studies have indicated that after processing emotional stimuli, our brains then engage areas associated with cognitive and attentional tasks (e.g., the anterior cingulate cortex) to manage emotional reaction. For example, heightened activity of the amygdala —a site commonly linked to the processing of emotional information—is followed by prefrontal cortex activity to regulate the amygdala. Thus, in general, recent trends have been to move away from pitting emotion regulation against cognitive regulatory skills (Zelazo et al., 2002), toward a conceptualization of these two sets of processes as interactive and reciprocally regulating. This argument parallels our claim that adaptive behavior in school depends not just on children's overall emotional reactivity but also on their managing extreme reactions through directing their attention and ultimate behavior. The theme of achieving an optimal balance of reactions and regulation of those reactions is further reflected in research on temperament, another child factor implicated in self-regulation.

Temperament

How a child reacts and regulates his or her reactions has biological origins in a construct known as temperament, which presages later personality tendencies (Kochanska, Murray, & Harlan, 2000). In general, the term *temperament* broadly refers to levels of reactivity and the regulation of that reactivity in early development. One factor, effortful control, contributes to the degree to which children can manage and direct their own actions in cognitive, social, emotional, and behavioral domains (e.g., Rothbart & Rueda, 2005). For example, effortful control helps children inhibit a behavior (e.g., grabbing for a cookie) and control their emotional reactivity (e.g., stop from having a tantrum). Effortful control also shapes how children relate to others, including conscience development (e.g., Kochanska, Murray, & Harlan, 2000) and social outcomes (e.g., Eisenberg et al., 2004; Eisenberg et al., 2005).

As shown in brain research with adults, the anterior attentional systems underlie children's effortful control, which predicts both emotional and behavioral regulation (Rothbart et al., 2006; Rueda, Posner, & Rothbart, 2005). Rothbart et al. have placed particular emphasis on the role of executive attention in effortful control, noting how some infants are more likely to selectively orient their attention as a means of soothing their distress. For example, at seeing a colorful, multiarmed mobile, one child might become distressed, communicating this by crying, fussing, and kicking. However, the child might then look into his mother's face and slowly calm down. More frequent use of early attentional strategies, such as directing attention away from the stressful stimulus, predicts later levels of strong effortful control. To describe how early attentional strategies and later behavioral outcomes interrelate, Calkins (2007) proposed a hierarchical, interactive model of self-regulation in which physiological, attentional, and emotional regulation in the first 3 years of life form a network of reactive and regulatory tendencies, within which intentional regulatory functions emerge as children enter the early school years.

Parent–Child Attachment

Regulation of distress, attention, and behavior does not emerge in isolation; caregivers are immensely important in helping children learn to regulate themselves. Caregivers—most often parents—are infants' first indicators about the world. Through their actions, reactions, and interactions, parents help children learn whether the world is generally a safe, consistent place that can be reliably affected by signaling for help, distress, or happiness, or a scary, unpredictable place in which one's actions go unnoticed. Parents who match their infant's signals, with appropriate levels of help and soothing when the infant is distressed or with positive affect when the infant is happy, are more likely to develop a secure attachment with their child (De Wolff & van Ijzendoorn, 1997). A secure parent–child attachment is thus seen as enabling children to express emotion appropriately and develop strong behavioral regulation (Waters, Weinfield, & Hamilton, 2000). Studies of attachment have also highlighted the importance of the child's reactivity and responsiveness in shaping caregiver responses (Calkins, 2004). For example, infants with an easy temperament may encourage more parental interaction than infants who are reactive and negative (i.e., those with a difficult or slow-to-warm-up temperament). Despite these themes, connections among parenting, attachment, and the development of self-regulation are not consistent and require more research using a transactional lens.

Parenting Styles

As infants become toddlers with a will of their own, parenting behaviors to discipline or control their child's misbehavior add to factors contributing to the development of self-regulation. Studies show that authoritative parenting styles characterized by maintaining consistency, reasoning with the child about discipline decisions, and supporting the child's autonomy are linked with stronger behavioral regulation (Tudge, Odero, Hogan, & Etz, 2003). In one study, mothers who were physically controlling with their 4-year-olds during a regulation cleanup task had children who were more likely to cheat on a game at 56 months (Kochanska & Knaack, 2003). Furthermore, maternal power assertion predicted cheating even after the child's own behavior during the cleanup tasks (e.g., defiance) was controlled. Thus, parents may be both mediators and moderators of the relation between children's experiences and their developing behavioral regulation.

School Factors

So far, we have identified the importance of behavioral regulation for academic achievement, described how being able to direct attention is important for regulating emotional responses and subsequent behavior, and shown the role of biological and parenting behaviors in whether children appropriate regulatory strategies. The next section focuses more squarely on behavioral regulation situated within early school settings.

Child Factors Interacting With Early School Experiences

Similar to themes from parent–child research, children's behavioral regulation in school depends on multiple factors, including children's prior characteristics and experiences as well as characteristics of the classroom. For example, in one study, kindergarteners with poor parent-rated inhibitory control were rated by their teachers as having more difficulty in adjusting to the classroom. Furthermore, those with low inhibitory control, whose parents also reported lax parenting behaviors (e.g., letting their kindergartener decide what to eat and when to go to bed), had the most difficulty in adjusting. Lax parenting had no relation with adjustment for children with strong inhibitory control (Nathanson, Rimm-Kaufman, & Brock, in press).

Another study used observational measures to classify participants as socially bold or wary; bold infants showed little distress at the stranger's appearance, and wary children tended to cry or to look worriedly at their mothers (Rimm-Kaufman et al., 2002). In classrooms with sensitive teachers, the children classified as bold at 15 months exhibited stronger behavioral regulation, whereas such children were more often off-task and less self-reliant in classrooms with less sensitive teachers. In another study, children who were rated by their teachers as impulsive but engaged in more complex kinds of play had stronger behavioral regulation, measured by persistence during cleanup, 6 months later, compared with impulsive children engaging in less complex play. No such relation was found for children rated low on impulsivity (Elias & Berk, 2002).

All of the studies cited here have highlighted the role of child factors like temperament in school functioning and demonstrate how they interact with the environmental context. Together, they have suggested that caregivers, including preschool providers, contribute to children's developing behavioral regulation directly and through complex, yet systematic, interactions with child factors. In general, the literature has suggested that providing a secure base, communicating consistent expectations for behavior, and helping children develop their own regulatory strategies without being didactic or directive are associated with development of successful self-regulation. This conclusion dovetails nicely with theoretical work on the development of self-regulation, emphasizing the transition from "other" regulation by adults to eventually being able to control one's own actions and reactions (Grolnick & Farkas, 2002; Kopp, 1982). However, specific experiences may be more important for some children than others. The studies we reviewed indicated that children with a history of lax parenting or those with bold behavioral predispositions may be particularly sensitive to the experiences they have in classrooms and appear to benefit from extra time to practice behavioral regulation—as in complex play—and from teachers who are sensitive to their emotional signals and cues.

Observational Studies of Classroom Factors

In addition to teacher sensitivity and responsiveness, observational studies have demonstrated that teachers who provide organizational information about classroom rules, procedures, and activities have students with strong behavioral regulation (Pressley, Rankin, & Yokoi, 1996). Teacher organization may be especially important in the primary grades, when students are being socialized to classroom environments and learning how to regulate themselves in that context (Patrick, 1997; Wentzel, 1991). Cameron, Connor, and Morrison (2005) found that a pattern of classroom activity characterized by high amounts of teacher organization in the fall of first grade, which decreased as the year progressed, was associated with greater amounts of classroom-level independent work and word-reading skills in the spring (Cameron, Connor, Morrison, & Jewkes, 2008). Although direct measures of behavioral regulation were not gathered, these findings suggest that classroom organization at the beginning of the school year positively predicts growth of regulatory skills, and it may contribute to enhanced literacy achievement at the end of the year. However, children with low initial vocabulary levels had higher literacy scores when they were in classrooms practicing high organization in the fall and the winter, compared with children who had high vocabularies; these children achieved higher reading scores when they were in classrooms with high organization in the fall only (Cameron et al., 2008). This suggests that organization may be more important for some children than others.

A separate child-by-classroom interaction emerged in a study of chaos in preschool settings; boys but not girls in chaotic, disorganized settings exhibited lower levels of behavioral regulation than boys in well-organized settings (Wachs, Gurkas, & Kontos, 2004). Finally, in another study, stronger teacher organization interacted with child gender, such that boys in well-organized first-grade classrooms made greater gains in mathematics, whereas girls made progress regardless of the level of organization in their classrooms (Ponitz, Rimm-Kaufman, Brock, & Nathanson, in press). These last preliminary findings, which hint that girls do better than boys regardless of the organization levels of their classrooms, suggest there is something to be learned by looking more closely at sources of gender-by-organization interactions. Future research is needed, but it is possible that boys are particularly susceptible to environmental disorganization or that boys contribute to a chaotic setting whereas girls remain less affected.

Experimental and Quasi-Experimental Evidence

A second line of work using experiments and quasi-experiments complements naturalistic studies suggesting that schooling-related experiences can affect children's behavioral regulation (McCrea, Mueller, & Parrila, 1999). One recent study utilized the school cut-off technique, which separates developmental and schooling effects by studying children of similar age who, because of arbitrary school entry dates set by the state or district, enroll in different years in school. Burrage et al. (2008) used the Head-Toes-Knees-Shoulders Task (HTKS) as a measure of behavioral regulation and a separate working memory task, with prekindergarten and kindergarten children who were on average 2 months apart in chronological age. They found distinct schooling effects, such that working memory improved with both prekindergarten and kindergarten attendance. In contrast, overall behavioral regulation showed a marginally significant effect for prekindergarten only. These findings indicate that growth in behavioral regulation may be influenced by schooling, and also document how working memory and overall behavioral regulation may be differentially shaped by schooling influences (Miyake et al., 2000). Additional data confirm that regulatory skills can be improved through training in both laboratory and school-based settings (Klingberg, Fernell, & Olesen, 2005). Evidence also suggests that attention can be trained in early childhood and that, after training, changes occur in the underlying neurological networks responsible for attention (Rueda, Rothbart, McCandliss, Saccomanno, & Posner, 2005).

The extent to which skills taught in the laboratory transfer to real-world settings has been less clear, but recent efforts to develop classroom-based interventions are encouraging. In a quasi-experiment, Rimm-Kaufman and colleagues measured the effects of the Responsive Classroom Approach (RC; Elliot, 1995), which is a teacher intervention aimed at creating a sense of community within the classroom, establishing and maintaining rules and consequences, enhancing student independence, and minimizing problem behaviors. Students in RC settings exhibited better social skills, decreased problem behaviors, and higher academic performance compared with participants in control classrooms (Rimm-Kaufman & Chiu, 2007). There is evidence that the more students are exposed to RC practices within a school year and over multiple years, the more their behavior benefits (Rimm-Kaufman, Fan, Chiu, & You, 2007). In a recent true experiment, researchers evaluated a Vygotskian, classroom-based curriculum called Tools of the Mind, which is intended to enhance children's preschool behavioral regulation through classroom activities (e.g., buddy reading requiring children to take turns; Diamond, Barnett, Thomas, & Munro, 2007). Children in the Tools of the Mind classrooms for 1 or 2 years scored higher on behavioral regulation than did children with no program experience, and participation in the curriculum predicted better academic performance. Together, such studies have supported the view that behavioral regulation skills are amenable to school experiences; identifying the experiences and dosage required to see results are important next steps.

RISK FACTORS

Despite this promising work, many children remain at a critical disadvantage when it comes to learning the regulatory skills they need in school. In the United States, children experiencing risk because of socioeconomic disadvantage, family background, or neighborhood violence have poorer self-regulation and academic achievement than those not experiencing such risks (Fantuzzo et al., 2005; Howse, Lange, et al., 2003; McClelland et al., 2000; Wanless, Sektnan, & McClelland, 2007). For example, children from disadvantaged backgrounds have been shown to be less able to regulate their attention in goal-directed tasks than their more advantaged peers (Howse, Lange, et al., 2003). Another study found that disadvantaged Spanish-speaking children had significantly poorer behavioral regulation (assessed with the Spanish version of the HTT) in preschool and kindergarten than English-speaking participants had (Wanless et al., 2007). Although preliminary, these results suggest that low-income Spanish-speaking children may be at risk of developing poor behavioral regulation prior to school entry.

Research suggests how stressful early environments may shape particular patterns of brain activation and behavior (Shonkoff & Phillips, 2000). Stressful situations require constant attention to and maintenance of intense emotional information, leaving little opportunity for the intellectual exploration and learning that a stimuli-rich environment affords (Baumeister, Zell, & Tice, 2007). Examples of early stressors associated with poor developmental outcomes include severe stimulus deprivation; inconsistent or volatile parenting; frequent moves or change in caregivers; intense and frequent violence, abuse, or neglect; and membership in an underrepresented, historically disadvantaged ethnic minority group (Morales & Guerra, 2006).

Recently, being male has also surfaced as a potential risk factor for poor self-regulation, as survey data have documented the relatively large numbers of boys diagnosed with behavioral maladies such as attention-deficit/hyperactivity disorder (ADHD) and conduct disorder (e.g., Barkley, 2000; Clark, Prior, & Kinsella, 2002). New evidence placing boys at an educational disadvantage contrasts with past findings that classrooms and schools favored male students (Fergusson, Lloyd, & Horwood, 1991). For example, Matthews, Ponitz, and Morrison (in press) found that kindergarten boys scored significantly lower on self-regulation, measured objectively (by HTKS) as well as by teacher report in both fall and spring of the school year. Entwisle, Alexander, and Olson (2007) posited that although today's model student is perceived as female (e.g., studious, conscientious, compliant), more educated families are likely to support academic behaviors in both their male and female children. Indeed, among middle-class families, boys typically do as well as or better than girls on academic achievement measures (Entwisle et al., 2007). Poor families, however, are more likely to endorse and support stereotypes of boys as active and aggressive and girls as quiet and well-behaved, possibly giving girls overall an advantage in classroom settings. Thus, parents as well as teachers and students themselves may contribute to socializing poorly regulated behaviors in male students from socioeconomically disadvantaged backgrounds. Research by Duckworth and Seligman (2006) also shows that throughout the school years, girls demonstrate stronger self-discipline (e.g., spending more time doing homework) than boys do.

We do not yet understand how the beliefs and practices of preschool elementary teachers, who are predominantly female and of majority ethnic status, may translate into variation in classroom experiences of male students, or children in general of different backgrounds. Researchers have suggested that the priorities of teachers who are Caucasian and from middle- to upper-middle socioeconomic backgrounds may not match the priorities and characteristics of socioeconomically disadvantaged students (Delpit, 1993, 1995). Moreover, Rimm-Kaufman et al. (2000) showed that teachers' assessments of the number of children experiencing difficulty with aspects of behavioral regulation (e.g., following directions) increase when the responders are nonminority teachers in classrooms with a high proportion of minority children. These findings have encouraged us to take a complex view of the origins of poor self-regulation in many children, considering individual as well as environmental sources of the problem as well as possible solutions.

SOLVING THE PROBLEM: IMPLICATIONS FOR RESEARCH AND PRACTICE

The foregoing discussion documented multiple child and family contributors to the development of behavioral regulation while also strengthening the claim that behavioral regulation is amenable to experience. Yet clearly children and behavioral regulation do not develop in a vacuum, and some young students are at risk of developing ineffective ways of regulating their emotional reactions and directing their attention and behavior. On the basis of current findings, we propose three suggestions for future scientific and practical endeavors to promote behavioral regulation in the early school years.

First, specifying aspects of behavioral regulation that are particularly strong predictors of academic success is critical; a simultaneous goal must be to develop effective measures of these skills. One recent study found that after early mathematics achievement, preschool levels of attention were the strongest predictors of mathematics and reading achievement measured up to 9 years later (Duncan et al., 2007), leading some to suggest that educators should work to promote mathematics achievement in young children. However, achievement tests were given directly, whereas most attention measures relied on teacher or parent report. Developing sensitive, predictive, and longitudinally valid measures of behavioral regulation and related skills can help illuminate this issue. Until then, we will lack precise information on how behavioral regulation and achievement truly relate, and we will chase the "chicken or the egg" question of which skill (achievement or behavioral regulation) deserves our focus and funding.

Second, further research is needed to examine how child factors and classroom contexts interact. Our interest in such research is based on several accumulating studies indicating that social boldness or wariness, impulsivity, or gender—to name a few examples—interact with classroom factors to predict behavioral regulation (Ponitz et al., in press; Rimm-Kaufman et al., 2002; Wachs et al., 2004). Although still considered preliminary, research has indicated that boys in general and any children entering classrooms with poor behavioral regulation have more difficulty functioning adaptively, compared with girls in general and children who can better control their attention and behavior.

A third, related implication is that some children may need to be explicitly taught the behavioral regulation skills expected in the classroom and have the opportunity to practice them. Observational evidence, as well as experimental evidence, has provided the basis for this claim, indicating positive relations among certain experiences and children's development of behavioral regulation (Burrage et al., 2008; Cameron et al., 2005; Diamond et al., 2007; Rueda, Rothbart, et al., 2005). Spending time orienting children about the purposes of learning activities and offering information about how to complete tasks may help students behaviorally self-regulate and plan their future actions. Diamond's work (e.g., Diamond et al., 2007) also emphasizes the importance of giving children time to practice their attention, working memory, and inhibitory control skills. Although fairly new, the importance of strong teacher organization and behavioral regulation can be seen in the vast parenting literature documenting the regulatory benefit for children when their parents provide consistent, clear expectations about behavior and support their independence (Grolnick & Farkas, 2002). Moreover, research indicates that incorporating time to practice regulating need not detract from the other priorities of preschool. Children can benefit from practicing behavioral regulation in both whole-group and small-group settings, and activities can be built into a variety of curricula activities in developmentally appropriate ways (Stipek et al., 1998).

Promoting behavioral regulation in the classroom seems especially relevant given the mandates of the No Child Left Behind Act, which requires increased classroom time spent in instructional content earlier in children's school lives than in the past (Stipek, 2006). Although increasing the quantity and quality of instruction in content areas is important, the degree to which children can benefit from learning activities depends largely on their ability to respond to challenging and complex classroom settings in a regulated, deliberate manner.

CONCLUSION

In this chapter, we have identified four emerging themes of research on behavioral regulation. First, behavioral regulation and its underlying cognitive components are strongly linked to academic achievement. Second, compared with emotional regulation, children's behavioral regulation is most predictive of their achievement. This may be due to the importance of the attentional focusing aspects of behavioral regulation for learning to regulate emotional reactivity and behavior, as well as to direct relations among behavioral regulation skills and academic tasks. Third, in the parenting and emerging educational literature, environments and interactions that provide structure, organization, and opportunities for children to practice regulating are associated with positive behavioral regulation in the early school years. Fourth, children whose disruptive behavior does not allow them to participate adaptively in school are at significantly greater risk of school failure than are children who successfully regulate themselves.

Success early in school, which is founded on children's ability to regulate their overt behavior in practical tasks like remembering instructions and working independently, is highly predictive of later academic and social functioning (McClelland et al., 2006; Vitaro et al., 2005). A confluence of factors—including individual, parenting, and teacher characteristics—clearly work together to contribute to children's behavioral regulation. An overarching implication from these findings is that factors such as child attributes, as well as the classroom context, must be considered as possible influences on developing behavioral regulation skills and intervention efforts. However, directly teaching classroom expectations and giving all children time to practice their behavioral regulation skills will help ensure that children who enter formal schooling without strong self-regulation have the opportunity to hone this critical skill set.

REFERENCES

Alexander, K. L., Entwisle, D. R., & Dauber, S. L. (1993). First-grade classroom behavior: Its short- and long-term consequences for school performance. *Child Development, 64,* 801–814.

Barkley, R. A. (2000). Genetics of childhood disorders: XVII. ADHD, Part 1: The executive functions and ADHD. *Journal of the American Academy of Child & Adolescent Psychiatry, 39,* 1064–1068.

Baumeister, R. F., Zell, A. L., & Tice, D. M. (2007). How emotions facilitate and impair self-regulation. In J. J. Gross (Ed.), *Handbook of emotion regulation* (pp. 408–426). New York, NY: Guilford Press.

Belsky, J., Friedman, S. L., & Hsieh, K.-H. (2001). Testing a core emotion-regulation prediction: Does early attentional persistence moderate the effect of infant negative emotionality on later development? *Child Development, 72,* 123–133.

Blair, C. (2002). School readiness: Integrating cognition and emotion in a neurobiological conceptualization of children's functioning at school entry. *American Psychologist, 57,* 111–127.

Blair, C. (2003). Behavioral inhibition and behavioral activation in young children: Relations with self-regulation and adaptation to preschool in children attending Head Start. *Developmental Psychobiology, 42,* 301–311.

Blair, C., & Razza, R. P. (2007). Relating effortful control, executive function, and false belief understanding to emerging math and literacy ability in kindergarten. Child Development, 78, 647–663.

Bull, R., Espy, K. A., & Senn, T. E. (2004). A comparison of performance on the Towers of London and Hanoi in young children. Journal of Child Psychology and Psychiatry, 45, 743–754.

Burrage, M., Ponitz, C. C., McCready, E. A., Shah, P. R., Sims, B. C., Jewkes, A. M., et al. (2008). Age and schooling-related effects on executive functions in young children: A natural experiment. Child Neuropsychology, 1–15.

Calkins, S. D. (2004). Early attachment processes and the development of emotional self-regulation. In R. F. Baumeister & K. D. Vohs (Eds.), Handbook of self-regulation: Research, theory, and applications (pp. 324–339). New York: Guilford Press.

Calkins, S. D. (2007). The emergence of self-regulation: Biological and behavioral control mechanisms supporting toddler competencies. In C. A. Brownell & C. B. Kopp (Eds.), Socioemotional development in the toddler years: Transitions and transformations (pp. 261–284). New York: Guilford Press.

Calkins, S. D., Graziano, P. A., & Keane, S. P. (2007). Cardiac vagal regulation differentiates among children at risk for behavior problems. Biological Psychology, 74, 144–153.

Cameron, C. E., Connor, C. M., & Morrison, F. J. (2005). Effects of variation in teacher organization on classroom functioning. Journal of School Psychology, 43, 61–85.

Cameron, C. E., Connor, C. M., Morrison, F. J., & Jewkes, A. M. (2008). Effects of classroom organization on letter-word reading in first grade. Journal of School Psychology, 46, 173–192.

Clark, C., Prior, M., & Kinsella, G. (2002). The relationship between executive function abilities, adaptive behaviour, and academic achievement in children with externalising behaviour problems. Journal of Child Psychology & Psychiatry & Allied Disciplines, 43, 785–796.

Delpit, L. D. (1993). The silenced dialogue: Power and pedagogy in educating other people's children. In L. Weis & M. Fine (Eds.), Beyond silenced voices: Class, race, and gender in United States schools (pp. 119–139). Albany: State University of New York Press.

Delpit, L. D. (1995). Other people's children: Cultural conflict in the classroom. New York: New York Press.

De Wolff, M., & van Ijzendoorn, M. H. (1997). Sensitivity and attachment: A meta-analysis on parental antecedents of infant attachment. Child Development, 68, 571–591.

Diamond, A., Barnett, W. S., Thomas, J., & Munro, S. (2007, November 30). Preschool program improves cognitive control. Science, 318, 1387–1388.

Diamond, A. (2000). Close interrelation of motor development and cognitive development and of the cerebellum and prefrontal cortex. Child Development, 71, 44–56.

Duckworth, A. L., & Seligman, M. E. P. (2006). Self-discipline gives girls the edge: Gender in self-discipline, grades, and achievement test scores. Journal of Educational Psychology, 98, 198–208.

Duncan, G. J., Dowsett, C. J., Claessens, A., Magnuson, K., Huston, A. C., Klebanov, P., et al. (2007). School readiness and later achievement. Developmental Psychology, 43, 1428–1446.

Eisenberg, N., Sadovsky, A., Spinrad, T. L., Fabes, R. A., Losoya, S. H., Valiente, C., et al. (2005). The relations of problem behavior status to children's negative emotionality, effortful control, and impulsivity: Concurrent relations and prediction of change. Developmental Psychology, 41, 193–211.

Eisenberg, N., Smith, C. L., Sadovsky, A., & Spinrad, T. L. (2004). Effortful control: Relations with emotion regulation, adjustment, and socialization in childhood. In R. F. Baumeister & K. D. Vohs (Eds.), *Handbook of self-regulation: Research, theory, and applications* (pp. 259–282). New York: Guilford Press.

Eisenberg, N., & Spinrad, T. L. (2004). Emotion-related regulation: Sharpening the definition. *Child Development, 75,* 334–339.

Elias, C. L., & Berk, L. E. (2002). Self-regulation in young children: Is there a role for sociodramatic play? *Early Childhood Research Quarterly, 17,* 216–238.

Elliot, S. N. (1995). *The Responsive Classroom approach: Its effectiveness and acceptability* (Final evaluation report). Washington, DC: Center for Systemic Educational Change, District of Columbia Public Schools.

Entwisle, D. R., Alexander, K. L., & Olson, L. S. (2007). Early schooling: The handicap of being poor and male. *Sociology of Education, 80,* 114–138.

Fantuzzo, J. W., Rouse, H. L., McDermott, P. A., Sekino, Y., Childs, S., & Weiss, A. (2005). Early childhood experiences and kindergarten success: A population-based study of a large urban setting. *School Psychology Review, 34,* 571–588.

Fergusson, D. M., Lloyd, M., & Horwood, L. J. (1991). Teacher evaluations of the performance of boys and girls. *New Zealand Journal of Educational Studies, 26,* 155–163.

Graziano, P. A., Reavis, R. D., Keane, S. P., & Calkins, S. D. (2006). The role of emotion regulation in children's early academic success. *Journal of School Psychology, 45,* 3–19.

Gilliam, W. S., & Shahar, G. (2006). Preschool and child care expulsion and suspension: Rates and predictors in one state. *Infants and Young Children, 19,* 228–245.

Golden, C. J. (1984). *Luria-Nebraska Neuropsychological Battery: Children's Revision.* Los Angeles: Western Psychological Services.

Griffin, J. (Chair). (2008, June). *Measurement in early childhood consortium.* Poster presented at the Ninth Annual Head Start National Research Conference, Washington, DC.

Grolnick, W. S., & Farkas, M. (2002). Parenting and the development of children's self-regulation. In M. H. Bornstein (Ed.), *Handbook of parenting: Vol. 5. Practical issues in parenting* (2nd ed., pp. 89–110). Mahwah, NJ: Erlbaum.

Henderson, H. A., & Fox, N. A. (1998). Inhibited and uninhibited children: Challenges in school settings. *School Psychology Review, 27,* 492–505.

Howse, R. B., Calkins, S. D., Anastopoulos, A. D., Keane, S. P., & Shelton, T. L. (2003). Regulatory contributors to children's kindergarten achievement. *Early Education & Development, 14,* 101–119.

Howse, R. B., Lange, G., Farran, D. C., & Boyles, C. D. (2003). Motivation and self-regulation as predictors of achievement in economically disadvantaged young children. Journal of *Experimental Education, 71,* 151–174.

Klingberg, T., Fernell, E., & Olesen, P. J. (2005). Computerized training of working memory in children with ADHD—A randomized, controlled trial. *Journal of the American Academy of Child & Adolescent Psychiatry, 44,* 177–186.

Kochanska, G., & Knaack, A. (2003). Effortful control as a personality characteristic of young children: Antecedents, correlates, and consequences. *Journal of Personality, 71*, 1087–1112.

Kochanska, G., Murray, K. T., & Harlan, E. T. (2000). Effortful control in early childhood: Continuity and change, antecedents, and implications for social development. *Developmental Psychology, 36*, 220–232.

Kopp, C. B. (1982). Antecedents of self-regulation: A developmental perspective. *Developmental Psychology, 18*, 199–214.

Lan, X., & Morrison, F. J. (2008, July). Inter-correlations among components of behavioral regulation and their relationship with academic outcomes in China. In M. M. McClelland & S. Wanless (Chairs), *Touching your toes in four cultures: Developing a new measure of behavioral regulation for young children*. Symposium conducted at the Biennial Meeting of the International Society for the Study of Behavioural Development, Würzburg, Germany.

Lewis, M. D., & Todd, R. M. (2007). The self-regulating brain: Cortical–subcortical feedback and the development of intelligent action. *Cognitive Development, 22*, 406–430.

Matthews, J. S., Ponitz, C. C., & Morrison, F. J. (in press). Early gender differences in self-regulation and academic achievement . *Journal of Educational Psychology*.

Mazzocco, M. M. M., & Kover, S. T. (2007). A longitudinal assessment of executive function skills and their association with math performance. *Child Neuropsychology, 13*, 18–45.

McClelland, M. M., Acock, A. C., & Morrison, F. J. (2006). The impact of kindergarten learning-related skills on academic trajectories at the end of elementary school. *Early Childhood Research Quarterly, 21*, 471–490.

McClelland, M. M., Cameron, C. E., Connor, C. M., Farris, C. L., Jewkes, A. M., & Morrison, F. J. (2007). Links between behavioral regulation and preschoolers' literacy, vocabulary, and math skills. *Developmental Psychology, 43*, 947–959.

McClelland, M. M., Cameron, C. E., Wanless, S. B., & Murray, A. (2007). Executive function, self-regulation, and social-emotional competence: Links to school readiness. In O. N. Saracho & B. Spodek (Eds.), *Contemporary perspectives on research in social learning in early childhood education*. (pp. 83–107). Charlotte, NC: Information Age.

McClelland, M. M., Morrison, F. J., & Holmes, D. L. (2000). Children at risk for early academic problems: The role of learning-related social skills. *Early Childhood Research Quarterly, 15*, 307–329.

McCrea, S. M., Mueller, J. H., & Parrila, R. K. (1999). Quantitative analyses of schooling effects on executive function in young children. *Child Neuropsychology, 5*, 242–250.

Miyake, A., Friedman, N. P., Emerson, M. J., Witzki, A. H., & Howerter, A. (2000). The unity and diversity of executive functions and their contributions to complex "frontal lobe" tasks: A latent variable analysis. *Cognitive Psychology, 41*, 49–100.

Morales, J. R., & Guerra, N. G. (2006). Effects of multiple context and cumulative stress on urban children's adjustment in elementary school. *Child Development, 77*, 907–923.

Morrison, F. J., Bachman, H. J., & Connor, C. M. (2005). *Improving literacy in America: Guidelines from research.* New Haven, CT: Yale University Press.

Müller, U., Dick, A. S., Gela, K., Overton, W. F., & Zelazo, P. D. (2006). The role of negative priming in preschoolers' flexible rule use on the Dimensional Change Card Sort task. *Child Development, 77*, 395–412.

Nathanson, L., Rimm-Kaufman, S. E., & Brock, L. L. (in press). Kindergarten adjustment difficulty: The contribution of children's effortful control and parental control. *Early Education & Development.*

National Institute for Child Health and Human Development Early Child Care Research Network. (2003). Do children's attention processes mediate the link between family predictors and school readiness? *Developmental Psychology, 39*, 581–593.

Patrick, H. (1997). Social self-regulation: Exploring the relations between children's social relationships, academic self-regulation, and school performance. *Educational Psychologist, 32*, 209–220.

Ponitz, C. C., McClelland, M. M., Jewkes, A. M., Connor, C. M., Farris, C. L., & Morrison, F. J. (2008). Touch your toes! Developing a direct measure of behavioral regulation in early childhood. *Early Childhood Research Quarterly, 23*, 141–158.

Ponitz, C. C., McClelland, M. M., Matthews, J. S., & Morrison, F. J. (2009). A structured observation of behavioral self-regulation and its contribution to kindergarten outcomes. *Developmental Psychology, 45*, 605–619.

Ponitz, C. C., Rimm-Kaufman, S. E., Brock, L. L., & Nathanson, L. (in press). Early adjustment, gender differences, and classroom organizational climate in first grade. *Elementary School Journal.*

Pressley, M., Rankin, J., & Yokoi, L. (1996). A survey of instructional practices of primary teachers nominated as effective in promoting literacy. *Elementary School Journal, 96*, 363–384.

Raver, C. C. (2004). Placing emotional self-regulation in sociocultural and socioeconomic contexts. *Child Development, 75*, 346–353.

Rimm-Kaufman, S. E., & Chiu, Y.-J. I. (2007). Promoting social and academic competence in the classroom: An intervention study examining the contribution of the Responsive Classroom approach. *Psychology in the Schools, 44*, 397–413.

Rimm-Kaufman, S. E., Early, D. M., Cox, M. J., Saluja, G., Pianta, R. C., Bradley, R. H., et al. (2002). Early behavioral attributes and teachers' sensitivity as predictors of competent behavior in the kindergarten classroom. *Journal of Applied Developmental Psychology, 23*, 451–470.

Rimm-Kaufman, S. E., Fan, X., Chiu, Y.-J. I., & You, W. (2007). The contribution of the Responsive Classroom Approach on children's academic achievement: Results from a three year longitudinal study. *Journal of School Psychology, 45*, 401–421.

Rimm-Kaufman, S. E., Pianta, R. C., & Cox, M. J. (2000). Teachers' judgments of problems in the transition to kindergarten. *Early Childhood Research Quarterly, 15*, 147–166.

Rothbart, M. K., Posner, M. I., & Kieras, J. (2006). Temperament, attention, and the development of self-regulation. In K. McCartney & D. Phillips (Eds.), *Blackwell handbook of early childhood development* (pp. 338–357). Walden, MA: Blackwell.

Rothbart, M. K., & Rueda, M. R. (2005). The development of effortful control. In U. Mayr, E. Awh, & S. W. Keele (Eds.), *Developing individuality in the human brain: A tribute to Michael I. Posner* (pp. 167–188). Washington, DC US: American Psychological Association.

Rueda, M. R., Posner, M. I., & Rothbart, M. K. (2005). The development of executive attention: Contributions to the emergence of self-regulation. *Developmental Neuropsychology, 28*, 573–594.

Rueda, M. R., Rothbart, M. K., McCandliss, B. D., Saccomanno, L., & Posner, M. I. (2005). Training, maturation, and genetic influences on the development of executive attention. *Proceedings of the National Academy of Sciences, 102*, 14391–14936.

Schunk, D. H., & Zimmerman, B. J. (1997). Social origins of self-regulatory competence. *Educational Psychologist, 32*, 195–208.

Shonkoff, J. P., & Phillips, D. A. (2000). *From neurons to neighborhoods: The science of early childhood development.* Washington, DC: National Academies Press.

Stipek, D. J. (2006). No Child Left Behind comes to preschool. *Elementary School Journal, 106*, 455–465.

Stipek, D. J., Feiler, R., Byler, P., Ryan, R., Milburn, S., & Salmon, J. M. (1998). Good beginnings: What difference does the program make in preparing young children for school? *Journal of Applied Developmental Psychology, 19*, 41–66.

Trentacosta, C. J., & Izard, C. E. (2007). Kindergarten children's emotion competence as a predictor of their academic competence in first grade. *Emotion, 7*, 77–88.

Tudge, J. R. H., Odero, D. A., Hogan, D. M., & Etz, K. E. (2003). Relations between the everyday activities of preschoolers and their teachers' perceptions of their competence in the first years of school. *Early Childhood Research Quarterly, 18*, 42–64.

Vitaro, F., Brendgen, M., Larose, S., & Trembaly, R. E. (2005). Kindergarten disruptive behaviors, protective factors, and educational achievement by early adulthood. *Journal of Educational Psychology, 97*, 617–629.

Wachs, T. D., Gurkas, P., & Kontos, S. (2004). Predictors of preschool children's compliance behavior in early childhood classroom settings. *Journal of Applied Developmental Psychology, 25*, 439–457.

Wanless, S. B., Sektnan, M., & McClelland, M. M. (2007, April). *Growth in behavioral self-regulation during the transition to kindergarten for English- and Spanish-speaking children.* Poster presented at the biennial meeting of the Society for Research in Child Development, Boston.

Waters, E., Weinfield, N. S., & Hamilton, C. E. (2000). The stability of attachment security from infancy to adolescence and early adulthood: General discussion. *Child Development, 71,* 703–706.

Wentzel, K. R. (1991). Social competence at school: Relation between social responsibility and academic achievement. *Review of Educational Research, 61,* 1–24.

Zelazo, P. D., Müller, U., Frye, D., & Marcovitch, S. (2003). The development of executive function in early childhood. *Monographs of the Society for Research in Child Development, 68.*

Zelazo, P. D., Müller, U., & Goswami, U. (2002). Executive function in typical and atypical development. In U. Goswami (Ed.), *Blackwell handbook of childhood cognitive development* (pp. 445–469). Malden, MA: Blackwell.

12

INTERSECTION OF EMOTION AND COGNITION IN DEVELOPMENTAL PSYCHOPATHOLOGY

JOEL T. NIGG, MICHELLE M. MARTEL, MOLLY NIKOLAS,
AND B. J. CASEY

In this chapter, we outline an approach to integrating cognition and emotion in a manner relevant to developmental psychopathology. This model is influenced by several specific priorities. First, the model should enable reference to multiple levels of analysis (i.e., types of measurement—experimental as well as observational, and behavioral as well as physiological). Second, it should enable reference to neural science—that is, to particular neural networks, as well as to biological and genetic sciences. That second element is important in enabling researchers to identify narrower phenotypes that may be components of complex disorders, so as to be able to connect levels of analysis. Finally, the model should enable a connection between typical and atypical development, so that measurements of the traits or components across different kinds of stress and risk shed light on how maladaptive development occurs.

Work described in this chapter was supported by National Institutes of Health Grants NIAAA 2 R01-AA12217, R21-MH70542–01A1, R01-MH63146, and R01-MH070004–01A2.

The model guiding our work thus begins with temperament, which in its historical roots and current formulations naturally points to interplay of cognitive and affective systems (Nigg, 2006). We then illustrate how the perspective we have taken can enrich understanding of psychopathology by highlighting relevant findings from both experimental and observational studies.

THEORETICAL FRAMEWORK

The theoretical framework draws on temperament theory, and we first explain why this is a powerful approach to thinking about the conjoined role of emotion and cognition. We then discuss how this framework also draws on recent neuroscience findings, thus considering theory from first a behavioral and then a neural perspective.

General Temperament Model

Temperament theory emphasized learning systems in the early work of Pavlov and his work subsequently influenced H. Eysenck and thus J. A. Gray. By the middle of the 20th century in America, the concept of temperament heavily emphasized not internal mechanisms but behavioral response styles in children (Thomas, Chess, & Birch, 1968; Thomas, Chess, Birch, Hertzig, & Korn, 1963;). Subsequently, numerous different structural models of basic temperament traits in children were suggested but with an increasingly prominent emphasis on affective response style. A body of work by Rothbart and colleagues (reviewed in Rothbart & Bates, 1998; Putnam, Ellis, & Rothbart, 2001) showed that in infancy, most parent rating scales of young children's temperament could be consolidated into five dimensions: *positive affect* (i.e., tendency to be cheerful), two kinds of *negative affect* (i.e., fear/anxiety and anger/irritability), *activity level*, and *rhythmicity* (which refers to the tendency to have regular sleep/wake and eating cycles). In infancy, a three-factor structure was defined by *surgency/extraversion* (i.e., the tendency to be outgoing, socially dominant, and energetic), *neuroticism/negative affect* (i.e., tendency to be fearful, worried, sad, anxious, or irritable), and *affiliation* (i.e., cuddliness and soothability, as well as orienting).

However, by toddlerhood and early to middle childhood, the third factor, affiliation, was anchored by attentional control (ability to deliberately control attention both to persevere in something difficult and to disengage from something attractive) and it was relabeled as *effortful control*. In adolescence, affiliation was separated as a fourth factor, distinct from effortful control. At that point, the resultant model of temperament traits had four factors. It had begun to closely resemble that proposed for adult personality, which is typically based on three, four, or five factors as well. Those adult

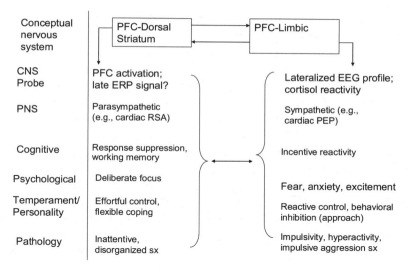

Conceptual nervous system	PFC-Dorsal Striatum	PFC-Limbic
CNS Probe	PFC activation; late ERP signal?	Lateralized EEG profile; cortisol reactivity
PNS	Parasympathetic (e.g., cardiac RSA)	Sympathetic (e.g., cardiac PEP)
Cognitive	Response suppression, working memory	Incentive reactivity
Psychological	Deliberate focus	Fear, anxiety, excitement
Temperament/ Personality	Effortful control, flexible coping	Reactive control, behavioral inhibition (approach)
Pathology	Inattentive, disorganized sx	Impulsivity, hyperactivity, impulsive aggression sx

Figure 12.1. Vertical integration and mutual influence model of regulatory control. Data from Nigg (2006). PFC = prefrontal cortex; CNS = central nervous system; EEG = electroencephalograph; PNS = peripheral nervous system; RSA = respiratory sinus arrythmia; PEP = preejection period; sx = symptoms.

personality models all tended to emphasize three factors that could be labeled, respectively, *extraversion/surgency, neuroticism/negative affect,* and *conscientiousness/control* (for a review, see Nigg, 2006). Some models also added a factor for *agreeableness* (i.e., tendency to get along with others, similar to childhood affiliation), and for *openness.*

Other important models of temperament have been influential in psychopathology research. The Rothbart and Bates (1998) model just described was partially integrated with alternative models such as that of Kagan and Snidman (2004) and that of Eisenberg and colleagues (e.g., 2005), although we do not wish to overstate the integration. Nonetheless, a workable integration can be derived for purposes of conceptualizing links between these traits and psychopathology.

An important aspect of addressing our topic is that the basic traits can be conceptualized at different levels of analysis: as behavioral traits, neural systems, and psychological processes. As noted by several authors (e.g., Calkins & Fox, 2002), such traits can be measured in the central nervous system (CNS) by imaging key brain circuits or via electroencephalograph recordings. They can also be measured in the peripheral nervous system (PNS) typically with cardiac or other physiological measures. Finally, they can be measured as psychological operations by laboratory tasks, or as behavioral tendencies by observations or ratings of behavior. Figure 12.1 schematically illustrates this general conceptual framework as we interpret it, showing how cognitive and affective components are partially distinct yet interrelated and able to be assessed at multiple levels of analysis. This proposed "vertical integration" across levels of analysis remains to be demonstrated, but it can serve as a framework to guide research.

Figure 12.1 suggests two fundamental functions, one that demands mental and cognitive resources and is perceived as top-down because it often reflects neural activation in PFC, with corresponding suppression in posterior or subcortical activation. Effortful control is seen when a child can wait without responding to a tempting toy or can persist on a difficult problem. Parents rate such a child as having low impulsivity and good attentional control. In the laboratory, effortful control (or its converse, poor attentional control) is expected to relate to experimental reaction-time measures such as set shifting, response interruption, and executive functioning (Calkins & Fox, 2002; Nigg, 2000; Rothbart & Bates, 1998). In the CNS, it is expected to be associated with neural activation in PFC. In the PNS, it is hypothesized to reflect key cardiac measures, such as vagal tone. This type of control may be seen as a "cognitive" operation in that it reflects mental resources and diversion of attention, and it taxes response control.

Effortful control may be contrasted with measures of immediate incentive response, indicated in Figure 12.1 by measures of limbic system, sympathetic cardiac activation, and ratings of emotional response style. Behaviorally, these responses include behaviors such as getting very excited by a possible reward or very fearful about a possible punishment. These responses tend to be viewed as "affective" in that they do not demand cognitive resources (though they obviously can interfere with cognition), are relatively spontaneous, and are thought to be "bottom-up" in the sense that they emanate from subcortical brain regions (modulated and evaluated by way of relevant cortical connections).

We call these multilevel constructs *traits* for the sake of simplicity. Extreme standing on one or more traits may be related to behavioral disorder. If so, then the patterning of these traits may shed light on the taxonomy of behavioral problems.

A Neural Account

Cognitive control enables people to maintain attention and behavior in response to a goal held in mind (working memory) while disregarding other immediate incentive signals. Limbic brain regions (e.g., amygdala, nucleus accumbens) are traditionally associated with affective processing of various kinds. In this chapter, *affective process* refers to behavioral and physiological processes that are strengthened with signals of impending incentive in the form of reward—pleasure—or in the form of psychological or physical pain, triggering avoidance. As a result, cognitive control modulates affective responding and vice versa. Together, these systems generate regulation of behavior and affect. For example, the ability to suppress a response can occur through cognitive and top-down mechanisms or, in contrast, through emotional and bottom-up mechanisms that influence top-down effects (Casey, Tottenham, Liston, & Durston, 2005; Nigg, 2000; Nigg & Casey, 2005).

Cognitive Control

Cognitive control, by suppressing irrelevant information or action, enables one to deliberately direct attention or response to serve a goal held in working memory. It thus supports incentives represented in working memory by protecting them from interference. Those incentives, in effect, are distal in time, whereas the bottom-up affective responding draws attention to immediate incentives. An example of cognitive control is to ignore the sounds of people talking in order to concentrate on what the teacher is saying. Cognitive control sometimes requires rapid shifts in behavior as the context signals change, in order to maintain progress on a goal (picture a baseball batter checking her swing as a pitch breaks wide of the plate: The swing begins, then is interrupted because the context has suddenly changed). This type of control, when viewed via neuroimaging in adults, involves activation in regions of PFC, including anterior cingulate (activated when contending with conflicting information and goals), dorsolateral PFC (activated when information must be protected in mind), and ventral and orbital PFC (activated when responses must be suppressed; Casey et al., 2005; Botvinick et al., 2004).

In turn, these activations appear to coincide with suppression of activity in the posterior cortex—regions that become active when one is orienting to new information (Nobre, 2004). Even more important for our discussion, this activity is correlated with decreased activation in amygdala when one is ignoring negative information (Hariri, Mattay, Tessitore, Fera, & Weinberger, 2003; Hare et al., 2008) and in nucleus accumbens when one is contending with attractive information (Hariri, Bookheimer, & Mazziotta, 2000).

The neural model that emerges is that subcortical or bottom-up responses to positive or attractive experiences may disrupt cognitive control (at a macro level, imagine a child breaking from his recess line to run over to a friend getting out of a car, or a faculty member during a dull meeting being distracted by a view of blue sky that evokes thoughts of the vacation starting the next day). Conversely, cognitive control can also suppress activations related to immediate incentives so as to maintain effort on a rewarding distal goal held in working memory (at the macro level, picture a child who, to earn the privilege of playing with his friends later, manages to stay quietly in line despite the temptation offered by apparently fun clowning around by misbehaving children nearby). Of course, the same story can be told about negative bottom-up responding. The speaker anxious about signs of disapproving audience reactions suddenly forgets what he was talking about (bottom-up interruption of goal-directed behavior) but then manages to suppress this concern and refocus on the topic of the talk (cognitive control suppresses bottom-up signals of threat to achieve a goal).

Incentive Response and Affective Regulation

The developmental framework advocated here draws as well on the psychobiology of personality and temperament, bodies of work integrated over the past 2 decades. A generation ago, Gray (1982) reframed the basic dimensions of personality in terms of affective, incentive response. Thus, according to Gray, anxiety and fear (on one hand) and excitement and hope (on the other) were supported by extensively described limbic circuitry. These systems learned cues for reward or negative consequences and anticipated events accordingly, interrupting other behavioral programs with this affective information. Individual differences in the reactivity of these systems underlay individual differences in optimal learning context and in personality and temperament.

At the most basic behavioral level, positive emotional valence (or expectation of reward) is related to approach, whereas negative valence (or expectation of nonreward) is associated with avoidance and withdrawal (Hare et al., 2008). Thus, interactions between cognitive and emotional processes play an important role in regulation of behavior in different incentive contexts. Although the neural basis of these interactions is not yet understood, reciprocal neural connections exist between prefrontal control regions and subcortical regions involved in affective response (Haber, Kunishio, Mizobuchi, & Lynd-Balta, 1995).

Human neuroimaging studies of affective control show a role for top-down prefrontal modulation of subcortical regions (Hariri et al., 2000; 2003; Hare et al., 2008; Ochsner et al., 2004). These studies show greater activation in the ventral amygdala when approaching negative information (i.e., fearful faces; Hare, Tottenham, Davidson, Glover, & Casey, 2005; Hare et al., 2008; Thomas et al., 2001). The greater the amygdala activity, the slower the reaction times in detecting (approaching) negative information (e.g., fearful faces; Hare et al., 2005). Compared to fearful expressions, happy expressions elicit greater activity in the nucleus accumbens, a region associated with reward and appetitive behavior (Schultz, Tremblay, & Hollerman, 2000). Imaging studies have shown an inverse correlation between prefrontal cortical activation and amygdala activity, which can be interpreted as reflecting top-down modulation of emotional processes (Hare et al., 2008).

Thus, when emotional information is irrelevant or contrary to the current goal, top-down connections from the PFC to subcortical regions are critical for regulating the effects of affective information on behavior. Their ability to do so obviously depends both on the integrity of those top-down systems and on the intensity or strength of the affective response.

Developmental Considerations and Mutually Influencing Cognition and Affect

The development of cognitive control may be thought of as presuming intact affect response systems and vice versa, because of the interdependent nature of these circuits functionally and their reciprocal communication during development (Rothbart & Bates, 1998), all modulated by socialization experiences. Developmentally, these systems appear in their measurable influence on behavior and cognition at different points, and they also functionally mature at different times. Affective systems appear somewhat earlier, and they also mature somewhat earlier, apparently coinciding with puberty, whereas prefrontal systems appear somewhat later and exhibit protracted development with age and experience.

As explained by Rothbart and Bates (1998), behavior early in life is largely stimulus driven, as midbrain systems come online and direct attention reflexively. By some time in infancy, limbic systems begin to associate stimulus and outcome, and rewards or their loss begin to be anticipated on the basis of signals in the environment. Thus, incentive response and, in turn, individual variation in affective responding each take on a role in shaping behavior. These two systems interplay, as illustrated in our earlier examples, and so influence one another during early development. By the toddler years, children show the first precursive signs of strategic control over behavior—effortfully maintaining attention on information that is relevant to a goal while ignoring immediately salient but irrelevant material (Putnam et al., 2001). It is important to note that even in the 1st year of life, infants can apparently regulate their emotions by turning their gaze away from disturbing information (as in the still-face procedure). Such regulatory removal of gaze from an upsetting stimulus may be precursive to control, but it remains distinct from moving attention away from an attractive stimulus to achieve a goal—the latter ability emerging around 18 months of age.

In addition to showing an onset of influence on behavior at different points in early development, each of these systems matures at different times later, too. Reflexive attention systems are functioning at essentially adult levels by early to middle childhood (Huang-Pollock, Carr, & Nigg, 2002). However, top-down cognitive control is still maturing into late adolescence and early adulthood, congruent with maturation of PFC and its associated connectivity throughout the brain. Behaviorally, top-down control develops rapidly between the ages of 3 and 6 years (Aksan & Kochanska, 2004). During that period there is rapidly increasing specialization of neural networks (Casey et al., 2005), and that is also when most externalizing disorders of childhood, including attention-deficit/hyperactivity disorder (ADHD), are diagnosed. Cognitive control continues to develop throughout childhood, yielding steady progress in the ability to ignore competing stimulus-driven responses over the second- to fourth-grade years (Huang-Pollock et al., 2002) and the ability to inhibit primary responses over the ages of about 5 to 7 years and beyond (Carver, Livesey, & Charles, 2001). Neurally, however, myelination and pruning continue through adolescence and beyond, while the brain gains efficiency in cognitive processing and affective regulation.

The affective systems probably continue to mature into adolescence, whereas control of these systems does not mature until early adulthood (Casey, Jones, & Hare, 2008; Luciano, 2006) with cognitive control. Luciano and colleagues (for a review, see Luciano, 2006) found that *cool* cognitive control (i.e., the simple ability to control complex response patterns) matured by around the age of 17 years, but *hot* cognitive control (the ability to maintain cognitive focus under strong countervailing incentives) did not mature until at least the early 20s. Thus, we can speculate that behavior early in life is heavily governed by stimulus and incentive responding, but that gradually cognitive control takes on a greater role, at least in typically developing children and adults. However, some nonlinearity is apparent in adolescence as incentive responding matures ahead of cognitive control. Risk of the emergence of psychopathology may be greater in the preschool years, when affective systems come online ahead of control systems, and again in adolescence, when affective systems mature ahead of control systems.

For example, Casey et al. (2008) suggested that the type of risk-taking behavior seen in adolescence may be related to limbic (bottom-up incentive response) systems reaching maturity prior to the full maturation of cortical (top-down control) neural systems. A recent study by Galvan, Hare, Voss, Glover, and Casey (2006) supported this perspective. Adolescents, compared with children and adults, showed an exaggerated response in the limbic system (nucleus accumbens) in anticipation of reward. However, both children and adolescents showed a less mature response in prefrontal control regions than did adults. These data suggest distinct developmental trajectories for these regions.

LINKING COGNITION AND EMOTION WITH DEVELOPMENTAL PSYCHOPATHOLOGY

The importance of linking cognition and emotion in understanding developmental psychopathology is apparent from reflection on the clinical phenomena. Most clinical problems are not easily explained by reference solely to a cognitive process or solely to an affective process. For example, anxiety (an emotion) can disrupt attention and concentration (cognitions) in children with anxiety and/or attention problems (Eysenck, Derakshan, Santos, & Calvo, 2007); depressed mood (emotion) interacts with cognitive control (cognition) in depression (Lonigan, Vasey, Phillips, & Hazen, 2004); and low empathy and poor verbal reasoning abilities intersect in antisocial behavior (Blair. 2005). Moreover, clinical assessment in one domain clearly is affected by the other. For example, attention is modulated by emotional arousal to varying degrees in different people.

As the preceding paragraph indicates, examples of the interplay of emotion and cognition in psychopathology are many. To constrain the scope of this discussion, however, our focus now turns to ADHD and disruptive behavior problems. *Disruptive behavior problems* refer to defiance, aggression, and conduct problems and are also called *externalizing problems*. They often co-occur with ADHD and attention problems yet have partially distinct correlates and outcomes. Further specifying their distinctions is important to setting up strong heuristics for clinical understanding.

Attention-Deficit/Hyperactivity Disorder and Disruptive Behaviors From an Integrated Cognitive–Affective Perspective

How do cognition and affect relate in the case of child disruptive behaviors? ADHD is characterized by developmentally excessive activity, impulsivity, and disorganized, off-task behaviors. Associated problems later in development can include excess traffic accidents, marital problems, employment difficulties, and injuries, as well as antisocial behaviors, alcohol and substance abuse and dependence, and aggression. The *Diagnostic and Statistical Manual of Mental Disorders* (4th ed., DSM–IV; American Psychiatric Association, 1994) specifies three subtypes: primarily inattentive, primarily hyperactive-impulsive, and combined. Neurobiological, and etiological heterogeneity are probable. Nevertheless, because of the extensive ADHD literature documenting weaknesses in a variety of cognitive domains and the disorder's strong implications for educational attainment, ADHD is often viewed as a cognitive disorder or as a learning disability (Pennington, 1991). This viewpoint has both clinical and experimental support. For example, children with ADHD are more likely than other children to have a bona fide learning disability (Hinshaw, 1992). Moreover, even when they do not have learning disabilities, children with ADHD are more likely to experience academic underachievement, indicating a pathway to long-term poorer life outcomes independent of externalizing and disruptive behavior disorders and independent of affective disturbances such as anxiety and depression (J. Breslau et al., 2009; N. Breslau et al., in press; Duncan et al., 2007).

Furthermore, a massive literature has conclusively demonstrated that youth with ADHD, at the level of group comparison with non-ADHD youth, have weakened executive functioning (Willcutt, Doyle, Nigg, Faraone, & Pennington, 2005). Indeed, there is considerable interest in beginning to apply interventions for training executive functioning in youth with learning disability, brain injury, and ADHD (Posner & Rothbart, 2007). However, ADHD also co-occurs beyond chance levels with anxiety and depression, and children with ADHD have difficulty with anger, mood, and affect regulation (Pliszka, Carlson, & Swanson, 1999). These clinical findings seem congruent with the idea of interdependent systems in cognition and affect.

Another complexity is that although landmark reviews 20 years ago established a partial distinction between ADHD and antisocial behavior or conduct problems (Hinshaw, 1987; Loney, 1987), the overlap of ADHD with oppositional defiant disorder is so extensive in clinical practice that ADHD can scarcely be studied without consideration of oppositional defiant disorder (ODD). ODD may be a developmental bridge linking ADHD to cognitive disorder (Lahey et al., 2002; Lahey, McBurnett, & Loeber, 2000). Yet ODD is typically viewed not as a cognitive disorder, as is ADHD, but as an emotional problem; these children are angry, defiant, defensive, and irritable, with irritability being one proposed core feature (Nigg, Goldsmith, & Sachek, 2004; Sanson & Prior, 1999). Indeed, oppositional behavior in youth often co-occurs with irritability, and it appears that a subset of these youngsters may go on to depression (Burke, Loeber, Lahey, & Rathouz, 2005) or another mood disorder. Unlike youth with ADHD, children with ODD are not noted for having extensive learning or cognitive problems apart from ADHD (although oppositional children without ADHD are difficult to find and rarely studied). An irritable temperament is theorized to lie at the root of oppositional behavior and an antisocial trajectory (Lahey, Waldman, & McBurnett, 1999). Oppositional behaviors frequently lead into conduct disorder; conduct disorder almost invariably is preceded by ODD (Lahey & Loeber, 1994).

A temperamental or personality perspective could be helpful in testing some guesses about how these problems develop in relation to the development of supposed psychological systems. We undertook investigations to clarify two key problems in the taxonomy of externalizing problems: (a) the distinction between inattention and hyperactivity–impulsivity, and (b) the distinction between oppositional defiant behavior and ADHD problems. From a temperamental perspective, is hyperactivity more closely related to inattention or to oppositional defiant behavior? Is oppositional defiant behavior more closely related to hyperactivity or to conduct disorder? Finally, what is the validity of the multilevel model depicted in Figure 12.1 with regard to the cognitive and emotional components of ADHD?

A Temperament-Based Approach: Recent Work at the Michigan State University Attention-Deficit/Hyperactivity Disorder Project

As hinted at in Figure 12.1, the questions raised in the previous section can be approached in several ways, such as using experimental measures of emotion and cognition, physiological measures, and neuroimaging (Calkins & Fox, 2002; Nigg & Casey, 2005). Recently, we have been approaching these issues using personality and temperament traits, following the logic presented earlier. Here, because we are discussing studies of children, adolescents, and adults, for convenience we use the term *personality* to refer to a range of commonly identified traits found in children and in adults, rather than the awkward *temperament or personality*. Readers should recognize that some theorists would consider some of these common traits to be aspects of temperament when they are measured in children. However, our argument here is that the core neurobiological systems related to these traits map onto the general framework we have outlined.

Personality Traits and Attention-Deficit/Hyperactivity Disorder in Adults

In an initial study that pooled data across several research centers on more than 1,600 adults (parents of children with ADHD, college students with ADHD, and adults with ADHD), Nigg, Blaskey, Huang-Pollock, and John (2002) examined the Big Five personality traits: Neuroticism, Extraversion, Openness, Agreeableness, and Conscientiousness. Symptoms of ADHD in adulthood and as recalled from childhood were associated systematically with particular personality traits. These mapped meaningfully onto ADHD symptom domains. ADHD symptoms of inattention and disorganization were related to low Conscientiousness (which connotes poor planfulness and is related to our concept of top-down control) and, to a lesser extent, with Neuroticism (which connotes anxiety, moodiness, and reactivity of negative affect). Hyperactivity–impulsivity, in contrast, was correlated with low Agreeableness (i.e., hostility; however, this effect was partially explained by the overlap of ADHD with antisocial behavior; Nigg, John, et al., 2002). This initial large sample study of adults seemed to suggest that we might be able to use personality to map a dual-process model of ADHD that involves cognitive control and affective response tendencies.

Temperament and Attention-Deficit/Hyperactivity Disorder in Children and Adolescents

We followed up the adult study with a study of children, relying primarily on parent and teacher ratings to measure personality and behavior (Martel & Nigg, 2006; Martel, Nigg, & Lucas, 2008; Martel, Nigg, & Von Eye, 2009; Martel et al., 2009). In a sample of clinically diagnosed children with ADHD and non-ADHD youth, we examined major personality traits (resiliency, reactive control, effortful control, and negative affectivity) derived from Eisenberg et al.'s (2005) model . Associations between personality traits and clinical symptoms were broadly consistent with the model in Figure 12.1. Inattention and hyperactivity symptoms had distinct personality correlates. Inattention/disorganization in turn was uniquely related to low resiliency (i.e., flexibility of control in response to context demands) and, in parent but not teacher data, low effortful control. *Effortful control* indicates thoughtful or deliberate self-regulation and so is related to our idea of cognitive control as described earlier. Hyperactivity–impulsivity was uniquely related to low reactive control (i.e., reflexive control, closely related to impulse control), but inattention and oppositional behaviors were not—a finding that was replicated using teacher report. In contrast, oppositional-defiant symptoms were related to negative emotionality, but not uniquely so (negative emotionality was also related to inattention and hyperactivity-impulsivity) and only in parent data.

Thus, it appeared that from a temperament perspective, one could argue that the roots of hyperactivity-impulsivity are distinct from both the inattention and the oppositional symptoms identified in the *DSM–IV*, even though all of these symptoms frequently co-occur. Inattention appears to be most uniquely related to top-down or cognitive control response tendencies, whereas hyperactivity-impulsivity and oppositional behaviors are related to bottom-up or affective response tendencies. Oppositional behavior problems have the added feature of being related to negative emotionality, and they could represent the confluence of negative emotionality and low reactive control. These behavior disorders may co-occur because of the extensive reciprocal interaction between these neural and psychological systems during childhood development.

To pursue this type of dissociation, we conducted a further analysis. In the same sample of 179 children, we conducted a factor analysis and created two factor scores that we deemed particularly relevant to our hypothesis. One factor was anchored by effortful control and included conscientiousness. The other factor was anchored by low reactive control and included extraversion; we called it the *affective* or *incentive* approach. In children, a clean double dissociation was noted in that control (but not approach) was related to inattentive ADHD symptoms, whereas approach (but not control) was related to hyperactive-impulsive ADHD symptoms.

We then attempted to replicate this in a sample of 184 adolescents ages 13 to 18 (109 boys, 87 with ADHD). The picture was similar but not so differentiated as in the children. Both low reactive control and low conscientiousness were related to inattentive ADHD symptoms, whereas only low reactive control was significantly related to hyperactive-impulsive ADHD symptoms. That could suggest that affective systems have more influence on behavior in adolescence, consistent with our general framework that includes an extra risky period in adolescence while incentive systems mature earlier than control systems.

Returning a final time to the question of the distinction between the ADHD symptom dimensions, we applied the top-down cognitive control and bottom-up affective responding idea in a formal structural equation model in 363 youths between the ages of 7 and 18 years (pooled across the samples just described). To anchor the cognitive control factor, we included two well-validated laboratory measures of cognitive control. The Logan Stop Signal Task yields stop signal reaction time as a measure of response suppression. That measure is consistently associated with ADHD (Willcutt et al., 2005), and neuroimaging findings link it to activation in PFC (Rubia et al., 2005). The Trailmaking Task from the Halstead Reitan Neuropsychological Battery (HRNB) is extensively used as a measure of prefrontal and executive functioning. Trails B time was the outcome measure. Teachers rated inattentive and hyperactive-impulsive ADHD symptoms using the Conners Parent Rating Scale (Conners, Sitarenios, Parker, & Epstein, 1997), a well-validated, nationally normed instrument. Thus, we had up to 10 trait scores, two cognitive test scores, and two ADHD symptom domains for our latent variable model fitting. A two-group structural equation model was fit to evaluate the hypothesized top-down (cognitive) and bottom-up (affective) domains (as in Figure 12.1). The model fit the data better than a one-factor model and fit very well. The top-down factor was associated with ADHD inattentive symptoms (as rated by teachers), and the affective factor was associated with ADHD hyperactive symptoms (as rated by teachers). Adding the cross paths— top-down on hyperactivity and bottom-up on inattention—failed to improve the model fit, supporting the hypothesis that top-down control and bottom-up affect have specific relations to inattention (cognitive problems) versus hyperactivity-impulsivity (incentive response problems). It is suggested that these two symptom domains co-occur often (but not invariably) because of the close interdependence of the underlying neural systems in maturation during childhood. Further, deficits in one or both of these pathways appear to lead to the behavioral disorder we currently refer to as *ADHD*.

Relevant Biological Systems and Genetics

Moving to a different level of analysis, one can consider biological systems that might be in some sense distinguishable along the same lines. We have argued that ADHD and CD may reflect distinct neurobiological systems (Nigg, 2003). That argument follows several others in the field. Luciano and colleagues (reviewed by Luciano, 2006) have argued that dopamine neurotransmitters, and therefore dopamine receptor genes, are important in modulating top-down cognitive control. Serotonergic neural transmission, and therefore serotonin-related genes, are important in affective control. Newcorn and Halperin (2000) argued from a similar perspective that aggression in children is underpinned by serotonergic mechanisms, whereas ADHD is related to dopaminergic systems.

Taking these preliminary ideas a step further, we suggest here that ADHD symptoms, particularly inattention, may be specifically related to catecholamine genes expressed in striatum and PFC, whereas disruptive behaviors, especially oppositional defiant and conduct symptoms, are related to serotonergic genes expressed throughout the brain and the limbic system. Preliminary studies provide some circumstantial support. For example, key dopamine and noradrenergic genes, expressed in prefrontal–striatal circuits, have been associated with deficits in cognitive control and response inhibition in ADHD samples (Bellgrove, Hawi, Kirley, Gill, & Robertson, 2005; Cornish et al., 2005; Waldman et al., 2006). Conversely, the low-functioning short allele of the 44bp promoter polymorphism of the serotonin transporter gene (5HTT) has been linked with problems in affect regulation, perhaps explaining its association to a range of clinical phenotypes, including mood disorders (Preisig, 2006) and antisocial behavior (Hallikainen et al.,

1999) in adults, as well as conduct disorder and persistent aggression in children (Beitchman et al., 2006; Sakai et al., 2006). The opposite finding appeared for ADHD.

The *long* allele of the 44-bp promoter polymorphism of 5HTT was related to ADHD (see Faraone et al., 2005). This different genetic effect may reflect differences in the contribution of 5HTT to these types of impulse control disorders (in other words, it would suggest that impulsivity in ADHD is of a kind different from impulsivity in conduct or bipolar disorder).

To explore this, we pooled three dopaminergic and noradrenergic gene markers (one marker each from dopamine transporter gene, dopamine DRD4 receptor gene, and noradrenergic alpha 2A receptor gene) to create a catecholamine risk genotype. The serotonin transporter 44-pb marker served as a serotonin genetic risk variable based on high and low expression (we arbitrarily collapsed this into two groups, rather than the three genotypes, so as to maximize statistical power). In a sample of 206 children ages 6 through 13 years (134 with ADHD), a double dissociation was revealed: Catecholamine genotype was specifically related to inattentive and hyperactive symptoms, whereas 5HTT was specifically related to CD symptoms.

CONCLUDING DISCUSSION

It is important for readers to recognize that many other domains of cognition are relevant to an emotion-plus-cognition account of psychopathology. Although cognitive control is often related to attention, relatively little discussion of other kinds of attention, memory, or language was pursued herein. Also bypassed in this chapter was a substantial treatment literature relying on use of attributions (types of cognition) to change mood in children and adults. Also bypassed were several bodies of literature that examine the etiological relation of cognition and affect in adult psychopathology using experimental methods. For example, Mineka and Sutton (1992) proposed that, in anxiety, emotion disrupts attention (and attention sustains negative emotion), whereas in depression, emotion distorts memory in a mutually sustaining loop. Eysenck and Calvo (1992) laid out their processing efficiency theory of anxiety (itself building on earlier, similar theories). In its most updated form, and resting on a body of work by M. Eysenck and colleagues, that theory posits that anxiety interferes with cognitive control (in the form of response inhibition and shifting) by redirecting mental resources to stimulus-driven rather than cognitive control–driven responses (Eysenck et al., 2007). Perhaps most influential was Clark and Watson's (1991) theory that top-down control moderates the relationship between negative affect and depression or anxiety. Similarly, a body of work on antisocial behavior in adults addresses attentional biases (Hiatt, Schmitt, & Newman, 2004; Vitale et al., 2005). Lonigan et al (2004) applied the Clark and Watson

Hussey-Mayfield Memorial Public Library
HMMPL

Check Out

03:40 PM   2010/04/08

Child development at the intersection of emotion
cognition
46002277890   Due: 2010-04-22 00:00:00

al 1 article(s).

al number of items checked-out: 1

Thank you for visiting Hussey-Mayfield Memorial
Public Library.

u can renew items on line at evergreen lib in us, by
one at 317-873-3149 or at a Self-check station at a
branch near you.

model to children. That work showed that temperamental control moderates the relation of negative affect to anxiety symptoms in children as well.

Furthermore, whereas we only touched briefly here on Genotype × Environment effects, examining Gene × Environment effects across development will be essential. Doing so may move researchers away from the idea of static risk alleles for psychopathology because some genotypes or alleles may be protective during one developmental period and a risk factor during another. For example, Casey et al. (in press) found that the variant $BDNF_{Met}$ with decreased regulated secretion was related to learning biases early in development but not in later adolescence. Likewise, alterations in gene expression and gene regulation will need to be examined across developmental periods and contexts.

What implications might the present approach have for developmental theory? First, it suggests that neither emotion nor cognition develops in unitary fashion but rather that each has components that may develop at different rates. Second, emotion and cognition do not develop in isolation from one another. Although they may in some respects come online or mature at different times, they are intertwined throughout development. Third, following from the idea of partially differential rates of maturation, the intersection of emotion and cognition relevant to psychopathology may depend on the developmental stage or age. Particularly important is the transition from preschool to school age (when cognitive demands sharply increase) and the pubertal transition (when affective processes develop somewhat "ahead" of cognitive control operations). Finally, we have noted here an individual differences approach that can be used to begin to describe variations related to psychopathology. It is important for developmental theory to include exceptions to the rule—atypical developmental routes.

With regard to psychopathology, integration of cognition and emotion began long ago in the field of adult internalizing disorders and to some extent externalizing disorders. More recently, developmental conceptions have been applied to how psychopathology evolves in childhood. Disruptive behavior disorders in children pose one of the most important taxonomic puzzles for the field and were a focus in this chapter. Application of an integrated emotion and cognition approach to psychopathology can begin at a descriptive level with temperament and personality studies of children with disruptive behavior disorders; the review and data summarized here point to some taxonomic conclusions from such an approach. These data can be integrated with experimental measures, and then specific hypotheses can be tested using biological measures such as neuroimaging and molecular genetic methods.

We conclude that inattention is quite distinct from oppositional defiant behavior, although hyperactivity–impulsivity and oppositional defiant behavior are more closely related. Inattention, hyperactivity, oppositional, and conduct problems appear to reflect varying kinds of breakdown of cognitive and affective systems. Inattention is related to breakdown in cognitive control, a top-down operation dependent on late-maturing prefrontal neural circuitry. Hyperactivity–impulsivity is related to excessive activation of bottom-up incentive responding, perhaps in an approach system related to the brain region called the *nucleus accumbens*. Oppositional defiant behavior is related to excess activation of negative affectivity. Because these systems are mutually influencing during development, the problem domains often co-occur. However, distinct developmental inputs are likely in temperament.

REFERENCES

Aksan, N., & Kochanska, G. (2004). Links between systems of inhibition from infancy to preschool years. *Child Development, 75,* 1477–1490.

American Psychiatric Association. (1994). *Diagnostic and statistical manual of mental disorders* (4th ed.). Washington, DC: American Psychiatric Association.

Beitchman, J. H., Baldassarra, L., Mik, H., DeLuca, V., King, N., Bender, D., et al. (2006). Serotonin transporter polymorphisms and persistent, pervasive childhood aggression. *American Journal of Psychiatry, 163,* 1103–1105.

Bellgrove, M. A., Hawi, Z., Kirley, A., Gill, M., & Robertson, I. H. (2005). Dissecting the attention deficit hyperactivity disorder phenotype: Sustained attention, response variability, and spatial attentional asymmetries in relation to dopamine transporter (DAT1) genotype. *Neuropsychologia, 43,* 1847–1857.

Blair, R. J. (2005). Applying a cognitive neuroscience perspective to the disorder of psychopathy. *Development and Psychopathology, 17,* 865–891.

Botvinick, M., Braver, T. S., Yeung, N., Ullsperger, M., Carter, C. S., & Cohen, J. D. (2004). Conflict monitoring: Computational and empirical studies. In M.I. Posner (Ed.), *Cognitive Neuroscience of Attention* (pp.91–102). New York: Guilford Press.

Breslau, J., Miller, E., Breslau, N., Bohnert, K., Lucia, V., & Schweitzer, J. (2009). The impact of early behavior disturbances on academic achievement in high school. *Pediatrics, 123,* 1472–1476.

Breslau, N., Breslau, J., Peterson, E., Miller, E., Lucia, V. C., Bohnert, K., & Nigg, J. T. (in press). Change in teachers' ratings of attention problems and subsequent change in academic achievement: a prospective analysis. *Psychological Medicine.*

Burke J. D., Loeber, R, Lahey, B. B., & Rathouz, P. J. (2005). Developmental transitions among affective and behavioral disorders in adolescent boys. *Journal of Child Psychology and Psychiatry, 46,* 1200–1210.

Calkins, S. D., & Fox, N. A. (2002). Self-regulatory processes in early personality development: a multilevel approach to the study of childhood social withdrawal and aggression. Development and Psychopathology, 14, 477–498.

Canli, H. (2004). Functional brain mapping of extraversion and neuroticism: Learning from individual differences in emotion processing. *Journal of Personality, 72,* 1105–1132.

Carver, A. C., Livesey, D. J., & Charles, M. (2001). Age related changes in inhibitory control as measured by stop signal task performance. *International Journal of Neuroscience, 107,* 43–61.

Casey, B. J., Glatt, C. E., Tottenham, N., Soliman, F., Bath, K., Amso, D., et al. (in press). BDNF as a Model System for examining Gene by Environment Interactions across development. *Neuroscience.*

Casey, B .J., Jones, R., & Hare, T. A. (2008). The adolescent brain. In A. Kingstone & M. B. Miller (Eds.), *Annals of the New York Academy of Sciences: Vol. 1124. The year in cognitive neuroscience* (pp. 111–1126). New York: New York Academy of Sciences.

Casey, B. J., Tottenham, N., Liston, C., & Durston, S. (2005). Imaging the developing brain: What have we learned about cognitive development? *Trends in Cognitive Science, 9,* 104–110.

Clark, L. A., & Watson, D. (1991). Tripartite model of anxiety and depression: Psychometric evidence and taxonomic implications. *Journal of Abnormal Psychology, 100,* 316–336.

Conners, C. K., Sitarenios, G., Parker, J. D. A., & Epstein, J. N. (1998). The Revised Conners' Parent Rating Scale (CPRS-R): Factor structure, reliability, and criterion validity. *Journal of Abnormal Child Psychology, 26,* 257–268.

Cornish. K. M., Manly, T., Savage, R., Swanson, J., Morisano, D., Butler, N., et al. (2005). Association of the dopamine transporter (DAT1) 10/10 repeat genotype with ADHD Symptoms and response inhibition in a general population sample. *Molecular Psychiatry, 10,* 686–698.

Duncan, G., Dowsett, C., Claessens., A., Magnuson, K., Huston, A. C., Klebanov, P., et al. (2007). School readiness and later achievement. *Developmental Psychology, 43,* 1428–1446.

Eisenberg, N., Sadovsky, A., Spinrad, T., Fabes, R. A., Losoya, S., Valiente, C., et al. (2005). The relations of problem behavior status to children's negative emotionality, effortful control, and impulsivity: Concurrent relations and prediction of change. *Developmental Psychology, 41,* 193–211.

Eysenck, M. W., & Calvo, M. G.(1992) Anxiety and performance: The processing efficiency theory. *Cognition and Emotion, 6,* 409–434.

Eysenck, M. W., Derakshan, N., Santos, R., & Calvo, M. G. (2007). Anxiety and cognitive performance: attentional control theory. *Emotion, 7,* 336–353.

Faraone, S. V., Perlis, R. H., Doyle, A. E. , Smoller, J. W., Goralnick, J. J., Holmgren, M. A., & Sklar, P. (2005). Molecular genetics of attention-deficit/hyperactivity disorder. *Biological Psychiatry, 57,* 1313–1323.

Galvan, A., Hare, T., Voss, H., Glover, G., & Casey, B.J. (2006). Earlier development of the accumbens relative to orbitofrontal cortex might underlie risk-taking behavior in adolescents. *Journal of Neuroscience, 26,* 6885–92.

Gray, J. A. (1964). *Pavlov's typology: Recent theoretical and experimental developments from the laboratory of B. M. Teplov.* New York: Macmillan.

Gray, J. A. (1982). *The neuropsychology of anxiety: An enquiry into the functions of the septo-hippocampal system*. New York: Oxford University Press.

Haber, S. N., Kunishio, K., Mizobuchi, M., & Lynd-Balta, E. (1995). The orbital and medial prefrontal circuit through the primate basal ganglia. *Journal of Neuroscience, 15*, 4851–4867.

Hallikainen, T., Saito, T., Lachman, H. M., Volavka, J., Pohjalainen, T., Ryynanen, O., et al. (1999). Association between low-activity serotonin transporter genotype and early onset alcoholism with habitual impulsive violent behavior. *Molecular Psychiatry, 4*, 385–388.

Hare, T. A., Tottenham, N., Davidson, M. C., Glover, G. H., & Casey, B. J. (2005). Contributions of amygdala and striatal activity in emotion regulation. *Biological Psychiatry, 57*, 624–632.

Hare, T. A., Tottenham, N., Galvan, A., Voss, H. U., Glover, G. H., & Casey, B. J. (2008). Biological substrates of emotional reactivity and regulation in adolescence during an emotional go-nogo task. *Biological Psychiatry, 63*, 927–934.

Hariri, A.R., Bookheimer, S.Y., & Mazziotta, J.C. (2000). Modulating emotional responses: effects of a neocortical network on the limbic system. *NeuroReport, 11*, 43–8.

Hariri, A. R., Mattay, V. S., Tessitore, A., Fera, F., & Weinberger, D. R. (2003). Neocortical modulation of the amygdala response to fearful stimuli. *Biological Psychiatry, 53*, 494–501.

Hiatt, K. D., Schmitt, W. A., & Newman, J. P. (2004). Stroop tasks reveal abnormal selective attention among psychopathic offenders. *Neuropsychology, 18*, 50–59.

Hinshaw, S. P. (1992). Academic underachievement, attention deficits, and aggression: comorbidity and implications for intervention. *Journal of Consulting and Clinical Psychology, 60*, 893–903.

Huang-Pollock, C.L., Carr, T. H., & Nigg, J. T. (2002). Development of selective attention: Perceptual load influences early versus late attentional selection in children and adults. *Developmental Psychology, 38*, 363–375.

Kagan, J., & Snidman, N. (2004). *The long shadow of temperament*. Cambridge, MA: Harvard University Press.

Lahey, B. B. & Loeber, R. (1994). Framework for a developmental model of oppositional defiant disorder and conduct disorder. In D. K. Routh (Ed.), *Disruptive behavior disorders in childhood* (pp.139–180). New York: Plenum Press.

Lahey, B. B., Loeber, R., Burke, J., Rathouz, P. J., & McBurnett, K. (2002). Waxing and waning in concert: Dynamic comorbidity of conduct disorder with other disruptive and emotional problems of 7 years among clinic-referred boys. *Journal of Abnormal Psychology, 111*, 556–567.

Lahey, B. B., McBurnett, K., & Loeber, R. (2000). Are attention deficit/hyperactivity disorder and oppositional defiant disorder developmental precursors to conduct disorder? In A. Sameroff, M. Lewis, & S. M. Miller (Eds.), *Handbook of developmental psychopathology* (2nd ed., pp. 431–446). New York: Plenum Press.

Lahey, B. B., Waldman, I. D., & McBurnett, K. (1999). Annotation: The development of antisocial behavior: An integrative causal model. *Journal of Child Psychology and Psychiatry, 40*, 669–682.

Lonigan, C. J., Vasey, M. W., Phillips, B. M., & Hazen, R. A (2004). Temperament, anxiety, and the processing of threat-relevant stimuli. *Journal of Clinical Child and Adolescent Psychology, 33*, 8–20.

Luciano, M. (2006). Cognitive neuroscience and the prefrontal cortex: Normative development and vulnerability to psychopathology. In D. Cicchetti & D. Cohen (Eds.), *Developmental psychopathology* (Vol. 2, 2nd ed., pp. 292–331). Hoboken, NJ: Wiley.

Martel, M. M., & Nigg, J. T. (2006). Child ADHD and personality/temperament traits of reactive and effortful control, resiliency, and emotionality. *Journal of Child Psychology and Psychiatry, 47*, 1175–1183.

Martel, M. M., Nigg, J. T., & Lucas, R. (2008). Trait mechanisms in youth with and without attention-deficit/hyperactivity disorder. *Journal of Research in Personality, 42*, 895–913.

Martel, M. M., Nigg, J. T., & von Eye, A. (2009). Top-down and bottom-up personality trait mechanisms in attention-deficit/hyperactivity disorder (ADHD). *Journal of Abnormal Child Psychology, 37*, 337–348.

Martel, M. M., Pierce, L., Nigg, J. T., Jester, J. M., Wong, M., Buu, A., et al. (2009). Temperament pathways to childhood disruptive behavior and adolescent substance abuse: Testing a cascade model. *Journal of Abnormal Child Psychology, 37*, 363–373.

Mineka, S., & Sutton, S. K. (1992). Cognitive biases and emotional disorders. *Psychological Science, 3*, 65–69.

Newcorn, J. H., & Halperin, J. M. (2000). Attention-deficit disorders with oppositionality and aggression. In T. E. Brown (Ed.), *Attention-deficit disorders and comorbidities in children, adolescents, and adults* (pp. 171–208). Washington, DC: American Psychiatric Association.

Nigg, J. T. (2000). On inhibition/disinhibition in developmental psychopathology: View from cognitive and personality psychology and a working inhibition taxonomy. *Psychological Bulletin, 126*, 220–246.

Nigg, J. T. (2003). Toward a multiprocess conception of etiological heterogeneity for ADHD combined type and conduct disorder early-onset type. In J. A. King, C. F. Ferris, & I. I. Lederhendler (Eds.), *Annals of the New York Academy of Sciences: Vol. 1008. Roots of mental illness in children* (pp. 170–182). New York: New York Academy of Sciences.

Nigg, J. T. (2006). *What causes ADHD? Toward a multi-path model for understanding what goes wrong and why.* New York: Guilford Press.

Nigg, J. T., Blaskey, L. B., Huang-Pollock, C., & John, O.P. (2002). ADHD and personality traits: Is ADHD an extreme personality trait? *The ADHD Report, 10*, 6–11.

Nigg, J. T., & Casey, B. J. (2005). An integrative theory of attention-deficit/hyperactivity disorder based on the cognitive and affective neurosciences. *Development and Psychopathology, 17*, 785–806.

Nigg, J. T., Goldsmith, H. H., & Sachek, J. (2004). Temperament and attention deficit hyperactivity disorder: The development of a multiple pathway model. *Journal of Clinical Child and Adolescent Psychology, 33*, 42–53.

Nigg, J. T., John, O. P., Blaskey, L. G., Huang-Pollock, C. L., Willcutt, E. G, Hinshaw, S. P., & Pennington, B. (2002). Big Five dimensions and ADHD symptoms: Links between personality traits and clinical symptoms. *Journal of Personality and Social Psychology, 83*, 451–469.

Nobre, A. C. (2004). Probing the flexibility of attentional orienting in the human brain. In M. I. Posner (Ed.), *Cognitive neuroscience of attention* (pp.157–179). New York: Guilford Press.

Pennington, B (1991). *Neuropsychology of learning disorders.* New York: Guilford Press.

Pliszka, S. R., Carlson, C. L., & Swanson, J. M. (1999). *ADHD with comorbid disorders.* New York: Guilford Press.

Posner, M. I., & Rothbart, M. K. (2007). *Educating the human brain.* Washington, DC: American Psychological Association.

Preisig, M. (2006). Genetics of bipolar disorder: A review. *Schweizer Archiv fur Neurologie und Psychiatrie, 157*(8), 366–377.

Putnam, S. P., Ellis, L. K., & Rothbart, M. K. (2001). The structure of temperament from infancy through adolescence. In A. Eliasz & A. Anglietner (Eds.), *Advances in research on temperament* (pp. 164–182). Lengerich, Germany: Pabst Science Publishers.

Rothbart, M. K. & Bates, J. E. (1998). Temperament. In W. Damon (Series Ed.) & N. Eisenberg (Vol. Ed.), *Handbook of child psychology: Social, emotional, and personality development* (Vol. 3, pp. 105–176). New York: Wiley.

Rubia, K., Lee, F., Cleare, A. J., Tunstall, N., Fu, C. H. Y., Brammer, M., & McGuire, P. (2005). Tryptophan depletion reduces right inferior prefrontal activation during response inhibition in fast, event-related fMRI. *Psychopharmacology, 179*, 791–803.

Sakai, J., Young, S. E., Stallings, M. C., Timberlake, D., Smolen, A., Stetler, G. L., et al. (2006). Case-control and within-family tests for an association between conduct disorder and 5HTTLPR. *American Journal of Medical Genetics, 141*, 825–832.

Sanson, A., & Prior, M. (1999). Temperament and behavioral precursors to oppositional-defiant disorder and conduct disorder. In H. C. Quay & A. E. Hogan (Eds.), *Handbook of disruptive behavior disorders* (pp. 397–417). New York: Kluwer Academic/Plenum Press.

Schultz, W., Tremblay, L., & Hollerman, J. R. (2000). Reward processing in primate orbitofrontal cortex and basal ganglia. *Cerebral Cortex, 10*, 272–284.

Thomas, A., Chess, S., Birch, H. G., Hertzig, M. E., & Korn, S. (1963). *Behavioral individuality in early childhood.* New York: New York University Press.

Thomas, A., Chess, S., & Birch, H. G. (1968). *Temperament and behavior disorders in children.* New York: New York University Press.

Thomas, K. M., Drevets, W. C., Dahl, R. E., Ryan, N. D., Birmaher, B., Eccard, C. H., et al. (2001). Amygdala response to fearful faces in anxious and depressed children. *Archives of General Psychiatry, 58*, 1057–1063.

Vitale, J. E., Newman, J. P., Bates, J. E., Goodnight, J., Dodge, K. A., & Petit, G. S. (2005). Deficient behavioral inhibition and anomalous selective attention in a community sample of adolescents with psychopathic traits and low-anxiety traits. *Journal of Abnormal Child Psychology, 33,* 461–470.

Waldman, I., D., Nigg, J. T., Gizer, I. R., Park, L., Rappley, M. D., & Friderici, K. (2006). The adrenergic receptor alpha-2A gene (ADRA2A) and neuropsychological executive functions as putative endophenotypes for childhood ADHD. *Cognitive, Affective, and Behavioral Neuroscience, 6,* 18–30.

Willcutt, E. G., Doyle, A. E., Nigg, J. T., Faraone, S. V., & Pennington, B. F. (2005). Validity of the executive function theory of ADHD: Meta-analytic review. *Biological Psychiatry, 57,* 1336–1346.

AFTERWORD: INTEGRATING EMOTION AND COGNITION IN DEVELOPMENTAL RESEARCH

MARTHA ANN BELL AND SUSAN D. CALKINS

Emotion–cognition integration is a rapidly evolving area of research in psychology that has implications for basic and applied approaches to the study of development. Our aim in this volume is to highlight the different ways in which developmental science is conceptualizing this integration with respect to behavior and biology and to extend these ideas to better understand children's functioning in real-world settings. By no means do we consider this volume to be the definitive treatment of the interrelations between emotion and cognition in childhood, however. We hope that its chapters will motivate theoretical and empirical efforts to investigate this significant area of work. We strive to further encourage this work by posing the following questions and offering tentative suggestions for future research designed to answer them.

WHAT CONCEPTUAL FRAMEWORKS GUIDE THE STUDY OF THE INTEGRATION OF EMOTION AND COGNITION?

Although all of the authors contributing to this volume endorse the value of studying emotion and cognition in a more integrated fashion, there are different ways of thinking about how best to organize and study these processes over time. For example, a framework that emphasizes the regulatory or control dimension of these processes highlights the need to identify common psychological and biological processes that link emotion and cognition (Bell & Deater-Deckard, 2007). A self-regulatory framework has the advantage of isolating one particular function of emotion and cognition, but what may be lost is an appreciation of the other functions that emotion and cognition may play in children's adaptation.

Children acquire ways of thinking about their world in both emotional and cognitive terms. Emotion understanding is associated with recognizing and labeling the emotions of self and others, leading to appropriate emotion communication and enhancing social competence (Denham et al., 2003). Cognitive understanding allows children to appreciate the mental states of self and others and view situations from different perspectives, also leading to more effective communication with others (Astington, 2003). Clearly, both emotion control and understanding, along with cognitive control and understanding, appear to be critical for early socioemotional competence and academic readiness (Leerkes, Paradise, O'Brien, Calkins, & Lange, 2008). Thus, there is a need to further explore and organize potential component processes associated with emotion and cognition integration.

Another approach to conceptualizing emotion and cognitive processes emphasizes their organization at a neural level (Lewis, 2005; Thompson, Lewis, & Calkins, 2008). Neural models note the deficiency of thinking about a purely emotional or purely cognitive brain, emphasizing the neural connections that make parsing such activity a challenge. A further step in this direction is the characterization of the *social brain*, which implies that the human brain is specialized for the processing of social information and that parts of the brain communicate different types of information in the service of integrated functioning. Clearly, different ways of thinking about how to frame emotion and cognition integration are important to consider as they clearly influence how these processes are measured and studied across time.

HOW DO EMOTION AND COGNITION INFLUENCE ONE ANOTHER ACROSS DEVELOPMENT?

Much research has been devoted to the study of emotional development and cognitive development in children, but how separable are emotion and cognition in the study of development? We propose that it is important to consider the simultaneous development of emotion and cognitive processes and their mutual influences. Moreover, an extension of the conceptual framework for studying emotion and cognition integration is how to think about—and measure—their integration or mutual influence (Grey, 2004). Traditional approaches focus on top-down versus bottom-up perspectives. There may or may not be a value in placing a primacy of one process over the other. We note that developmental and neural considerations can help to resolve this issue. More data are needed, however, that can speak to the influence of one process over the other across time.

There are at least two time courses that must be considered: the in-the-moment relations between emotion and cognition, and the longer-term relations that evolve as a function of growth in each domain. This latter issue raises important questions about differential development and periods of vulnerability that may be a function of greater skill in one area than another (Steinberg, 2008). Adding to this complexity is the idea that the degree of mutual influence may vary as a function of developmental period. Many important ideas about development have been raised that cannot be easily addressed without more longitudinal studies that measure these processes over time.

WHAT IS THE ROLE OF CONTEXT IN EMERGING EMOTION–COGNITION RELATIONS?

Context is a powerful contributor to both emotional and cognitive development. Our understanding of the ways in which first relationships shape children's understanding of their social and physical worlds has changed dramatically, in part as a function of the appreciation of the interrelations of emotion and cognition. The world to which the social brain is exposed provides many opportunities for emotion–cognition interactions to be engaged, as most ostensibly social tasks require language and specific cognitive skills such as understanding of others, monitoring behavior, controlling affect, and attention. Real-world tasks in the home, school, and peer environment have both emotionally and motivationally significant elements. More work on the moderational role of various important contexts is needed before one can really appreciate the nature of contextual effects on emotion–cognition integration.

WHAT ARE THE IMPLICATIONS OF DEVELOPING EMOTION–COGNITION INTEGRATION FOR INTERVENTION RESEARCH?

Understanding emotion and cognition integrative processes in typically developing children is critical for understanding the development of extremes in self-regulation and associated complexities in emotional and cognitive processing (Cicchetti & Posner, 2005). Thus, research on the integration of cognition and emotion, as well as possible atypical development, has implications for clinical and education research (Blair, 2002). As we noted in the introduction to this volume, most of the current work on predictors of mental health and school performance has focused on specific emotion or cognitive predictors of particular clinical disorders or failing academic skills. There are indications, however, that children's school performance problems and psychopathology may provide greater cause for concern if there are difficulties in both emotion and cognitive processing (e.g., Pennington & Ozonoff, 1996). Thus, the merging of cognition and emotion research in intervention science has the potential for critical impact on treatment outcomes.

The contributors to this unique volume have focused exclusively on emotion–cognition relations in childhood. They have examined basic behavioral, neuropsychological and genetic, and applied areas of study, as well as the integration of these three areas, in studying the emergence of emotion–cognition relations. Each chapter author is conducting highly innovative, cutting-edge work. Nevertheless, work remains to be done at both a conceptual level and in terms of empirical efforts to study these dynamic and mutually influential processes. We are eager to see how the work of these researchers influences the evolving field of emotion and cognition integration in child development.

REFERENCES

Astington, J. W. (2003). Sometimes necessary, never sufficient: False-belief understanding and social competence. In B. Repacholi & V. Slaughter (Eds.), *Individual differences in theory of mind: Implications for typical and atypical development* (pp. 13–39). New York: Psychology Press.

Bell, M. A., & Deater-Deckard, K. (2007). Biological systems and the development of self-regulation: Integrating behavior, genetics, and psychophysiology. *Journal of Developmental & Behavioral Pediatrics, 28*, 409–420.

Blair, C. (2002). School readiness: Integrating cognition and emotion in a neurobiological conceptualization of children's functioning at school entry. *American Psychologist, 57*, 111–127.

Cicchetti, D., & Posner, M. I. (2005). Editorial: Cognitive and affective neuroscience and developmental psychopathology. *Development and Psychopathology, 17*, 569–575.

Denham, S. A., Blair, K. A., DeMulder, E., Levitas, J., Sawyer, K. S., Auerbach-Major, S. T., et al., (2003). Preschool emotional competence: Pathway to social competence. *Child Development, 74*, 238–256.

Gray, J. R. (2004). Integration of emotion and cognitive control. *Current Directions in Psychological Science, 13*, 46–48.

Leerkes, E. M., Paradise, M., O'Brien, M., Calkins, S.D., & Lange, G. (2008). Emotion and cognition processes in preschool children. *Merrill-Palmer Quarterly, 54*, 102–124.

Lewis, M.D. (2005). Bridging emotion theory and neurobiology through dynamic systems modeling (target article). *Behavioral and Brain Sciences, 28*, 169–194.

Pennington, B. F. & Ozonoff, S. (1996). Executive functions and developmental psychopathology. *Journal of Child Psychology and Psychiatry and Allied Disciplines*, *37*, 51–87.

Steinberg, L. (2008). A social neuroscience perspective on adolescent risk-taking. *Developmental Review*, 28, 78–106.

Thompson, R. A., Lewis, M. D., & Calkins, S. D. (2008). Reassessing emotion regulation. *Child Development Perspectives*, *2*, 124–131.

INDEX

Object manipulation, 167
ODD. *See* Oppositional defiant disorder
OFC. *See* Orbitofrontal cortex
Olson, L. S., 215
Openness, 235
Oppositional defiant disorder (ODD), 45, 234, 239
Optimal balance, 19
Orbitofrontal cortex (OFC), 99–102, 118, 187–191
Organization, classroom, 212–213
Outerdirectedness, 27

Panksepp, J., 177
Parasympathetic nervous system, 43
Parental scaffolding, 62, 141
Parent–child attachment, 210–211
Parent–child conversation, 83–89
Parent–child relationship, 22
Parenting, lax, 211–212
Parenting styles, 211
Parietal lobe, 44
Parkinson's disease, 189
Parrot, W., 177
Peripheral nervous system (PNS), 227–228
Persistence, 140, 212
Personality development, 175, 194
Personality traits, 228, 235
Pettit, G. S., 45
PFC. *See* Prefrontal cortex
Physiological response, 39
Planning, 40
PLDs (point-light-displays), 167
Pleiotropic genes, 146
PNS (peripheral nervous system), 227–228
Point-light-displays (PLDs), 167
Ponitz, C. C., 215
Porge, S. W., 120
Positive reaction tendencies, 27
Posner, M. I., 44, 117, 145
Posterior parietal cortex, 122, 229
Poverty, 89
Prefrontal cortex (PFC), 18, 20, 24–25, 42, 99, 101–102, 104–106, 121–122, 187–189, 191–192, 229–231
Prencipe, A., 103–104
Price, C. J., 156
Private speech, 66
Probabilistic epigenesis, 156
Problem solving, 29, 82
Proffitt, D., 167
Psychobiological mechanisms, 115–128

autonomic nervous system measures of, 120–121
central nervous system measures of, 117–120
in emotion regulation, 122–123
and relation between cognitive and emotion control, 123–127
in temperament-based attentional control, 116–117
in working memory/inhibitory control, 121–122
Psychopathology, 47. *See also* Developmental psychology
Pulvinar, 159
Puppets, 86

Qu, L., 105
Quality of life, 26

Raikes, H. A., 82
Razza, R. P., 46, 205
Readiness for school, 22–25, 205
Regression analyses, 89
Regulation. *See also* Emotion regulation; Self-regulation
affective, 230
behavioral, 204–207
vagal, 43
Reid, V. M., 167, 168
Relationships, 79–92
challenging circumstances, construction of understanding in, 89–91
and construction of mental working models, 83–85
influence of, on emotional growth/understanding, 80
internal working models and conceptualizing of, 81–82
and parent–child conversation, 85–89
Representational capacity, 40
Responsive Classroom Approach, 214
Rhythmicity, 226
Riggs, N. R., 47
Risk-taking behavior, 232
Rohrer, L., 102
Rothbart, M. K., 44, 116, 145, 210, 226–227
Rutter, M., 46

Schacter, A., 4
Schmidt, M., 86
Schneider, R., 45
Script theory, 82

ABOUT THE EDITORS

Susan D. Calkins, PhD, is professor of human development, family studies, and psychology at the University of North Carolina at Greensboro, where she directs the Child and Family Research Network. She conducts longitudinal research funded by the National Institute of Mental Health (NIMH), the National Institute of Child Health and Human Development, and the National Science Foundation on the development of biological and behavioral indicators of self-regulation across infancy, childhood, and adolescence. She is a fellow of American Psychological Association Division 7 (Developmental Psychology), a recipient of an NIMH Research Scientist Career Development Award, and an associate editor of the journal *Developmental Psychology*.

Martha Ann Bell, PhD, is associate professor of psychology at Virginia Polytechnic Institute and State University, Blacksburg. Her research specialization is developmental cognitive neuroscience, and she examines developmental change in frontal lobe functioning using both behavioral and electrophysiological methods. Her current work, funded by the National Institutes of Health and the National Institute of Child Health and Human Development, focuses on individual differences in the development of executive function and emotion regulation across infancy and early childhood. Dr. Bell is a fellow of American Psychological Association Division 7 (Developmental Psychology) and the editor of the journal *Infancy*.